THE SCARECROW AUTHOR BIBLIOGRAPHIES

CHARLOTTE PERKINS GILMAN:
A Bibliography

by
GARY SCHARNHORST

Scarecrow Author Bibliographies, No. 71

The Scarecrow Press, Inc.
Metuchen, N.J., and London
1985

Library of Congress Cataloging in Publication Data

Scharnhorst, Gary.
    Charlotte Perkins Gilman, a bibliography.

    (Scarecrow author bibliographies ; no. 71)
    Includes index.
    1. Gilman, Charlotte Perkins, 1860-1935--Biography.
I. Title. II. Series.
Z8342.415.S32   1985   016.818'409   84-27625
[PS1744.G57]
ISBN 0-8108-1780-2

To Sandy and Emily once again.

Contents

INTRODUCTION

Despite recent scholarship, the publications of the long-neglected Charlotte Perkins Stetson Gilman (1860-1935) are still largely inaccessible. Like Herman Melville before the "Melville revival" of the 1920s, Gilman was virtually forgotten until 1971, when the Schlesinger Library at Radcliffe College acquired her papers, totaling twenty-nine boxes of diaries, scrapbooks, correspondence, and clippings. Over the past decade, Gilman's life has been explored in detail by several biographers, though no previous bibliographer systematically searched the magazines, many of them ephemeral, for which she wrote. No one attempted to trace the original appearances of the works she clipped for her personal files, reprintings of her works in other periodicals, or translations of her works into other languages. Many of her contributions, especially early poems and essays, were lost in a bibliographical blindspot.

Unfortunately, the sorry state of the Gilman bibliography demonstrably affected critical assessments of her work. Even the most careful of the recent Gilman scholars commit egregious errors of fact in their publications. In her biography Charlotte Perkins Gilman: The Making of a Radical Feminist (item 2312), for example, Mary A. Hill asserts that the early story "The Unexpected" was "significantly, never published" (p. 287) when, in fact, the story was published three times, first in 1890 in Kate Field's Washington (item 493). Moreover, Hill confuses the New York Nation with the Boston New Nation (p. 170), the former an organ of Liberal Republicanism, the latter of the Nationalism of Edward Bellamy. Not surprisingly, she fails to locate several pieces Charlotte Perkins Stetson contributed to the short-lived New Nation and in turn underestimates Stetson's enthusiasm for Bellamy's movement.

Thus to set straighter the record of Gilman's publications, I have attempted to compile a reliable bibliography of her works. The moment is ripe for such a tool to promote the critical revaluation of her career. In addition to identifying hitherto unknown publications, the present compilation provides indices to the Impress and the

vii

<u>Forerunner</u>, two magazines Gilman edited, and it identifies by complete bibliographical citation many of the items collected among her papers. The compilation proves, if nothing else, that Gilman was as incredibly prolific as she claimed. She published hundreds of poems during her career, only a fraction of which were collected in her verse anthology <u>In This Our World</u>. By her own estimate, she published the equivalent of twenty-five volumes of material, including scores of articles, reviews, poems, and short stories. Many of these pieces are identified here for the first time. I have attempted to locate the first appearances of her works as well as the most significant and accessible reprintings, a task complicated by Gilman's tendency to reuse such titles as "Masculine, Feminine, and Human" and "The Woman of Fifty." I have also collected reports of Gilman's unpublished lectures and prepared a bibliography of the most important criticism of her works. I have omitted private verse only recently published by her biographers.

For the record, I do not claim that this bibliography is definitive, merely that it is both reliable and virtually complete. Gilman listed in her diaries and logs a few works that were accepted for publication over the years which either failed to reach print or, more likely, were issued in journals so obscure I failed to find them.

I am indebted for their cooperation in this project to the following individuals: Jack Bales, Reference Librarian, Mary Washington College; Vickie Bullock, Interlibrary Loan Office, University of Texas at Dallas; Elizabeth Shenton, Assistant to the Director, Schlesinger Library, Radcliffe College; Gene DeGruson, Special Collections Librarian, Pittsburg State University; Anne Middleton, Serials Librarian, New Orleans Public Library; James P. Danky, Newspapers and Periodicals Librarian, the State Historical Society of Wisconsin; Charles Bryant, Reference Librarian, Yale University; Betty Haupt, Center for Research Libraries; Cole Dawson; Gilbert K. Westgard II; Touko Siltala; Daniel Fitzgerald; Zsuzsanna Ozsvath; Nancy Down; and Stephen Wee. I also wish to acknowledge receipt of an Organized Research Grant from the University of Texas at Dallas, a Travel to Collections Grant from the National Endowment for the Humanities, and a Radcliffe Research Support Program Grant from Radcliffe College for the purpose of compiling this bibliography.

1 November 1984   Gary Scharnhorst
                                    University of Texas at Dallas
                                    Richardson, Texas

Abbreviations

CPS	Charlotte Perkins Stetson
CPG	Charlotte Perkins Gilman
CWS	Charles Walter Stetson
Charlotte Perkins Gilman Reader	item 676
Concerning Children	item 1088
His Religion and Hers	item 2142
In This Our World, I	item 49
In This Our World, II	item 106
In This Our World, III	item 122
In This Our World, IV	item 170
Hill	item 2312
Living	item 2165
Suffrage Songs and Verses	item 320
Women and Economics	item 1045

Part I

Works by Charlotte Perkins Stetson Gilman

VERSE

1884

1. "In Duty Bound," Woman's Journal," 12 Jan 1884, p. 14.
    1st line: "In duty bound, a life hemmed in"
      Rpt. in In This Our World, I, 27; II, 30; III, 30; IV,
        33-34.
      Excerpted in Bookman, 1 (June 1895), 336.
      Rpt. in Woman's Tribune, 22 June 1895, p. 100.
      Rpt. in Woman's Tribune, 13 Nov 1895, p. 145.
      Rpt. in Living, pp. 76-77.
      Rpt. in Hill, pp. 95-96.

2. "My View," Buffalo Christian Advocate, 17 Jan 1884, p. 1.
    1st line: "From my high window the outlooker sees"
      Rpt. in Living, pp. 68-69.

3. "One Girl of Many," Alpha, 1 Feb 1884, p. 15.
    1st line: "One girl of many. Hungry from her birth"

4. "Young Allan Black," ca. spring 1884.
    1st line: "There was a youth who had a horse"
      MS dated 18 Oct 1883 in folder 193, CPG Papers.
      Clipping signed "Charlotte A. Perkins" in vol. 7, CPG
      Papers, with inscription in CPG's hand: "In an Old
      South Church entertainment in Boston Uncle Edward Hale
      actually printed this absolute nonsense." (Quoted by
      permission of the Schlesinger Library, Radcliffe
      College.)

5. "Sketches," Buffalo Christian Advocate, 19 June 1884, p.
    2.
      1st line: "I can see straight ahead as I lie on the
      grass"

1886

6. "On the Pawtuxet," printed under pseudonym "C. A. Paget"
in Providence Journal, 1 Aug 1886, 4:6.
   1st line: "Broad and blue is the river, all bright in
   the sun"
   Rpt. in In This Our World, I, 7; II, 9; III, 7; IV,
   92-93.

7. "The Answer," Woman's Journal, 2 Oct 1886, p. 313.
   1st line: "A man would build a house, and found a
   place"
   Rpt. in Boston Sunday Herald, 10 Oct 1886, 18:4.
   Rpt. in the Walton, N.Y., Chronicle, 21 Oct 1886, 1:4.
   Rpt. under title "Nature's Answer" in In This Our
   World, I, 14-15; II, 17-18; III, 16-17; IV, 2-4.
   Excerpted in Bookman, 8 (Sept 1898), 51.
   Excerpted in Hill, p. 136.

8. "Nevada," Providence Journal, 7 Nov 1886, 4:6.
   1st line: "An aching, blinding, barren, endless plain"
   Rpt. in Woman's Journal, 15 Jan 1887, p. 22.
   Rpt. under title "A Nevada Desert" in In This Our
   World, I, 20; II, 23; III, 22; IV, 75-76.
   Excerpted in Bookman, 1 (June 1895), 336.
   Rpt. in Wave, 30 Nov 1895, p. 5.
   Excerpted in Dial, 1 Sept 1898, p. 134-135.

9. "A Use of Memory," Woman's Journal, 18 Dec 1886, p. 406.
   1st line: "Why should I think of dragging clouds"
   Rpt. in Brookline, Mass., Chronicle, 22 Jan 1887, p.
   30.

1887

10. "The Sarcasm of Destiny," Boston Evening Traveller, 19
Feb 1887, 3:1.
   1st line: "The sunlight is mine! And the sea!"
   Rpt. under title "The Ship" in In This Our World, I,
   8; II, 10; III, 15; IV, 67.

1889

11. "Girls of To-day," Woman's Journal, 6 July 1889, p. 209.
   1st line: "Girls of to-day! Give ear!"
   Rpt. in Woman's Column, 13 July 1889, p. 2.
   Rpt. in In This Our World, I, 35-36; II, 39-40; III,
   36-37; IV, 147-148.
   Rpt. in Housekeeper's Weekly, 10 June 1893, p. 4.
   Rpt. in Chicago Tribune, 14 Dec 1895, 16:4.

Rpt. in Suffrage Songs and Verses, pp. 12-13.

12. "A Common Inference," Boston Evening Traveller, 5 Oct
    1889, 14:3.
    1st line: "A night: mysterious, tender, quiet, deep"
    Rpt. in In This Our World, I, 4; II, 4-5; IV, 8-9.
    Rpt. in An American Anthology 1787-1900, ed. Edmund C.
        Stedman (Boston and New York: Houghton Mifflin,
        1900), p. 663.
    Rpt. in Woman's Journal, 2 July 1904, p. 209.
    Rpt. in The World's Great Religious Poetry, ed.
        Caroline Miles Mills (New York: Macmillan, 1926),
        pp. 147-148.
    Rpt. in Lyric America, ed. Alfred Kreymborg (New
        York: Coward-McCann, 1930), pp. 220-221.

13. "She Walketh Veiled and Sleeping," Woman's Journal, 12
    Oct 1889, p. 326.
    1st line: "She walketh veiled and sleeping"
    Rpt. in In This Our World, I, 33; II, 37; III, 35;
        IV, 125.
    Excerpted in Current Literature, 25 (Feb 1899), 116.
    Rpt. in Cosmopolitan, 27 (Aug 1899), 453.
    Rpt. in Deseret Evening News, 2 Dec 1899, 22:4.
    Rpt. in Chautauqua Assembly Herald, 25 Aug 1904, p.
        1.
    Rpt. in Suffrage Songs and Verses, p. 3.
    Rpt. in Current Literature, 51 (July 1911), 70.
    Rpt. in Progressive Woman, 5 (March 1912), 8.
    Rpt. in The World Split Open: Four Centuries of
        Women Poets in England and America 1552-1950, ed.
        Louise Bernikow (New York: Vintage, 1974), p. 224.
    Rpt. in Hill, pp. 188-189.

14. "Thanksgiving Hymn for California," Pacific Monthly, 1
    (Nov 1889), 49.
    1st line: "Our forefathers gave thanks to God"
    Rpt. under title "Thanksgiving Hymn" in In This Our
        World, I, 16; II, 19; III, 10.
    Rpt. in Wave, 30 Nov 1895, p. 5.
    Rpt. under original title in In This Our World, IV,
        51-52.
    Rpt. in Grizzly Bear, 4 (Dec 1908), 10.
    Rpt. in San Francisco Call and Post, 24 Nov 1921, p.
        16.

1890

15. "Similar Cases," Nationalist, 2 (April 1890), 165-166.
    1st line: "There was once a little animal"

Rpt. in New England Magazine, NS 3 (Sept 1890), 134-135.

Rpt. Roxbury, Mass.: South End Industrial School Press, 1891. 8 pp.

Rpt. in Current Literature, 6 (March 1891), 348-351.

Rpt. in Woman's Journal, 16 April 1892, p. 128. See also Katherine Lente Stevenson, "'Similar Cases,'" Woman's Journal, 30 April 1892, p. 143.

Rpt. in Woman's Journal, 10 Dec 1892, p. 400.

Rpt. in Woman's Column, 10 Dec 1892, p. 2.

Rpt. in In This Our World, I, 75-79; II, 76-80; III, 72-76; IV, 95-100.

Rpt. in Woman's Journal, 23 May 1896, p. 166.

Excerpted in American Fabian, 3 (Jan 1897), 2.

Rpt. in Appeal to Reason, 14 May 1898, p. 3.

Excerpted in St. Louis Observer, 18 Aug 1898, p. 14.

Excerpted in Cosmopolitan, 27 (Aug 1899), 454.

Rpt. in Deseret Evening News, 2 Dec 1899, 22:1.

Rpt. in A Book of American Humorous Verse (Chicago: Herbert S. Stone & Co., 1904), pp. 89-94.

Rpt. in Woman Worker (London), 14 July 1909, p. 46.

Rpt. in The Home Book of Verse, ed. Burton Stevenson (New York: Henry Holt and Co., 1912), pp. 1823-1826.

Rpt. with comment by Lester Ward in Glimpses of the Cosmos (New York and London: G. P. Putnam's Sons, 1917), vol. V, pp. 337-340. See also Ward's comment in American Journal of Sociology, 2 (May 1897), 815n.

Excerpted in New York Times, 8 Oct 1919, 18:6. See also "A Correction Followed by Apologies," New York Times, 9 Oct 1919, 14:5.

Rpt. in Poems of Evolution, People's Pocket Series No. 71 (Girard, Kans.: Appeal to Reason, [1920]), pp. 15-18. See also "Notes to 'Similar Cases,'" p. 38.

Rpt. in Poems of Evolution, ed. by Emanuel Haldeman-Julius, Ten Cent Pocket Series No. 71 (Girard, Kans.: Haldeman-Julius Co., [1922]), pp. 25-28. See also "Notes to 'Similar Cases,'" p. 60.

Rpt. in Poems of Evolution, ed. by Emanuel Haldeman-Julius, Little Blue Book No. 71 (Girard, Kans.: Haldeman-Julius Co., n.d.), pp. 12-15. See also "Notes to 'Similar Cases,'" pp. 31-32.

Rpt. in The World's One Thousand Best Poems, ed. Berton Braley (New York and London: Funk & Wagnalls Co., 1929), vol. IV, pp. 139-143.

Excerpted in The Home Book of Quotations, ed. Burton Stevenson (New York: Dodd, Mead, and Co., 1934), pp. 303-304, 585.

Rpt. in Zona Gale, "Foreword" to <u>Living</u>, pp. xxxiv-
xxxvii.
Rpt. in W. M. Parrish, <u>Reading Aloud</u> (New York:
Thomas Nelson and Sons, 1941), pp. 143-146.
Adapted to music in Jean Berger, "Birds of a Feather:
An Entertainment in One Act Based on the poem
'Similar Cases'" (Hackensack, NJ: Sheppard Music
Press, 1971). 84 pp.

16. "Ode to a Fool," <u>Kate Field's Washington</u>, 4 June 1890, p.
363.
   1st line: "Singular insect! Here I watch thee spin"
   Rpt. in <u>In This Our World</u>, II, 128-129.
   Rpt. in <u>Forerunner</u>, 1 (Feb 1910), 26.

17. "Women of To-day. (To the Remonstrants)," <u>Woman's
Journal</u>, 7 June 1890, p. 177.
   1st line: "You women of to-day who fear so much"
   Rpt. in <u>Woman's Column</u>, 7 June 1890, p. 1.
   Rpt. without subtitle in <u>In This Our World</u>, I, 34;
      II, 37-38; III, 38; IV, 128-129.
   Rpt. in <u>Woman's Tribune</u>, 22 June 1895, p. 100.
   Rpt. in <u>Suffrage Songs and Verses</u>, pp. 4-5.
   Rpt. in <u>Regionalism and the Female Imagination</u>, 4
      (Winter 1979), 36.

18. "An Obstacle," <u>Boston Budget</u>, 1 June 1890, p. 10.
   1st line: "I was climbing up a mountain path"
   Rpt. in <u>Woman's Journal</u>, 14 June 1890, p. 185.
   Rpt. in <u>Woman's Column</u>, 14 June 1890, p. 1.
   Rpt. under title "Prejudice" in <u>Homemaker</u>, 7 (Nov
      1891), 637.
   Rpt. in <u>In This Our World</u>, I, 84-85; II, 85-86; III,
      80-81; IV, 102-103.
   Rpt. under title "A Prejudice: I Was Climbing" in
      <u>Outlook</u>, 24 March 1894, p. 565.
   Rpt. in <u>Overland Monthly</u>, 23 (May 1894), 555.
   Rpt. in <u>Appeal to Reason</u>, 23 Nov 1895, p. 2.
   Rpt. in <u>Woman's Tribune</u>, 1 Feb 1896, p. 12.
   Rpt. in <u>Woman's Journal</u>, 16 May 1896, p. 158.
   Rpt. in <u>Woman's Column</u>, 16 May 1896, p. 2.
   Rpt. in <u>American Fabian</u>, 2 (June 1896), 10.
   Rpt. under title "A Prejudice" in Ruskin, Tenn.,
      <u>Coming Nation</u>, 31 Oct 1896, p. 3.
   Rpt. in <u>Outlook</u>, 2 April 1898, p. 864.
   Rpt. in <u>Deseret Evening News</u>, 2 Dec 1899, 22:3-4.
   Rpt. in <u>Ruskin, Tenn., Coming Nation</u>, 17 March 1900,
      p. 3.
   Rpt. in <u>Progressive Woman</u>, 3 (July 1909), 4.
   Rpt. in <u>Woman Worker</u> (London), 4 Aug 1909, p. 107.

Excerpted in John Davidson, The Man Forbid and Other
Essays (Boston: Ball Pub. Co., 1910), p. 80.
Published in Hungarian translation under title "Az
Akadály" in A Nó és a társadalom, 1 Nov 1911, p.
191.
Rpt. in West Coast, 13 (Oct 1912), 80.
Excerpted in New York Times Book Review, 7 Feb 1932,
p. 23.
Rpt. in Zona Gale, "Foreword" to Living, pp. xxxiii-
xxxiv.

19. "Ballade of the Young Editor," Kate Field's Washington,
18 June 1890, p. 397.
1st line: "In the days when I struggled to earn"
Rpt. under title "Ballade of the New Editor" in
Forerunner, 5 (April 1914), 108.

20. "Reassurance," Woman's Journal, 5 July 1890, p. 214.
1st line: "Can you imagine nothing better, brother"
Rpt. in Woman's Column, 5 July 1890, p. 1.
Rpt. in In This Our World, I, 42; II, 46-47; III, 45-
46; IV, 138-139.
Excerpted in Bookman, 1 (June 1895), 337.
Rpt. in Woman's Journal, 6 June 1896, p. 184.
Excerpted in Cosmopolitan, 27 (Aug 1899), 454.
Rpt. in Suffrage Songs and Verses, p. 15.
Excerpted in Hill, p. 215.

21. "Wedded Bliss," Kate Field's Washington, 30 July 1890, p.
69.
1st line: "'O come and be my mate!' said the Eagle to
the Hen"
Rpt. in Woman's Tribune, 30 Aug 1890, p. 214.
Rpt. in In This Our World, I, 86-87; II, 87-88; III,
87-88; IV, 157-158.
Rpt. in Woman's Journal, 6 Jan 1894, p. 6.
Rpt. in Woman's Column, 6 Jan 1894, p. 2.
Rpt. in Deseret Evening News, 2 Dec 1899, 22:5.
Published in German translation by Emma Clausen under
title "Ehealüd" in Der arme Teufel, 23 June 1900,
p. 252.
Rpt. in Woman's Journal, 15 July 1911, p. 224.
Rpt. in Suffrage Songs and Verses, pp. 9-10.
Rpt. in The Home Book of Verse, ed. Burton Stevenson
(New York: Henry Holt & Co., 1912), pp. 1830-1831.
Rpt. in Regionalism and the Female Imagination, 4
(Winter 1979), 37-38.

22. "The Cup," Boston Budget, 3 Aug 1890, p. 10.
1st line: "And yet, saith he, ye need but sip"

Rpt. in In This Our World, I, 6; II, 8; III, 6; IV, 58.

23. "What Then?" Boston Budget, 7 Sept 1890, p. 10.
    1st line: "Suppose you write your heart out till the world"
    Rpt. in In This Our World, I, 19; II, 22; III, 20, IV, 59.

24. "To Man," Woman's Journal, 13 Sept 1890, p. 294.
    1st line: "In dark and early ages, through the primal forests faring"
    Rpt. in Woman's Column, 13 Sept 1890, p. 3.
    Rpt. in In This Our World, I, 70-73; II, 72-74; III, 68-70; IV, 125-128.
    Rpt. in Woman's Tribune, 19 Feb 1894, p. 37.
    Rpt. in Woman's Tribune, 22 June 1895, p. 97.
    Rpt. under title "Proem" in Women and Economics, pp. ii-iv.
    Published in Danish translation by U. Birkedal under title "Forenede--skilte--genforenede" in Kvinden og Samfundet (Copenhagen), 14 Aug 1900, pp. 1-2.

25. "Why Nature Laughs," Pacific Monthly, 2 (Nov 1890), 184.
    1st line: "In a very lonely forest"

26. "For Sweet Charity's Sake. (An Anti-Nationalist Wail)," New England Magazine, NS 3 (Dec 1890), 543.
    1st line: "Oh, dear!"
    Rpt. under title "The Anti-Nationalist Wail" in In This Our World, I, 90-92; II, 91-93.
    Rpt. under title "Christian Virtues" in In This Our World, III, 84-86; IV, 210-213.

1891

27. "Another Conservative," Pacific Monthly, 3 (March 1891), 105-106.
    1st line: "Upon a broad and placid beach"
    Rpt. in Woman's Journal, 9 July 1904, p. 218.

28. "The Survival of the Fittest," Boston New Nation, 14 March 1891, p. 161.
    1st line: "In northern zones the ranging bear"
    Rpt. in In This Our World, I, 93-94; II, 94-95; III, 78-79; IV, 208-209.
    Rpt. in Appeal to Reason, 27 Sept 1902, p. 3.
    Adapted to music by Caroline L. Goodenough in Melodies of the People (Des Moines: privately printed, n.d.), pp. 21-22.

Excerpted in Judith Nies, Seven Women (New York: Viking Press, 1977), p. 136.

29. "The Amiable Elephant," Wasp, 6 June 1891, p. 5.
    1st line: "In slumber's calm, untroubled joys"

30. "She Who is to Come," Woman's Tribune, 20 June 1891, p. 193.
    1st line: "A woman--in so far as she beholdeth"
    Rpt. in Woman's Tribune, 12 Nov 1892, p. 232.
    Rpt. in In This Our World, I, 74; II, 75; III, 71; IV, 146.
    Rpt. in San Francisco Call, 28 May 1893, 11:6.
    Rpt. in San Francisco Call, 3 Dec 1893, 15:3.
    Rpt. in Woman's Journal, 17 Feb 1894, p. 54.
    Rpt. in Woman's Column, 17 Feb 1894, p. 1.
    Rpt. in Woman's Tribune, 21 Feb 1894, p. 45.
    Rpt. in Topeka State Journal, 13 June 1896, p. 6.
    Rpt. in Arena, 22 (Aug 1899), 263.
    Rpt. in Deseret Evening News, 2 Dec 1899, 22:4.
    Rpt. in Women in Professions, vol. 3 of International Congress of Women of 1899, ed. Countess of Aberdeen (London: T. Unwin Fisher, 1900), p. 156.
    Rpt. in Chautauqua Assembly Herald, 25 Aug 1904, p.8.
    Rpt. in Woman's Journal, 21 Nov 1908, p. 188.
    Rpt. in Suffrage Songs and Verses, p. 24.
    Rpt. in The Cry for Justice, ed. Upton Sinclair (Philadelphia: John C. Winston Co., 1915), p. 877.
    Rpt. in Equal Rights, 1 July 1938, p. 286.

31. "What's That?" Boston New Nation, 10 Oct 1891, p. 584.
    1st line: "I met a little person on my land"
    Rpt. in In This Our World, I, 88-89; II, 89-90; III, 82-83; IV, 213-215.
    Rpt. in Girard, Kans., Coming Nation, 23 Dec 1911, p. 14.

32. "The Prophets," Century, 43 (Nov 1891), 168.
    1st line: "Time was we stoned the prophets. Age on age"
    Rpt. in In This Our World, I, 10; II, 13; III, 26; IV, 95.
    Rpt. in Bookman, 1 (June 1895), 336.
    Rpt. in The World Split Open: Four Centuries of Women Poets in England and America, 1552-1950, ed. Louise Bernikow (New York: Vintage, 1974), p. 226.

33. "'Feminine Vanity,'" Kate Field's Washington, 18 Nov 1891, p. 332.
    1st line: "Feminine Vanity! O ye Gods! Here to this man!"

Rpt. in In This Our World, I, 46-47; II, 51-52; III,
48-49; IV, 164-166.
Excerpted in Bookman, 1 (June 1895), 337.
Rpt. in Regionalism and the Female Imagination, 4
(Winter 1979), 40-41.

34. "Rockefeller's Prayer," Wasp, 21 Nov 1891, p. 2.
1st line: "By his bedside, bowed in prayer"
Rpt. in In This Our World, I, 102-103; II, 102-104;
III, 96-97.

35. "Where Memory Sleeps/Rondeau," Harper's Bazar, 28 Nov
1891, p. 915.
1st line: "Where memory sleeps the soul doth rise"
Rpt. in Woman's Journal, 12 Dec 1891, p. 404.
Rpt. in In This Our World, I, 12; II, 15; III, 14;
IV, 81.

36. "We, as Women," Wasp, 5 Dec 1891, p. 2.
1st line: "There's a cry in the air about us--"
Rpt. in In This Our World, I, 40-41; II, 44-45; III,
42-43; IV, 148-150.
Rpt. in Woman Worker (London), 24 Feb 1909, p. 170.
Rpt. in Suffrage Songs and Verses, pp. 11-12.
Excerpted in Glasgow, Scotland, Forward, 12 Sept
1925, p. 4.

37. "The Changeless Year/Southern California," Harper's
Bazar, 19 Dec 1891, p. 978.
1st line: "Doth Autumn remind thee of sadness?"
Rpt. without subtitle in In This Our World, I, 13;
II, 16; III, 13; IV, 80.

1892

38. "The Old-Time Wail," Boston New Nation, 23 Jan 1892, p.
53.
1st line: "Still Dives hath no peace. Broken his
slumber"
Rpt. in In This Our World, I, 107-109; II, 107-109;
III, 98-99; IV, 184-186.
Rpt. in Appeal to Reason, 2 Oct 1897, p. 3.

39. "A Conservative," Life, 4 Feb 1892, p. 68.
1st line: "The garden beds I wandered by"
Rpt. in Woman's Journal, 20 Feb 1892, p. 64.
Rpt. in In This Our World, I, 82-83; II, 83-84; III,
76-78; 100-101.
Rpt. in Harper's Weekly, 25 Jan 1896, p. 18.
Rpt. in Chicago Tribune, 7 March 1896, 16:4.

Rpt. in <u>Saturday Review</u> (London), 7 March 1896, p. 253.

Rpt. in Outlook, 4 April 1896, p. 647.

Rpt. in <u>Literary Digest</u>, 4 April 1896, p. 671.

Rpt. in <u>Woman's Journal</u>, 23 May 1896, p. 161.

Rpt. in <u>Woman's Column</u>, 23 May 1896, p. 2.

Rpt. in <u>Current Literature</u>, 20 (August 1896), 647.

Rpt. in <u>An American Anthology</u> 1787-1900, ed. Edmund C. Stedman (Boston and New York: Houghton Mifflin, 1900), pp. 663-664.

Published in German translation by Emma Clausen under title "Ein Conservativer" in <u>Der arme Teufel</u>, 21 July 1900, p. 284.

Rpt. in <u>Woman Worker</u> (London), 6 Jan 1909, p. 7.

Rpt. in <u>Vocal Expression in Speech</u>, ed. Henry Evarts Gordon and Rollo F. Lyman (Boston: Ginn and Co. 1911), pp. 41-42.

Rpt. in <u>The Home Book of Verse</u>, ed. Burton Stevenson (New York: Henry Holt and Co., 1912), pp. 1822-1823.

Rpt. in <u>Modern American Poetry</u>, ed. Louis Untermeyer (New York: Harcourt, Brace and Co., 1921), pp. 78-80.

Rpt. in Glasgow, Scotland, <u>Forward</u>, 12 Sept 1925, p. 4.

Rpt. in <u>The Standard Book of British and American Verse</u>, ed. Nella Bruddy Henney (Garden City: Garden City Pub. Co., 1932), pp. 665-667.

Excerpted in <u>The Home Book of Quotations</u>, ed. Burton Stevenson (New York: Dodd, Mead and Co., 1934), p. 2244.

40. "The Dead Level," Boston <u>New Nation</u>, 9 April 1892, p. 228.

1st line: "There is a fear among us as we strive"

Rpt. in Woman's Journal, 7 May 1892, p. 152.

Rpt. in <u>In This Our World</u>, I, 113-114; II, 113-114; III, 103-104; IV, 203-204.

41. "The Cart Before the Horse," Boston <u>New Nation</u>, 21 May 1892, p. 325.

1st line: "Our business system has its base"

Rpt. in <u>In This Our World</u>, I, 97; II, 97; III, 94; IV, 204-205.

Excerpted in Arena, 14 (Oct 1895), 274.

Rpt. in <u>Appeal to Reason</u>, 3 Jan 1903, p. 6.

Rpt. in <u>Appeal to Reason</u>, 24 Jan 1914, p. 3.

42. "Ballad of the Summer Sun," <u>Californian Illustrated</u>, 2 (June 1892), 151.

1st line: "It is said that human nature needeth

hardship to be strong."
Rpt. in In This Our World, III, 113-115; IV, 71-74.

43. "'The Poor Ye Have Always With You,'" Boston New Nation,
4 June 1892, p. 356.
1st line: "The poor ye have always with you--therefore
why"
Rpt. in In This Our World, I, 98; II, 98; III, 95.

44. "Females," Woman's Journal, 18 June 1892, p. 200.
1st line: "The female fox she is a fox"
Rpt. in In This Our World, I, 48-49; II, 53-54; III,
50-51; IV, 169-171.
Excerpted in John Davidson, The Man Forbid and Other
Essays (Boston: Ball Pub. Co., 1910), p. 82.
Rpt. in Suffrage Songs and Verses, pp. 10-11.
Excerpted in Glasgow, Scotland, Forward, 12 Sept
1925, p. 4.

45. "Unsexed," Woman's Journal, 9 July 1892, p. 224.
1st line: "It was a wild, rebellious Drone"
Rpt. in In This Our World, I, 50-51; II, 55-56; III,
52-53; IV, 168-169.

46. "The Amoeboid Cell," Boston New Nation, 30 July 1892, p.
484.
1st line: "Said the Specialized Cell to the Amoeboid
Cell"
Rpt. in In This Our World, I, 99-101; II, 99-101;
III, 91-93; IV, 205-208.

47. "The Nation," Cosmopolitan, 13 (Nov 1892), 58.
1st line: "The nation is a unit. That which makes"
Rpt. in Boston New Nation, 5 Nov 1892, p. 664.
Rpt. under title "Nationalism" in In This Our World,
I, 120; II, 120; III, 108-109; IV, 197-198.

1893

48. "Free Land is Not Enough," Boston New Nation, 22 April
1893, p. 204.
1st line: "Free land is not enough. In earliest days"
Rpt. in In This Our World, I, 118-119; II, 118-119;
III, 106-107; IV, 186-187.
Rpt. in Arena, 10 (Oct 1894), 642.

49. In This Our World, 1st ed. Oakland: McCombs & Vaughn,
1893. 120 pp.
Reviewed in San Francisco Call, 3 Dec 1893, 15:3.
Reviewed by Alice Stone Blackwell in Woman's Journal,

30 Dec 1893, p. 412.
Reviewed in Unity, 18 Jan 1894.
Reviewed by Ambrose Bierce in San Francisco Examiner, 4
    Feb 1894, 6:4-5. See also "Bierce and Stetson,"
    Stockton Mail, 6 Feb 1894, 2:3.
Reviewed in Overland Monthly, 23 (May 1894), 554-555.
Reviewed by Henry Norman in the London Chronicle. Rpt.
    in Impress, 17 Nov 1894, p. 10.

50. "The Rock and the Sea," in In This Our World, I, 1-2.
    1st line: "I am the Rock, presumptuous Sea!"
        Rpt. in In This Our World, II, 1-3; III, 1-3; IV, 9-
            12.
        Rpt. in Woman's Tribune, 22 June 1895, p. 97.
        Rpt. in Woman's Journal, 7 March 1896, p. 78.
        Excerpted in Current Literature, 21 (April 1897),
            299.
        Rpt. in Current Literature, 24 (July 1898), 6.
        Published in German translation by Emma Clausen under
            title "Der Fels und das Meer" in Der arme Teufel, 4
            Nov 1899, p. 404.

51. "A Moonrise," in In This Our World, I, 3.
    1st line: "The heavy mountains, lying huge and dim"
        Rpt. in In This Our World, II, 4; III, 15; IV, 93.

52. "Songs," in In This Our World, I, 5-6.
    1st line: "O world of green, all shining, shifting!"
        Rpt. in In This Our World, II, 6-7; III, 5-6; IV, 69-
            70.

53. "A Prayer," in In This Our World, I, 8.
    1st line: "O God! I cannot ask thee to forgive"
        Rpt. in In This Our World, II, 10; III, 14; IV, 50.
        Rpt. in Athenaeum, 30 Dec 1899, p. 893.

54. "Christmas Carol (For Los Angeles)," in In This Our
    World, I, 9-10.
        1st line: "On the beautiful birthday of Jesus"
        Rpt. in In This Our World, II, 11-12; III, 11-12; IV,
            52-54.
        Rpt. without subtitle in Woman's Journal, 24 Dec
            1904, p. 414.

55. "Heaven," in In This Our World, I, 11.
    1st line: "Thou bright mirage, that o'er man's arduous
    way"
        Rpt. in In This Our World, II, 13; III, 9; IV, 71.

56. "Pioneers," in In This Our World, I, 11-12.

1st line: "Long have we sung our noble pioneers"
Rpt. in In This Our World, II, 14; III, 8; IV, 74.

57. "Among the Gods," in In This Our World, I, 17-18.
1st line: "How close the air of valleys, and how close"
Rpt. in In This Our World, II, 20-21; III, 18-19; IV, 67-69.

58. "The Heart of the Water," in In This Our World, I, 20.
1st line: "O the ache in the heart of the water that lies"
Rpt. in In This Our World, II, 23; III, 22; IV, 66-67.
Rpt. in Woman's Journal, 27 Jan 1894, p. 25.
Rpt. in Woman's Column, 27 Jan 1894, p. 2.

59. "The Lion Path," in In This Our World, I, 21-22.
1st line: "I dare not!"
Rpt. in In This Our World, II, 24-25; III, 24-25; IV, 12-13.
Rpt. in Woman's Journal, 20 Jan 1894, p. 17.
Rpt. in Woman's Column, 20 Jan 1894, p. 2.
Rpt. in Overland Monthly, 23 (May 1894), 555.
Rpt. in It Can Be Done: Poems of Inspiration, ed. Joseph Morris Bachelor and St. Clair Adams (Toronto: Ryerson Press, 1921), p. 24.
Rpt. in A Book of Living Poems, ed. William R. Bowlin (Chicago: Albert Whitman & Co., 1934), pp. 116-117.

60. "Too Much," in In This Our World, I, 22.
1st line: "There are who die without love, never seeing"
Rpt. in In This Our World, II, 25; III, 26; IV, 57-58.
Published in German translation by Emma Clausen under title "Zu Viel" in Der arme Teufel, 11 Nov 1899, p. 412.
Excerpted in Hill, p. 215.

61. "Baby Love," in In This Our World, I, 23.
1st line: "Baby Love came prancing by"
Rpt. in In This Our World, II, 26; III, 25; IV, 174.
Rpt. in St. Louis Observer, 18 Aug 1898, p. 14.
Published in German translation by Emma Clausen under title "Bübchen Liebe" in Der arme Teufel, 11 Nov 1899, p. 412.
Rpt. in Athenaeum, 30 Dec 1899, p. 893.

62. "For Us," in In This Our World, I, 24.
    1st line: "If we have not learned that God's in man"
      Rpt. in In This Our World, II, 27; III, 28; IV, 43-
        44.
      Rpt. in Woman's Tribune, 19 Dec 1903, p. 140.
      Rpt. in Woman's Tribune, 26 Dec 1903, p. 144.
      Rpt. in Woman's Journal, 2 Jan 1904, p. 6.
      Excerpted in Canadian Magazine, 61 (Aug 1923), 335.
      Rpt. in Quotable Poems: An Anthology of Modern
        Verse, ed. Thomas Curtis Clark and Esther A.
        Gillespie (Chicago and New York: Willett, Clark &
        Colby, 1928), p. 171.
      Rpt. in Poems for Special Days and Occasions, ed.
        Thomas Curtis Clark (New York: Richard R. Smith,
        Inc., 1930), pp. 48-49.
      Rpt. in 1000 Quotable Poems: An Anthology of Modern
        Verse, ed. by Thomas Curtis Clark (Chicago:
        Willett, Clark & Co., 1937), vol. 1, p. 171.

63. "Why Not?" in In This Our World, I, 25.
    1st line: "Why not look forward far as Plato looked"
      Rpt. in In This Our World, II, 28; III, 21; IV, 35-
        36.
      Rpt. in Woman's Journal, 22 Sept 1894, p. 302.
      Rpt. in Woman's Tribune, 23 Nov 1895, p. 145.

64. "Desire," in In This Our World, I, 26.
    1st line: "Lo, I desire! Sum of the ages' growth--"
      Rpt. in In This Our World, II, 29; III, 29; IV, 34-
        35.

65. "The Modern Skeleton," in In This Our World, I, 28.
    1st line: "As kings of old in riotous royal feasts"
      Rpt. in In This Our World, II, 31; III, 23; IV, 39-
        40.
      Rpt. in Woman's Journal, 10 March 1894, p. 78.

66. "Reinforcements," in In This Our World, I, 29.
    1st line: "Yea, we despair. Because the night is
    long"
      Rpt. in In This Our World, II, 32; III, 27; IV, 13-
        14.
      Rpt. in Woman's Tribune, 16 June 1894, p. 109.

67. "The Lesson of Death/To S.T.D.," in In This Our World, I,
    30-33.
    1st line: "In memory of one whose breath"
      Rpt. in In This Our World, II, 33-36; III, 31-34; IV,
        40-43.

68. "To Mothers," in In This Our World, I, 37-39.
    1st line: "In the name of your ages of anguish!"
    Rpt. in In This Our World, II, 41-43; III, 39-41.
    Excerpted in Bookman, 1 (June 1895), 337.
    Rpt. under title "The Burden of Mothers: A Clarion
    Call to Redeem the Race" (Mt. Lebanon, N.Y.:
    Shaker Press, n.d.). 4 pp.
    Rpt. in Woman Worker (London), 20 Oct 1909, p. 371.
    Excerpted under title "Mothers" in Progressive Woman,
    3 (Dec 1909), 6.
    Rpt. under title "We, the Mothers of Men" and
    pseudonym "M. C. Smith" in Woman's Journal, 2 May
    1914, p. 144.
    Excerpted under title "Mothers" in Woman's Voice: An
    Anthology, ed. Josephine Conger-Kaneko (Boston:
    Stratford Co., 1918), p. 120.

69. "Six Hours a Day," in In This Our World, I, 43.
    1st line: "Six hours a day the woman spends on food!"
    Rpt. in In This Our World, II, 48; III, 44; IV, 136-
    137.
    Excerpted in Bookman, 1 (June 1895), 336.
    Rpt. in American Kitchen Magazine, 12 (Feb 1900),
    cover. See also Lisbeth Canning, "An Answer to
    Mrs. Stetson," American Kitchen Magazine, 12 (March
    1900), 220.
    Rpt. in On Common Ground: A Selection of Hartford
    Writers, ed. Alice DeLana and Cynthia Reik
    (Hartford, Conn.: Stowe-Day Foundation, 1975), p.
    116.
    Rpt. in Regionalism and the Female Imagination, 4
    (Winter 1979), 39-40.

70. "Ballade of ye Gentil Mayde," in In This Our World, I,
    44-45.
    1st line: "Shee was a mayde, a gentil mayde"
    Rpt. in In This Our World, II, 49-50; III, 46-47.

71. "The Holy Stove," in In This Our World, I, 52-53.
    1st line: "O the soap-vat is a common thing!"
    Rpt. in In This Our World, II, 57-58; III, 54-55; IV,
    158-160.
    Excerpted in Bookman, 1 (June 1895), 336-337.
    Excerpted in Bookman, 8 (Sept 1898), 52.
    Rpt. in Progressive Woman, 4 (March 1910), 10.

72. "A Brood Mare," in In This Our World, I, 54-57.
    1st line: "I had a quarrel yesterday"
    Rpt. in In This Our World, II, 59-61; III, 56-58; IV,
    161-164.

Rpt. in Woman's Journal, 10 Feb 1894, p. 46.
Rpt. in Woman's Column, 10 Feb 1894, p. 2.
Excerpted in John Davidson, The Man Forbid and Other
Essays (Boston: Ball Pub. Co., 1910), p. 80-81.

73. "To the Young Wife," in In This Our World, I, 58-59.
1st line: "Are you content, you pretty three-years'
wife?"
Rpt. in In This Our World, II, 62-63; III, 60-61; IV,
129-131.
Excerpted in Bookman, 1 (June 1895), 337.
Excerpted in Bookman, 8 (Sept 1898), 51.
Excerpted in Regionalism and the Female Imagination,
4 (Winter 1979), 38.

74. "An Old Proverb," in In This Our World, I, 60-61.
1st line: "No escape, little creature! The earth hath no
place"
Rpt. in In This Our World, II, 64-65; III, 62-63; IV,
137-138.
Published in German translation by Emma Clausen under
title "Ein altes Sprichwort" in Der arme Teufel, 7
July 1900, p. 268.

75. "False Play," in In This Our World, I, 62.
1st line: "'Do you love me?' asked the mother of her
child"
Rpt. in In This Our World, II, 66; III, 59; IV, 131-
132.
Rpt. in Woman's Journal, 3 Feb 1894, p. 33.
Rpt. in Woman's Column, 3 Feb 1894, p. 1.

76. "The Child Speaks," in In This Our World, I, 63-65.
1st line: "Get back! Give me air! Give me freedom and
room"
Rpt. in In This Our World, II, 67-68; III, 63-65; IV,
26-28.
Rpt. in Chautauqua Assembly Herald, 26 Aug 1904, p.
8.

77. "Mother to Child," in In This Our World, I, 66-69.
1st line: "How best can I serve thee, my child! My
child!"
Rpt. in In This Our World, II, 69-71; III, 65-67; IV,
140-142.
Rpt. in Woman's Tribune, 15 Feb 1896, p. 17.
Rpt. in Woman's Journal, 29 Feb 1896, p. 66.
Rpt. in Arena, 22 (Aug 1899), 270-271.
Published in Danish translation by J. Christian Bay
under title "Mit Barn" in Dannebrog, 24 Dec 1899.

Rpt. in Chautauqua Assembly Herald, 26 Aug 1904, p.
8.
Excerpted in John Davidson, The Man Forbid and Other
Essays (Boston: Ball Pub. Co., 1910), pp. 84-85.
Rpt. in Suffrage Songs and Verses, pp. 6-8.
Rpt. in Forerunner, 4 (June 1913), 144-145.
Rpt. in Bulletin of the Child Welfare League of
America, 12 (June 1933), 2.

78. "Vain Tears," in In This Our World, I, 80-81.
1st line: "O fools and blind! Are ye so wed to pain"
Rpt. in In This Our World, II, 81-82.

79. "The Sweet Uses of Adversity," in In This Our World, I,
95-96.
1st line: "In Norway fiords, in summer-time"
Rpt. in In This Our World, II, 95-96; III, 88-89; IV,
105-106.

80. "A Hope," in In This Our World, I, 105-106.
1st line: "Are you tired, patient miner?"
Rpt. in In This Our World, II, 105-106; III, 89-90.

81. "Poor Human Nature," in In This Our World, I, 110.
1st line: "I saw a meagre, melancholy cow"
Rpt. in In This Our World, II, 110; III, 100; IV,
111.

82. "Charity," in In This Our World, I, 111.
1st line: "Came two young children to their mother's
shelf"
Rpt. in In This Our World, II, 111; III, 101; IV,
217.
Rpt. in Railway Times, 16 April 1894, p. 2.
Rpt. under title "O 'Blessed Charity'" in Railway
Times, 15 Aug 1894, p. 6. See also E. E. Evans,
"In Reverse ('Oh, Blessed Charity')," Railway
Times, 15 Sept 1894, p. 1.
Rpt. in Railway Times, 15 Sept 1894, p. 2.
Rpt. in American Fabian, 3 (Jan 1897), 3.
Rpt. in Ruskin, Tenn., Coming Nation, 8 May 1897, p.
4.
Rpt. under title "Sweet Charity" in Appeal to Reason,
5 June 1897, p. 4.
Rpt. in Current Literature, 22 (Aug 1897), 191.
Rpt. in Chicago Social Democrat, 19 Aug 1897, p. 2.
Rpt. in Appeal to Reason, 11 Sept 1897, p. 3.
Rpt. in Ruskin, Tenn., Coming Nation, 24 June 1899,
p. 4.
Rpt. in Woman's Journal, 7 Nov 1903, p. 358.

Rpt. in Public, 13 Sept 1919, p. 987.
Rpt. in Glasgow, Scotland, Forward, 12 Sept 1925, p. 4.

83. "Division of Property," in In This Our World, I, 112.
   1st line: "Some sailors were starving at sea"
   Rpt. in In This Our World, II, 112-113; III, 102; IV, 209-210.

84. "Waste," in In This Our World, I, 115.
   1st line: "Doth any man consider what we waste"
   Rpt. in Boston New Nation, 6 Jan 1894, p. 4.
   Rpt. in In This Our World, II, 115; III, 107-108; IV, 63-64.

85. "The Looker-On," in In This Our World, I, 116-118.
   1st line: "The world was full of the battle"
   Rpt. in Woman's Journal, 24 Feb 1894, p. 62.
   Rpt. in In This Our World, II, 116-118; III, 104-106; IV, 181-184.
   Rpt. in Open Gates, ed. Susan Thompson Spaulding and Francis Trow Spaulding (Boston and New York: Houghton Mifflin, 1924), pp. 325-327.

1894

86. "The Wolf at the Door," Scribner's, 15 (Jan 1894), 31.
   1st line: "There's a haunting horror near us"
   Rpt. in In This Our World, II, 126-127; III, 148-149; IV, 177-178.
   Rpt. in Current Literature, 20 (Nov 1896), 391.
   Rpt. in American Fabian, 3 (Jan 1897), 3.
   Excerpted in American Fabian, 4 (June 1898), 12.
   Rpt. in Conservator, 9 (Sept 1898), 97.
   Rpt. in Current Literature, 25 (Jan 1899), 32.
   Published in German translation by Emma Clausen under title "Der Wolf vor der Tür" in Der arme Teufel, 2 Sept 1899, p. 329.
   Rpt. in Ruskin, Tenn., Coming Nation, 12 Jan 1901, p. 2.
   Rpt. in Progressive Woman, 3 (July 1910), 15.
   Excerpted in The Cry for Justice, ed. Upton Sinclair (Philadelphia: John C. Winston Co., 1915), pp. 200-201.
   Rpt. in Kirby Page, Living Creatively (New York: Farrar and Rinehart, 1932), p. 263.
   Excerpted in Hill, p. 216.

87. "The Modest Maid," Impress, 6 Oct 1894, p. 5.
   1st line: "I am a modest San Francisco maid"

Rpt. in In This Our World, III, 165-166; IV, 166-167.
Rpt. in Wave, 30 Nov 1895, p. 5.
Excerpted in Regionalism and the Female Imagination,
4 (Winter 1979), 37.

88. "The Pastellette," Impress, 13 Oct 1894, p. 3.
1st line: "The pastelle is too strong, said he"
Rpt. in In This Our World, II, 123; III, 175; IV,
108-109.

89. "Powell Street," Impress, 13 Oct 1894, p. 4.
1st line: "You start"
Rpt. in In This Our World, III, 160-162; IV, 82-85.

90. "News," Impress, 20 Oct 1894, p. 5.
1st line: "Crieth the empty public, greedily"
Rpt. in In This Our World, III, 174-175.

91. "Technique," Impress, 27 Oct 1894, p. 3.
1st line: "Cometh to-day the very skillful man"
Rpt. in In This Our World, III, 166-167; IV, 107-108.
Rpt. in American Fabian, 4 (June 1898), 12.

92. "Our San Francisco Climate," Impress, 3 Nov 1894, p. 4.
1st line: "Said I to my friend from the East--"
Rpt. in In This Our World, III, 178-179; IV, 111-113.

93. "Little Cell!" Impress, 10 Nov 1894, p. 2.
1st line: "Little Cell! Little Cell! with a heart as
big as heaven--"
Rpt. in In This Our World, II, 132; III, 164; IV, 25-
26.

94. "The Mother's Charge," Impress, 17 Nov 1894, p. 4.
1st line: "She raised her head. With hot and
glittering eye"
Rpt. in In This Our World, III, 167-168; IV, 160-161.
Rpt. in Regionalism and the Female Imagination, 4
(Winter 1979), 38-39.

95. "The Duty Farthest," Impress, 17 Nov 1894, p. 5.
1st line: "Finding myself unfit to serve my own"
Rpt. in Hill, p. 257.

96. "Thanksgiving," Impress, 24 Nov 1894, p. 1.
1st line: "Well is it for that land whose people,
yearly"
Rpt. in In This Our World, III, 146; IV, 44.

97. "Step Faster, Please," Impress, 24 Nov 1894, p. 4.

1st line: "Of all the most aggravating things"
Rpt. in In This Our World, II, 131; III, 177; IV, 23.

98. "Tassels," Impress, 1 Dec 1894, p. 4.
1st line: "Don't you remember the tassels that hung"

99. "From Russian Hill," Impress, 1 Dec 1894, p. 5.
1st line: "A strange day--bright and still"
Rpt. in In This Our World, III, 159-160; IV, 85-86.

100. "Unmentionable," Impress, 8 Dec 1894, p. 5.
1st line: "There is a thing of which I fain would speak"
See also "A Western Habit," Impress, 8 Dec 1894, p. 5.
Rpt. in In This Our World, III, 172-173; IV, 118-120.

101. "A New Creation," Impress, 15 Dec 1894, p. 5.
1st line: "What is that mother? A head my child"
Rpt. in In This Our World, III, 169.

102. "Christmas Hymn," Impress, 22 Dec 1894, p. 3.
1st line: "Listen not to the word that would have you believe"
Rpt. in In This Our World, III, 145-146; IV, 44-46.

103. "Christmas Time," Impress, 22 Dec 1894, p. 5.
1st line: "'Tis Christmas time, my little son"
Rpt. in In This Our World, III, 179-180.

104. "New Year's Day/Rondeau," Impress, 29 Dec 1894, p. 4.
1st line: "On New Year's Day he plans a cruise"
Rpt. in In This Our World, III, 173; IV, 116-117.

105. "The Hills," Impress, 29 Dec 1894, p. 5.
1st line: "The flowing waves of our warm sea"
Rpt. in In This Our World, III, 155-156; IV, 88-89.

1895

106. In This Our World, British edition. London: T. Fisher Unwin, 1895. 132 pp.

107. "Ideas. (After Emerson)," in In This Our World, II, 121.
1st line: "We do not make ideas: they flow"

108. "The Teacher," in In This Our World, II, 122.
1st line: "Who leads the world in its long upward

way?"

109. "The Keeper of the Light," in In This Our World, II,
     124.
         1st line: "A lighthouse keeper, with a loving heart"
         Rpt. in In This Our World, III, 143-144; IV, 61-62.

110. "It is Good To Be Alive," in In This Our World, II, 125.
         1st line: "It is good to be alive when the trees
     shine green"
         Rpt. in In This Our World, III, 144; IV, 79.
         Rpt. in Land of Sunshine, 3 (Aug 1895), 117.
         Rpt. in Woman's Journal, 26 Nov 1898, p. 382.

111. "If a Man May Not Eat Neither Can He Work," in In This
     Our World, II, 130-131.
         1st line: "How can he work? He never has been taught"
         Rpt. in In This Our World, IV, 189-190.

112. "A New Year's Reminder," Impress, 5 Jan 1895, p. 4.
         1st line: "Better have a tender conscience for the
     record of your house"
         Rpt. in In This Our World, III, 163-164; IV, 23-24.

113. "'An Unusual Rain,'" Impress, 5 Jan 1895, p. 5.
         1st line: "Again!"
         Rpt. in In This Our World, III, 157-159; IV, 86-88.

114. "Connoisseurs," Impress, 12 Jan 1895, p. 4.
         1st line: "'No,' said the Cultured Critic, gazing
     haughtily"
         Rpt. in In This Our World, III, 170; IV, 106-107.

115. "En Banc (California)," Impress, 19 Jan 1895, p. 5.
         1st line: "Associate Justices of Court Supreme!"
         Rpt. in In This Our World, III, 183-184.

116. "City's Beauty," Impress, 26 Jan 1895, p. 4.
         1st line: "Fair, O fair are the hills uncrowned"
         Rpt. in In This Our World, III, 156-157; IV, 89-90.

117. "The San Francisco Hen," Impress, 26 Jan 1895, p. 5.
         1st line: "The San Francisco house-mama"
         Rpt. in In This Our World, III, 182-183.

118. "In re 'Andromaniacs,'" Impress, 2 Feb 1895, p. 4.
         1st line: "Pankhurst says that woman is superior"
         Rpt. in Woman's Journal, 16 Feb 1894, p. 49.
         Rpt. in Woman's Column, 16 Feb 1894, p. 4.
         Rpt. in In This Our World, III, 181.

119. "My Cyclamen," Impress, 9 Feb 1895, p. 4.
     1st line: "A little dull brown bulb from somewhere"
     Rpt. in In This Our World, III, 152.

120. "Work and Wages," Impress, 9 Feb 1895, p. 4.
     1st line: "John Burns receives in weekly pay"
     Rpt. in In This Our World, III, 176-177.

121. "A Type," Impress, 16 Feb 1895, p. 4.
     1st line: "I am too little, said the Wretch"
     Rpt. in In This Our World, III, 171; IV, 20-21.
     Rpt. in Overland, NS 27 (Jan 1896), 124.

122. In This Our World, 2nd edition. San Francisco: Press
     of James H. Barry, 1895. 184 pp.
     Reviewed by Henry Austin in Bookman, 1 (June 1895),
        335-337.
     Reviewed by Lida Calvert Obenchain in Louisville
        Courier-Journal. Rpt. in Woman's Tribune, 22 June
        1895, pp. 97, 99.
     Reviewed by Charles F. Lummis in Land of Sunshine, 3
        (Oct 1895), 239.
     Reviewed in Woman's Tribune, 23 Nov 1895, p. 147.
     Reviewed by John Bonner in Wave, 30 Nov 1895, p. 5.
     Reviewed in Overland Monthly, NS 27 (Jan 1896), 124.
     Reviewed by W. D. Howells in Harper's Weekly, 25 Jan
        1896, p. 79.

123. "Wings," in In This Our World, III, 116-117.
     1st line: "A sense of wings--"
     Rpt. in In This Our World, IV, 64-66.
     Rpt. in Current Literature, 24 (Aug 1898), 102.

124. "Compromise," in In This Our World, III, 117-118.
     1st line: "It is well to fight and win--"
     Rpt. in In This Our World, IV, 21-22.
     Rpt. in Woman's Journal, 21 Jan 1899, p. 22.
     Rpt. in Appeal to Reason, 1 Nov 1913, p. 3.
     Rpt. in Open Gates, ed. Susan Thompson Spaulding and
        Francis Trow Spaulding (Boston and New York:
        Houghton Mifflin, 1924), pp. 331-332.

125. "As Flew the Cross," in In This Our World, III, 118.
     1st line: "As flew the fiery cross from hand to hand"
     Rpt. in In This Our World, IV, 193.

126. "Services," in In This Our World, III, 119-120.
     1st line: "She was dead. Forth went the word"
     Rpt. in In This Our World, IV, 142-144.

127. "Seeking," in In This Our World, III, 121-122.
1st line: "I went to look for Love among the roses, the roses"
Rpt. in In This Our World, IV, 55-56.

128. "New Duty," in In This Our World, III, 123-124.
1st line: "Once to God we owed it all,--"
Rpt. in In This Our World, 54.

129. "Ruined," in In This Our World, III, 124-125.
1st line: "I am ruined! sobbed the seed"

130. "Motherhood," in In This Our World, III, 126-129.
1st line: "Motherhood: First mere laying of an egg"
Rpt. in In This Our World, IV, 132-136.
Excerpted in John Davidson, The Man Forbid and Other Essays (Boston: Ball Pub. Co., 1910), pp. 78-79.
Rpt. in Antiphonal Readings for Free Worship, ed. L. Griswold Williams (Boston: Murray Press, 1933), item 31.

131. "Finding," In This Our World, III, 122-123.
1st line: "Out of great darkness and wide wastes of silence"
Rpt. in In This Our World, IV, 56-57.

132. "The Lost Game," in In This Our World, III, 130-132.
1st line: "Came the big children to the little ones"
Rpt. in In This Our World, IV, 179-181.
Rpt. in Appeal to Reason, 6 Aug 1898, p. 4.

133. "Who is to Blame?" in In This Our World, III, 132-134.
1st line: "Who was to blame in that old time"
Rpt. in In This Our World, IV, 187-189.

134. "Out of Place," in In This Our World, III, 135.
1st line: "Cell, poor little cell"
Rpt. in In This Our World, IV, 24-25.

135. "Out of the Gate," in In This Our World, III, 136-138.
1st line: "Out of the glorious city gate"
Rpt. in In This Our World, IV, 36-39.
Rpt. in Ruskin, Tenn., Coming Nation, 17 Sept 1898, p. 3.

136. "Limits," in In This Our World, III, 138.
1st line: "On sand--loose sand and shifting--"
Rpt. in In This Our World, IV, 82.
Rpt. in Woman's Journal, 16 July 1898, p. 230.

137. "An Economist," in In This Our World, III, 139-140.
    1st line: "The serene savage sitting in his tree"
    Rpt. in In This Our World, IV, 215-216.

138. "A Misfit," in In This Our World, III, 142-143.
    1st line: "O Lord, take me out of this!"
    Rpt. in In This Our World, IV, 115-116.

139. "Morning," in In This Our World, III, 147.
    1st line: "Think not of the morning as coming and
    going"

140. "The Living God," in In This Our World, III, 150-151.
    1st line: "The living God. The God that made the
    world"
        Rpt. in In This Our World, IV, 48-49.
        Published in German translation by Emma Clausen
            under title "Der lebendige Gott" in Der arme
            Teufel, 9 June 1900, p. 233.
        Rpt. in The World's Great Religious Poetry, ed.
            Caroline Miles Mills (New York: Macmillan, 1926),
            pp. 128-129.
        Excerpted in The Golden Book of Faith, ed. Thomas
            Curtis Clark (New York: Richard R. Smith, Inc.,
            1931), p. 24.

141. "Birth," in In This Our World, III, 153-154.
    1st line: "Lord, I am born!"
        Rpt. in In This Our World, IV, 1.
        Rpt. in Current Literature, 51 (July 1911), 67-68.

142. "The Pig and the Pearl," San Francisco Star, ca. 1895.
    1st line: "Said the Pig to the Pearl, 'Oh, fie!'"
        Rpt. in In This Our World, III, 140-142; IV, 109-
        110.

1896

143. "California Car Windows," Land of Sunshine, 4 (Jan
    1896), 59.
        1st line: "Lark songs ringing to heaven"
        Rpt. in In This Our World, IV, 81-82.
        Rpt. under title "From a California Train" in
            Sunset, 9 (May 1902), 76.

144. "Women to Men. Relatives and Otherwise," Woman's
    Journal, 1 Feb 1896, p. 33.
        1st line: "Dear father, from my cradle I acknowledge"
        Rpt. in Woman's Tribune, 1 Feb 1896, p. 9.
        Rpt. in Woman's Column, 1 Feb 1896, p. 1.

Rpt. without subtitle in <u>Suffrage</u> <u>Songs</u> <u>and</u> <u>Verses</u>,
pp. 13-15.
Rpt. in <u>Woman's</u> <u>Journal</u>, 3 June 1911, p. 170.

145. "An Invitation," <u>Land</u> <u>of</u> <u>Sunshine</u>, 5 (Aug 1896), 120.
1st line: "Aren't you tired of protection from the
weather?"
Rpt. under title "An Invitation from California" in
<u>In</u> <u>This</u> <u>Our</u> <u>World</u>, IV, 120-121.

146. "Our Sky," <u>Land</u> <u>of</u> <u>Sunshine</u>, 6 (Dec 1896), 22.
1st line: "They have a sky in Albion--"
Rpt. under title "Two Skies" in <u>In</u> <u>This</u> <u>Our</u> <u>World</u>,
IV, 90-91.

147. "Their Grass!" <u>Land</u> <u>of</u> <u>Sunshine</u>, 7 (July 1897), 64.
1st line: "They say we have no grass!"
Rpt. under title "Their Grass!--A Protest from
California" in <u>In</u> <u>This</u> <u>Our</u> <u>World</u>, IV, 93-95.

<u>1897</u>

148. "For the New Year," <u>American</u> <u>Fabian</u>, 3 (Jan 1897), 8.
1st line: "For the New Year"
Rpt. in <u>Woman's</u> <u>Journal</u>, 1 Jan 1898, p. 1.

149. "Women Do Not Want It," <u>Woman's</u> <u>Journal</u>, 23 Jan 1897, p.
30.
1st line: "When the woman suffrage argument first
stood upon its legs"
Rpt. in <u>Woman's</u> <u>Column</u>, 23 Jan 1897, p. 1.
Rpt. in <u>In</u> <u>This</u> <u>Our</u> <u>World</u>, IV, 154-157.
Rpt. in <u>Suffrage</u> <u>Songs</u> <u>and</u> <u>Verses</u>, pp. 21-22.
Rpt. in <u>Regionalism</u> <u>and</u> <u>the</u> <u>Female</u> <u>Imagination</u>, 4
(Winter 1979), 41-42.

150. "The King is Dead! Long Live the King!" <u>American</u> <u>Fabian</u>,
3 (Feb 1897), 9.
1st line: "When man, the hunter, winning in the race"
Rpt. in <u>In</u> <u>This</u> <u>Our</u> <u>World</u>, IV, 199-200.
Rpt. in <u>Ruskin</u>, <u>Tenn.</u>, <u>Coming</u> <u>Nation</u>, 20 May 1899,
p. 2.

151. "Wind and Leaves," <u>Land</u> <u>of</u> <u>Sunshine</u>, 6 (March 1897),
152.
1st line: "Wet winds that flap the sodden leaves!"
Rpt. in <u>In</u> <u>This</u> <u>Our</u> <u>World</u>, IV, 152.

152. "How Many Poor!" <u>American</u> <u>Fabian</u>, 3 (April 1897), 8.
1st line: "'Whene'er I take my walks abroad how many

poor I see!'"
>Rpt. in In This Our World, IV, 200-202.
Excerpted in Richard Hofstadter, Social Darwinism in American Thought (Philadelphia: Univ. of Pennsylvania Press, 1944), pp. 100-101. 2nd ed., (Boston: Beacon Press, 1955), p. 230.

153. "To the Preacher," American Fabian, 3 (May 1897), 7.
1st line: "Preach about yesterday, Preacher!"
Rpt. in In This Our World, IV, 19-20.
Rpt. in The Cry for Justice, ed. Upton Sinclair (Philadelphia: John C. Winston Co., 1915), pp. 421-422.

154. "On the Anti-Suffragists," Woman's Journal, 26 June 1897, p. 206.
1st line: "Fashionable women in luxurious homes"
Rpt. under title "The Anti-Suffragists" in In This Our World, IV, 152-154.
Rpt. in Suffrage Songs and Verses, pp. 17-19.
Rpt. in The World Split Open: Four Centuries of Women Poets in England and America 1552-1950, ed. Louise Bernikow (New York: Random House, 1974), pp. 224-226.
Rpt. in On Common Ground: A Selection of Hartford Writers, ed. Alice DeLana and Cynthia Reik (Hartford, Conn.: Stowe-Day Foundation, 1975), pp. 114-115.

155. "Our System," American Fabian, 3 (July 1897), 8.
1st line: "When our economic system wore the cowl"

156. "His Own Labor," American Fabian, 3 (August 1897), 6.
1st line: "Let every man be given what he earns!"
Rpt. under title "The Labor of One" in Ruskin, Tenn., Coming Nation, 23 Oct 1897, p. 1.
Rpt. under title "The Labor of One" in Appeal to Reason, 25 Dec 1897, p. 3.
Rpt. under original title in In This Our World, IV, 190-193.

157. "A Man Must Live," Chicago Social Democrat, 2 Sept 1897, p. 1.
1st line: "A man must live. We justify"
Rpt. in American Fabian, 3 (Nov 1897), 9.
Rpt. in Woman's Journal, 20 Nov 1897, p. 369.
Rpt. in Woman's Column, 20 Nov 1897, p. 2.
Rpt. in In This Our World, IV, 33.
Rpt. in Criterion, 25 June 1898, p. 22.
Rpt. in Bookman, 8 (Sept 1898), 51.

Rpt. in Dial, 1 (Sept 1898), 134.
Rpt. in Deseret Evening News, 2 Dec 1899, 22:4.
Rpt. in Vocal Expression in Speech, ed. Henry Evarts
    Gordon and Rollo L. Lyman (Boston: Ginn and Co.
    1911), p. 180.
Rpt. in Poems of the English Race, ed. Raymond
    Macdonald Alden (New York: Scribner's, 1921), pp.
    367-368.
Rpt. in Types of Poetry Exclusive of the Drama, ed.
    Howard J. Hall (Boston: Ginn and Co., 1927), p.
    317.
Rpt. in Ralph Spaulding Cushman, The Message of
    Stewardship (New York and Nashville: Abingdon-
    Cokesbury Press, 1929), p. 64.
Rpt. in Cynthia Pearl Maus, Youth and Creative
    Living (New York: Harper & Bros., 1932), pp. 142-
    143.

158. "The Four Travelers," Chicago Social Democrat, 2 Sept
    1897, p. 4.
    1st line: "She had found it dull in her city"
    Rpt. under title "Hardly a Pleasure" in In This Our
        World, IV, 195-197.
    Published in German translation by Martin Drescher
        under title "Reisen macht wenig Vergnügen" in Der
        arme Teufel, 20 Jan 1900, p. 73.

159. "To American Men," Chicago Social Democrat, 25 Nov 1897,
    p. 2.
    1st line: "Men! Men! Front of the foremost race!"
    Rpt. in Ruskin, Tenn., Coming Nation, 12 March 1898,
        p. 1.

160. "Christmas," American Fabian, 3 (Dec 1897), 3.
    1st line: "Slow--slow and weak"
    Rpt. in In This Our World, IV, 46-47.

1898

161. "To Labor," American Fabian, 4 (Jan 1898), 3.
    1st line: "Shall you complain who feed the world?"
    Rpt. in In This Our World, IV, 194.
    Rpt. under title "For You" in Woman's Journal, 7 Oct
        1905, p. 160.
    Rpt. in Progressive Woman, 3 (Aug 1910), 13.
    Rpt. in Current Literature, 51 (Oct 1911), 444-445.
    Rpt. in Appeal to Reason, 20 Sept 1913, p. 3.
    Rpt. in Survey, 3 Jan 1914, p. 412.
    Rpt. in The Cry for Justice, ed. Upton Sinclair
        (Philadelphia: John C. Winston Co., 1915), p.

      820.
      Rpt. in Socialism in Verse, ed. W. J. Ghent, Appeal
         Socialist Classics No. 12 (Girard, Kans.: Appeal
         to Reason, [1916]), p. 35.
      Rpt. under title "To the Workers" in Appeal to
         Reason, 15 April 1916, p. 3.
      Rpt. in Appeal to Reason, 30 Dec 1916, p. 3.
      Adapted to music by H. Walford Davies in The
         Fellowship Song Book, part 1 (London: J. Curwen &
         Sons, Ltd., and the Swarthmore Press, 1918), p.
         22.
      Rpt. in The Voice of Labor (Chicago: National
         Women's Trade Union League of America, 1919), p.
         17.
      Rpt. in Elegy in a Country Churchyard, People's
         Pocket Series No. 10 (Girard, Kans.: Appeal to
         Reason, [1919]), p. 10.
      Rpt. in Three Great Poems, People's Pocket Series
         No. 9, (Girard, Kans.: Appeal to Reason, 1919),
         p. 44.
      Rpt. in Three Great Poems, Ten Cent Pocket Series
         No. 9, ed. Emanuel Haldeman-Julius (Girard, Kans.:
         Haldeman-Julius Co., [1920]), p. 44.
      Rpt. in Socialist Ginger-Box, People's Pocket Series
         No. 149 (Girard, Kans.: Appeal to Reason,
         [1921]), p. 38.
      Rpt. in An Anthology of Revolutionary Verse, ed.
         "Marcus Graham" [Shmuel Marcus] (New York: Active
         Press, 1929), p. 191.
      Adapted to music by Caroline L. Goodenough, Melodies
         of the People (Des Moines: privately printed,
         n.d.), p. 20.

162. "Exiles," New England Magazine, NS 17 (Jan 1898), 642.
      1st line: "Exiled from home! The far sea rolls"
      Rpt. in Woman's Journal, 5 Feb 1898, p. 46.
      Rpt. in In This Our World, IV, 74-75.
      Rpt. in Current Literature, 23 (May 1898), 421.
      Published in German translation by Emma Clausen
         under title "Verbannte" in Der arme Teufel, 23
         June 1900, p. 252.

163. "The Beds of Fleur-de-lys," Atlantic Monthly, 81 (Feb
      1898), 167.
      1st line: "High-lying, sea-blown stretches of green
      turf"
      Rpt. in Woman's Journal, 5 March 1898, p. 78.
      Rpt. in Current Literature, 23 (April 1898), 296-
         297.
      Revised and rpt. in In This Our World, IV, 78-79.

Rpt. in An American Anthology 1787-1900, ed. Edmund
C. Stedman (Boston and New York: Houghton
Mifflin, 1900), p. 663.
Rpt. in Golden Songs of the Golden State, ed.
Marguerite Wilkinson (Chicago: A. C. McClurg &
Co., 1917), pp. 80-81.
Rpt. in Living, p. 188.

164. "Fire with Fire," Scribner's, 23 (Feb 1898), 233.
1st line: "There are creeping flames in the nearby
grass"
Rpt. in Woman's Journal, 2 April 1898, p. 110.
Rpt. in In This Our World, IV, 16-18.
Rpt. in Outlook, 21 Jan 1899, p. 176.

165. "Criticism," Chap-book, 1 February 1898, p. 242.
1st line: "The critic eyed the sunset as the umber
turned to gray"
Rpt. in In This Our World, IV, 113.

166. "The Commonplace," Time and the Hour, 26 Feb 1898, pp.
10-11.
1st line: "Life is so weary commonplace! Too fair"
Rpt. in In This Our World, IV, 4-7.

167. "Our Wealth," American Fabian, 4 (March 1898), 3.
1st line: "How poor I am! cries one whose hold"
Rpt. in Ruskin, Tenn., Coming Nation, 26 March 1898,
p. 1.

168. "Noblesse Oblige," American Fabian, 4 (April 1898), 7.
1st line: "I was well born"
Rpt. in Woman's Journal, 23 Sept 1899, p. 302.
Rpt. in Appeal to Reason, 7 April 1900, p. 3.
Rpt. in Comrade, 1 (Jan 1902), 84.
Rpt. in Woman's Journal, 6 Feb 1904, p. 42.

169. "The Fox Who Had Lost His Tail," Chap-book, 1 April
1898, p. 392.
1st line: "The fox who had lost his tail found out"
Rpt. in In This Our World, IV, 104-105.

170. In This Our World, 3rd ed. Boston: Small, Maynard &
Co., 1898. 217 pp.
2nd printing issued in Boston by Small, Maynard & Co.
in 1899. 1st British printing issued in London by G. P.
Putnam's Sons in 1899. 3rd American printing issued by
Small, Maynard & Co. in 1908, 4th in 1913, 5th in 1914.
Reviewed in American Fabian, 4 (June 1898), 12.
Reviewed in Criterion, 25 June 1898, p. 22.

Reviewed in Independent, 21 July 1898, p. 193.
Reviewed in New York Commercial Advertiser, 23 July 1898, 11:2.
Reviewed in St. Louis Observer, 18 Aug 1898, p. 14.
Reviewed by Harry Thurston Peck in Bookman, 8 (Sept 1898), 50-53.
Reviewed by Horace Traubel in Conservator, 9 (Sept 1898), 109.
Reviewed by Charles F. Lummis in Land of Sunshine, 9 (Sept 1898), 201.
Reviewed in Facts and Fiction, 7 (Sept 1898), 46.
Reviewed by William Morton Payne in Dial, 1 Sept 1898, pp. 134-135.
Reviewed in Boston Literary World, 3 Sept 1898, p. 284.
Reviewed by Helen A. Clarke in Poet-lore, 11 (Jan 1899), 124-128.
Reviewed in Book Notes, NS 2 (Jan 1899), 11-12.
Reviewed in Literature (American edition), 17 Jan 1899, p. 43.
Reviewed by W. D. Howells in North American Review, 168 (May 1899), 589-590.
Reviewed in Literature (English edition), 29 July 1899, p. 92.
Reviewed in Athenaeum, 30 Dec 1899, p. 893.
Reviewed by John Davidson, The Man Forbid and Other Essays (Boston: Ball Pub. Co., 1910), pp. 78-85.
Reviewed by H. F. Chettle in Common Cause, 15 Sept 1910, p. 375.

171. "Homes. A Sestina," in In This Our World, IV, 7-8.
1st line: "We are the smiling comfortable homes"

172. "Heroism," in In This Our World, IV, 14-16.
1st line: "It takes great strength to train"
Rpt. in Conservator, 9 (Aug 1898), 81.
Rpt. under title "Strength, Courage, Love" in Woman's Tribune, 11 May 1901, p. 36.
Rpt. under title "It Takes Strength" in New York Call, 24 Sept 1909, 5:1.
Rpt. in Progressive Woman, 5 (Dec 1911), 18.
Excerpted in Equal Rights, 1 July 1938, p. 286.
Excerpted under title "Love" (undated clipping in folder 256, CPG Papers).

173. "The Shield," in In This Our World, IV, 18-19.
1st line: "Fight! said the leader. Stand and fight!"
Published in German translation by Emma Clausen under title "Der Schild" in Der arme Teufel, 28 July 1900.

Rpt. in _Open Gates_, ed. Susan Thompson Spaulding and
Francis Trow Spaulding (Boston and New York:
Houghton Mifflin, 1924), p. 34.

174. "Part of the Battle," in _In This Our World_, IV, 22-23.
1st line: "There is a moment when with splendid joy"
Rpt. in _Criterion_, 25 June 1898, p. 22.

175. "To a Good Many," in _In This Our World_, IV, 28-29.
1st line: "O blind and selfish! Helpless as the
beast"
Excerpted in _Dial_, 1 Sept 1898, p. 134.

176. "How Would You?" in _In This Our World_, IV, 29-32.
1st line: "Half of our misery, half our pain"

177. "Give Way!" in _In This Our World_, IV, 50-51.
1st line: "Shall we not open the human heart"
Rpt. in _His Religion and Hers_, pp. 299-300.
Rpt. in _San Francisco Chronicle_, 30 April 1924, 5:5.
Rpt. in _The World's Great Religious Poetry_, ed.
Caroline Miles Mills (New York: Macmillan, 1926),
p. 148.
Rpt. in Cynthia Pearl Maus, _Youth and Creative
Living_ (New York: Harper & Bros., 1932), p. 68.
Rpt. in _American Friend_, 9 June 1932, p. 419.

178. "Our Loneliness," in _In This Our World_, IV, 60-61.
1st line: "There is no deeper grief than loneliness"
Rpt. in _Century Club Advance_, 1 (Jan-Feb 1903), 68.

179. "Immortality," in _In This Our World_, IV, 62-63.
1st line: "When I was grass, perhaps I may have wept"
Excerpted in _Poems of Evolution_, People's Pocket
Series No. 71 (Girard, Kans.: Appeal to Reason,
[1920]), p. 20.
Excerpted in _Poems of Evolution_, ed. Emanuel
Haldeman-Julius, Ten Cent Pocket Series No. 71
(Girard, Kans.: Haldeman-Julius Co., [1922]), p.
30.
Excerpted in _Poems of Evolution_, ed. Emanuel
Haldeman-Julius, Little Blue Book No. 71 (Girard,
Kans.: Haldeman-Julius Co., n.d.), pp. 16-17.
Excerpted in _Golden Book_, 2 (Aug 1925), 208.

180. "Tree Feelings," in _In This Our World_, IV, 76-77.
1st line: "I wonder if they like it--being trees?"
Rpt. Boothbay Harbor, Me.: Appalachee Camps,
192[0?].
Rpt. Winter Park, Fla.: Angel Alley Press, 193[0?].

181. "Monotony. From California," in In This Our World, IV,
     77-78.
     1st line: "When ragged lines of passing days go by."

182. "Another Creed," in In This Our World, IV, 113-114.
     1st line: "Another creed! We're all so pleased!"

183. "The Little Lion," in In This Our World, IV, 114-115.
     1st line: "It was a little lion lay--"

184. "Our East," in In This Our World, IV, 117-118.
     1st line: "Our East, long looking backward over seas"

185. "Resolve," in In This Our World, IV, 121.
     1st line: "To keep my health!"
         Rpt. in Woman's Journal, 28 May 1898, p. 169.
         Rpt. in Woman's Tribune, 14 July 1900, p. 53.
         Rpt. in American Kitchen Magazine, 16 (Jan 1902),
             128.
         Rpt. in It Can Be Done: Poems of Inspiration, ed.
             Joseph Morris Bachelor and St. Clair Adams
             (Toronto: Ryerson Press, 1921), p. 71.
         Rpt. in The World's Great Religious Poetry, ed.
             Caroline Miles Mills (New York: Macmillan 1926),
             p. 630.
         Rpt. in The Singing Choir, ed. Opal Wheeler and
             Helen deLong (Boston: C. C. Birchard & Co.,
             1933), p. 81.
         Rpt. in A Book of Living Poems, ed. William R.
             Bowlin (Chicago: Albert Whitman & Co., 1934), p.
             67.
         Rpt. in 1000 Quotable Poems: An Anthology of Modern
             Verse, ed. Thomas Curtis Clark (Chicago: Willett,
             Clark & Co., 1937), vol. II, p. 246.

186. "In Mother-Time," in In This Our World, IV, 144-146.
     1st line: "When woman looks at woman with the glory in
     her eyes"

187. "If Mother Knew," in In This Our World, IV, 150-152.
     1st line: "If mother knew the way I felt--"
     Excerpted in Hill, pp. 228-229.

188. "A Mother's Soliloquy," in In This Our World, IV, 171-
     173.
     1st line: "You soft, pink, moving thing!"

189. "They Wandered Forth," in In This Our World, IV, 173.
     1st line: "They wandered forth in springtime woods"

190. "Our Tomorrow," Land of Sunshine, 8 (May 1898), 251.
     1st line: "Back of our wide world-curving waste of
     land"
          Rpt. in Ruskin, Tenn., Coming Nation, 18 Feb 1899,
          p. 1.

191. "Up and Down," Arena, 20 (Oct 1898), 478-479.
     1st line: "Up, up, up! On and out and away"
     Rpt. in Public, 18 Jan 1908, pp. 998-999.
     Rpt. in Forerunner, 3 (Jan 1912), 17-18.

192. "Closed Doors," Scribner's, 24 (Nov 1898), 548.
     1st line: "When it is night and the house is still"

1899

193. "The Rats of Ruskin," Ruskin, Tenn., Coming Nation, 11
     Feb 1899, p. 4.
     1st line: "O Ruskin colony's fair to see"
     Published anonymously. Attributed to CPS on the
        basis of her diary entry for 1 Feb 1899.

194. "Queer People," Cosmopolitan, 27 (June 1899), 172.
     1st line: "The people people work with best are often
     very queer"

195. "Eternal Me," Cosmopolitan, 27 (Sept 1899), 477.
     1st line: "What an exceeding rest 'twill be"
     Rpt. in Current Literature, 26 (Oct 1899), 294.

1900

196. "The Earth, the World and I," Cosmopolitan, 28 (Feb
     1900), 383-384.
     1st line: "'Child,' said the Earth to me"
     Rpt. in Current Literature, 27 (March 1900), 201.

197. "A Protest," Appeal to Reason, 24 March 1900, p. 3.
     1st line: "Away with the hate of the idle rich"
     Rpt. in Ruskin, Tenn., Coming Nation, 16 Feb 1901,
        p. 3.

198. "The Calf Path," Appeal to Reason, 11 Aug 1900, p. 3.
     1st line: "One day through the primeval wood"
     Mistakenly attributed to CPS. Correctly attributed
        to Sam Walter Foss in Appeal to Reason, 22 Nov
        1902, p. 4.

199. "The Ladies' Sin," Woman's Journal, 17 Nov 1900, p. 366.
     1st line: "It was a lovely lady"

Rpt. under title "The Speakers' Sin" in <u>Forerunner</u>,
5 (June 1914), 148.
Rpt. in <u>Living</u>, pp. 279-280.
Rpt. in <u>Scholastic</u>, 15 May 1937, p. 13.

1903

200. "Two Callings," in <u>The Home</u>, pp. vii-xi.
1st line: I hear a deep voice through uneasy
dreaming"
Rpt. in <u>Vocal Expression in Speech</u>, ed. Henry Evarts
Gordon and Rollo L. Lyman (Boston: Ginn and Co.,
1911), pp. 116-119.
Rpt. in <u>Forerunner</u>, 2 (April 1911), 104-105.
Excerpted in <u>Progressive Woman</u>, 5 (Nov 1911), 12.
Rpt. in <u>The Oven Birds</u>, ed. Gail Parker (New York:
Doubleday, 1972), pp. 335-338.
Rpt. in <u>Women in America: A History</u>, ed. Carol
Berkin and Mary Beth Norton (Boston: Houghton
Mifflin, 1979), pp. 173-175.

201. "In Honor," <u>Woman's Journal</u>, 28 March 1903, p. 97.
1st line: "From that dim past where clouds of
darkness lower"
Rpt. in <u>Woman's Tribune</u>, 28 March 1903, p. 33.

202. "A Glimpse of New Orleans," <u>Woman's Journal</u>, 18 April
1903, p. 121.
1st line: "A city of gardens fair"

1904

203. "For This New Year," <u>Woman's Journal</u>, 2 Jan 1904, p. 2.
1st line: "As human creatures in a human world"

204. "The Clam and the Lark," <u>Woman's Journal</u>, 9 Jan 1904, p.
10.
1st line: "'I am happy,' said the clam"
Rpt. in <u>Woman's Column</u>, 9 Jan 1904, p. 1.
Rpt. in <u>Forerunner</u>, 4 (Oct 1913), 278.

205. "Coming," <u>Woman's Journal</u>, 16 Jan 1904, p. 18.
1st line: "Because the time is right, the age is
ready"
Rpt. in <u>Suffrage Songs and Verses</u>, p. 3.
Rpt. in <u>Forerunner</u>, 4 (Nov 1913), 289.

206. "The 'Old' Woman," <u>Woman's Journal</u>, 23 Jan 1904, p. 26.
1st line: "Don't talk to me of modern wives--"
Rpt. in <u>Woman's Column</u>, 23 Jan 1904, p. 3.

207. "Ode to the Cook," Woman's Journal, 30 Jan 1904, p. 34.
     1st line: "O Cook! Domestic cook! no exhumed stone"
     Rpt. in Forerunner, 6 (Aug 1915), 213.

208. "The Departing Housemaid," Twentieth Century Home, 1
     (Feb 1904), 23.
     1st line: "The housewife is held to her labors"

209. "A Valentine to the Bluestocking," Woman's Journal, 13
     Feb 1904, p. 50.
     1st line: "Lady whose pen is a power!"

210. "Her Answer," Woman's Journal, 13 Feb 1904, p. 50.
     1st line: "Have I a heart? and pray why should you
     doubt it?"

211. "Where Women Meet," Woman's Journal, 20 Feb 1904, p. 58.
     1st line: "Where women meet!--the village well"
     Rpt. in Woman's Tribune, 9 April 1904, p. 52.

212. "To the Indifferent Woman," Woman's Journal, 27 Feb
     1904, p. 66.
     1st line: "You are happy in a thousand homes"
     Rpt. in Suffrage Songs and Verses, pp. 19-20.

213. "My Lady's Hat," Twentieth Century Home, 1 (March 1904),
     43.
     1st line: "How wonderful my lady's hat"

214. "The Love of Human Kind," Woman's Journal, 5 March 1904,
     p. 74.
     1st line: "O fast we hold to those we love"
     Rpt. in Forerunner, 4 (Dec 1913), 315.

215. "The Purpose," Woman's Journal, 12 March 1904, p. 82.
     1st line: "Serene she sat, full grown in human power"

216. "Parent and Child," Woman's Journal, 19 March 1904, p.
     90.
     1st line: "Turn now and look your parents in the
     face"

217. "Missing the Way," Woman's Journal, 26 March 1904, p.
     98.
     1st line: "It is so dark! I must have lost my way!"

218. "Human Living," Woman's Journal, 2 April 1904, p. 106.
     1st line: "Living is doing: Doing the deeds that are
     human"

219. "The Primal Power," Woman's Journal, 9 April 1904, p. 114.
     1st line: "Would ye plant the world with new-made men?"
     Rpt. in Forerunner, 4 (Nov 1913), 297.
     Rpt. in His Religion and Hers, pp. 96-97.

220. "What Counts," Woman's Journal, 16 April 1904, p. 122.
     1st line: "You may stuff your brain till it jumps the pan"

221. "The Source," Woman's Journal, 23 April 1904, p. 130.
     1st line: "Behind us lies a long forgetfulness"

222. "Step by Step," Woman's Journal, 30 April 1904, p. 138.
     1st line: "Step by step you told me was the journey--"
     Rpt. in Forerunner, 5 (April 1914), 109.

223. "O 'Tis Love, 'Tis Love, 'Tis Love That Makes the World Go Round," Woman's Journal, 7 May 1904, p. 146.
     1st line: "Why should the people of to-day"
     Rpt. in Forerunner, 6 (Sept 1915), 236.

224. "The Fool-Killer," Woman's Journal, 14 May 1904, p. 154.
     1st line: "O Executioner long-sought on every side!"
     Rpt. in Forerunner, 6 (July 1915), 173.

225. "Faith and Fact," Woman's Journal, 21 May 1904, p. 162.
     1st line: "Have you lost your hold on God?"
     Rpt. in Forerunner, 4 (Sept 1913), 232.

226. "The Coming Day," Woman's Journal, 28 May 1904, p. 170.
     1st line: "As the strong sweet light of the morning"

227. "Whatever Is," Cosmopolitan, 37 (June 1904), 170.
     1st line: "Whatever is we only know"

228. "Where We Leave Off," Woman's Journal, 4 June 1904, p. 178.
     1st line: "Where we leave off and something else begins--"

229. "Pushing into the Days," Woman's Journal, 11 June 1904, p. 186.
     1st line: "Pushing into the days"
     Rpt. in Woman's Column, 11 June 1904, p. 1.

230. "For Each Day," Woman's Journal, 18 June 1904, p. 194.
     1st line: "For each day"

231. "In Alabama Woods," Woman's Journal, 25 June 1904, p. 201.
     1st line: "The wet dark woods--monotonous tall pines"
     Rpt. in Forerunner, 4 (Nov 1913), 284.

232. "Strange Lands," Cosmopolitan, 37 (July 1904), 338.
     1st line: "Of all strange lands whose luring charms we own"

233. "Motion," Woman's Journal, 2 July 1904, p. 210.
     1st line: "We all like motion. Why not grow to feel"

234. "I Am Human," Woman's Journal, 16 July 1904, p. 226.
     1st line: "I was deprived in childhood--robbed of my birthright fair"

235. "Climb a Tree," Woman's Journal, 13 Aug 1904, p. 258.
     1st line: "Look ahead! look ahead! as far as you can see"
     Rpt. in Forerunner, 4 (Dec 1913), 327.

236. "The Eternal Mother to the Bachelor Maid," Woman's Journal, 20 Aug 1904, p. 266.
     1st line: "Child! poor child! so little and so weak!"

237. "Human Pain," Woman's Journal, 27 Aug 1904, p. 274.
     1st line: "A world of joy! a world of light!"

238. "Heirlooms," Woman's Journal, 3 Sept 1904, p. 282.
     1st line: "To my child I have transmitted"
     Rpt. in Forerunner, 4 (Dec 1913), 317.

239. "The Proposal," Woman's Journal, 17 Sept 1904, p. 298.
     1st line: "To be a wife! . . . . He asks of me"

240. "A Protest," Woman's Journal, 22 Oct 1904, p. 338.
     1st line: "O mother! mother! cried the babe"

241. "Kitchen Women," Woman's Journal, 5 Nov 1904, p. 354.
     1st line: "A shallow creature, empty-minded weak"

1905

242. "Out of Doors," Cosmopolitan, 39 (May 1905), 2-3.
     1st line: "Just to be out of doors! So still! So green!"
     Rpt. in Woman's Journal, 20 May 1905, p. 77.
     Rpt. in Literary Digest, 27 May 1905, p. 796.
     Rpt. in Woman's Journal, 7 Sept 1907, p. 141.
     Rpt. in Canadian Magazine, 33 (July 1909), 275.

243. "Labor is Prayer," Out West, 22 (May 1905), 407.
     1st line: "What should I ask of God?"

244. "Freedom," Woman's Journal, 15 July 1905, p. 109.
     1st line: "Only in freedom are great virtues found"

1906

245. "I Would Fain Die a Dry Death," Independent, 14 June
     1906, p. 1401.
     1st line: "The American public is patient"

246. "High Sovereignty," Independent, 12 July 1906, p. 79.
     1st line: "I love to see my little dog"

1907

247. "The Little White Animals," Conservator, 18 (Oct 1907),
     116.
     1st line: "We who have grown human--house-bodied,
     cloth-skinned"
     Rpt. in Forerunner, 1 (Nov 1910), 7.

1908

248. "A Social Puzzle," Public, 15 Feb 1908, p. 1094.
     1st line: "Society sat musing, very sad"
     Rpt. in Forerunner, 7 (Oct 1916), 259.

249. "To the Wise--A Bargain," Public, 22 Feb 1908, p. 1116.
     1st line: "Said the Slumchild to the Wise--"
     Rpt. in Woman's Journal, 7 March 1908, p. 40.
     Rpt. under title "A Bargain" in New York Call, 15
       July 1908, 4:2.
     Rpt. in Socialist Woman, 2 (Aug 1908), 8.
     Rpt. in Progressive Woman, 5 (Nov 1911), 5.
     Rpt. in Forerunner, 5 (Jan 1914), 19.
     Rpt. in California Outlook, 18 July 1914, p. 12.
     Rpt. in Life and Labor, 5 (May 1915), 93.
     Rpt. in Proceedings of the National Conference of
       Social Work (1917), 14-15.
     Rpt. in Playground, 18 (Sept 1924), 370.
     Rpt. in Friends Intelligencer, 7 Nov 1931, p. 936.

250. "Little Leafy Brothers," Conservator, 19 (Aug 1908), 84-
     85.
     1st line: "Little, leafy brothers! You can feel"
     Rpt. in Forerunner, 1 (Feb 1910), 17-18.

1909

251. "Song for Equal Suffrage," Woman's Journal, 13 Feb 1909,
p. 28.
1st line: "Day of hope and day of glory! After
slavery and woe"
Rpt. in Suffrage Songs and Verses, pp. 22-23.
Rpt. in Suffrage Songs (1909), item 5, folder 256.

252. "Water-lilies," Harper's Bazar, 43 (Sept 1909), 887.
1st line: "I shall have water-lilies then--"
Rpt. in New York Evening Mail, 16 Sept 1909, 6:3-4.

253. "Then This," Forerunner, 1 (Nov 1909), i.
1st line: "The news-stands bloom with magazines"

254. "Arrears," Forerunner, 1 (Nov 1909), 4.
1st line: "Our gratitude goes up in smoke"

255. "How Doth the Hat," Forerunner, 1 (Nov 1909), 12.
1st line: "How doth the hat loom large upon her
head!"
Rpt. in Woman Worker (London), 1 Dec 1909, p. 497.
Published in Hungarian translation under title "A
Nagy Kalapok" in A Nó és a társadalom, 1 Jan 1911,
p. 13.

256. "Handicapped," Forerunner, 1 (Nov 1909), 13.
1st line: "One may use the Old Man of the Sea"

257. "Thanksgiving," Forerunner, 1 (Nov 1909), 19.
1st line: "I never thought much of the folks who
pray"

258. "Thanksong," Forerunner, 1 (Nov 1909), 27.
1st line: "Thankful are we for life"

259. "Love," Forerunner, 1 (Dec 1909), i.
1st line: "Not the child-god of our most childish
past"

260. "Steps," Forerunner, 1 (Dec 1909), 6.
1st line: "I was a slave, because I could not see"

261. "Child Labor," Forerunner, 1 (Dec 1909), 10.
1st line: "The children in the Poor House"
Excerpted in Progressive Woman, 4 (Feb 1910), 12.
Rpt. in Womans Era, 1 (March 1910), 88.
Rpt. in Woman's Journal, 31 Dec 1910, p. 254.
Published in Hungarian translation by Polgar Kalman

under title "Gyermekmunka" in A Nó és a
társadalom, 1 Oct 1911, p. 169.
Excerpted in Progressive Woman, 6 (July 1912), 12.
Excerpted in Woman's Journal, 6 Dec 1913, p. 386.
Excerpted in The Cry for Justice, ed. Upton Sinclair
  (Philadelphia: John C. Winston Co., 1915), p.
  662.
Excerpted in Poems of Child Labor (New York:
  National Child Labor Committee, 1924), p. 18.
Excerpted in The Home Book of Quotations, ed. Burton
  Stevenson (New York: Dodd, Mead and Co., 1934),
  p. 1249.
Excerpted in The Cry for Justice, abridged ed.
  (Girard, Kans.: Haldeman-Julius, 1944), p. 23.
Excerpted in The Cry for Justice, 2nd ed., by Upton
  Sinclair (New York: Lyle Stuart, 1963), p. 428.

262. "An Unnatural Daughter," Forerunner, 1 (Dec 1909), 11.
  1st line: "The brooding bird fulfills her task"

263. "His Crutches," Forerunner, 1 (Dec 1909), 18.
  1st line: "Why should the Stronger Sex require"

264. "Get Your Work Done," Forerunner, 1 (Dec 1909), 29.
  1st line: "Get your work DONE, to remember"

1910

265. "A Central Sun," Forerunner, 1 (Jan 1910), i.
  1st line: "Given a central sun--and a rolling world"

266. "Locked Inside," Forerunner, 1 (Jan 1910), 8.
  1st line: "She beats upon her bolted door"
  Rpt. in Woman's Journal, 5 Feb 1910, p. 21.
  Rpt. in Suffrage Songs and Verses, pp. 3-4.

267. ["With God Above--Beneath--Beside,"] Forerunner, 1 (Jan
  1910), 11.
  Rpt. under title "Now" in Suffrage Songs and Verses,
  p. 4.

268. "Here is the Earth," Forerunner, 1 (Jan 1910), 15.
  1st line: "Here is the earth; as big, as fresh, as
  clean"

269. "Breakers," Forerunner, 1 (Jan 1910), 16.
  1st line: "Duck! Dive! Here comes another one!"

270. "The 'Anti' and the Fly," Forerunner, 1 (Jan 1910), 22.
  1st line: "The fly upon the cartwheel"

Rpt. in Woman's Journal, 5 Feb 1910, p. 24.
Rpt. in Suffrage Songs and Verses, p. 19.

271. "The Melancholy Rabbit," Forerunner, 1 (Jan 1910), 30.
1st line: "A melancholy rabbit in distress"

272. "Two Prayers," Forerunner, 1 (Feb 1910), i.
1st line: "Only for these I pray"
Rpt. in The World's Great Religious Poetry, ed.
Caroline Miles Mills (New York: Macmillan, 1926),
p. 442.
Rpt. in 1000 Quotable Poems: An Anthology of Modern
Verse, ed. Thomas Curtis Clark (Chicago: Willett,
Clark & Co., 1937), vol. II, p. 95.

273. "Before Warm February Winds," Forerunner, 1 (Feb 1910),
6.
1st line: "Before warm February winds"

274. "A Crying Need," Forerunner, 1 (Feb 1910), 13.
1st line: "'Lovest thou me?' said the Fair Ladye"

275. "A Walk Walk Walk," Forerunner, 1 (Feb 1910), 25.
1st line: "I once went out for a walk, walk, walk"

276. "The Sands," Forerunner, 1 (March 1910), i.
1st line: "It runs--it runs--the hourglass turning"

277. "The Minor Birds," Forerunner, 1 (March 1910), 5.
1st line: "Shall no bird sing except the
nightingale?"

278. ["When the fig growns on the thistle,"] Forerunner, 1
(March 1910), 12.

279. "Water-lure," Forerunner, 1 (March 1910), 22.
1st line: "We who were born of water, in the warm
slow ancient years"

280. "Aunt Eliza," Forerunner, 1 (March 1910), 25.
1st line: "Seven days had Aunt Eliza"
A collaboration, probably with Martha A. Luther.

281. "The Cripple," Forerunner, 1 (March 1910), 26.
1st line: "There are such things as feet, human feet"

282. "When Thou Gainest Happiness," Forerunner, 1 (April
1910), i.
1st line: "When thou gainest happiness"

283. "For Fear," Forerunner, 1 (April 1910), 6.
     1st line: "For fear of prowling beasts at night"
     Rpt. in Woman's Journal, 5 Aug 1911, p. 242.
     Rpt. in Suffrage Songs and Verses, pp. 5-6.

284. "The Cynosure," Forerunner, 1 (April 1910), 12.
     1st line: "It's a singular thing that the commonest place"

285. ["I gave myself to God,"] Forerunner, 1 (April 1910), 16.

286. "His Agony," Forerunner, 1 (April 1910), 21.
     1st line: "A Human Being goes past my house"

287. "Brain Service," Forerunner, 1 (May 1910), i.
     1st line: "We offer our hearts to God, contrite and broken"

288. "The Kingdom," Forerunner, 1 (May 1910), 8-9.
     1st line: "'Where is Heaven?' asked the Person"

289. "Heaven Forbid," Forerunner, 1 (May 1910), 11.
     1st line: "When I was seventeen, you'd find"

290. "Heresy and Schism," Forerunner, 1 (May 1910), 12.
     1st line: "You may talk about religion with a free and open mind"
     Rpt. in Living, p. 286.

291. "The Puritan," Forerunner, 1 (June 1910), i.
     1st line: "'Where is God?' I cried. 'Let me hear!'"

292. "The Malingerer," Forerunner, 1 (June 1910), 9.
     1st line: "Exempt! She does not have to work!'"
     Rpt. in Suffrage Songs and Verses, 17.

293. "May Leaves," Forerunner, 1 (June 1910), 13.
     1st line: "My whole heart grieves"

294. "The Room at the Top," Forerunner, 1 (June 1910), 18.
     1st line: "There is room at the top"
     Excerpted in Living, p. 189.

295. "The Bawling World," Forerunner, 1 (July 1910), i.
     1st line: "Be not impatient with the bawling world!--"
     Published in Hungarian translation under title "Az Üvöltö Világ" in A Nö és a társadalom, 1 Jan 1911, p. 13.

296. "Shares," Forerunner, 1 (July 1910), 4.
     1st line: "To those who in leisure may meet"

297. "O Faithful Clay!" Forerunner, 1 (July 1910), 9.
     1st line: "O faithful clay of ancient brain!"

298. "Sleeping In," Forerunner, 1 (July 1910), 10.
     1st line: "Men have marched in armies, fleets have
     borne them"

299. "We Eat at Home," Forerunner, 1 (July 1910), 16.
     1st line: "We eat at home; we do not care"
     Rpt. in Progressive Woman, 3 (Aug 1910), 16.
     Rpt. in Woman's Era, 1 (Nov 1910), 656.
     Published in Hungarian translation under title
        "Otthon Eszunk" in A No es a tarsadalom, 1 Jan
        1911, p. 13.

300. "The Earth's Entail," Forerunner, 1 (Aug 1910), i.
     1st line: "No matter how we cultivate the land"

301. ["Sit up and think!"] Forerunner, 1 (Aug 1910), 7.

302. "Alas!" Forerunner, 1 (Aug 1910), 10.
     1st line: "Have those in monstrous hats no glimmering
     dream"

303. "Union House," Forerunner, 1 (Aug 1910), 12.
     1st line: "'We are weak!' said the Sticks, and men
     broke them"

304. "'The Outer Reef!'" Forerunner, 1 (Aug 1910), 16.
     1st line: "Who dares paint daylight?"

305. "To-morrow Night," Forerunner, 1 (Sept 1910), i.
     1st line: "Marginal mile after mile of smooth-running
     granite embankment"

306. "The Power of the Screw," Forerunner, 1 (Sept 1910), 7.
     1st line: "Your car is too big for one person to
     stir--"

307. "The Waiting Room," Forerunner, 1 (Sept 1910), 16.
     1st line: "The waiting room. With row on row"

308. "The Housewife," Forerunner, 1 (Sept 1910), 18.
     1st line: "Here is the House to hold me--cradle of
     all the race"

309. "Only Mine," Forerunner, 1 (Oct 1910), i.

1st line: "They told me what she had done--"

310. "A Question," Forerunner, 1 (Oct 1910), 5.
     1st line: "Why is it, God, that mothers' hearts are
     made"
       Rpt. in Suffrage Songs and Verses, p. 8.

311. "In How Little Time," Forerunner, 1 (Oct 1910), 9.
     1st line: "In how little time, were we so minded"

312. "Like a Banyan Tree," Forerunner, 1 (Oct 1910), 14.
     1st line: "The Earth-plants spring up from beneath"

313. "The Socialist and the Suffragist," Forerunner, 1 (Oct
     1910), 25.
     1st line: "Said the Socialist to the Suffragist"
       Rpt. in Suffrage Songs and Verses, p. 16.
       Rpt. in Woman's Journal, 21 Jan 1911, p. 24.
       Rpt. in Life and Labor, 2 (Feb 1912), 61.
       Rpt. in Survey, 9 March 1912, p. 1915.
       Rpt. in Appeal to Reason, 28 Sept 1912, p. 3.
       Rpt. in Socialist Revolution, no. 27 (Jan-March
         1976), 81-82.
       Rpt. in Flawed Liberation: Socialism and Feminism,
         ed. Sally M. Miller (Westport, Conn., and London:
         Greenwood Press, 1981), pp. 113-114.
       Rpt. in Mari Jo Buhle, Women and American Socialism
         1870-1920 (Urbana: Univ. of Illinois Press,
         1981), p. 214.

314. "Worship," Forerunner, 1 (Nov 1910), i.
     1st line: How does it feel?--"

315. "All This," Forerunner, 1 (Nov 1910), 11.
     1st line: "They laid before her conquering feet"

316. "Many Windows," Forerunner, 1 (Nov 1910), 21.
     1st line: "Many minds are many windows"

317. "Boys Will Be Boys," Forerunner, 1 (Nov 1910), 21.
     1st line: "'Boys will be boys,' and boys have had
     their day"
       Rpt. in Suffrage Songs and Verses, p. 5.

318. "In as Much," Forerunner, 1 (Dec 1910), i.
     1st line: "The Christian arose upon Christmas Day"

319. "Love's Highest," Forerunner, 1 (Dec 1910), 14.
     1st line: "Love came on earth, woke, laughed and

began his dominion"

1911

320. Suffrage Songs and Verses. New York: Charlton Co., 1911. 24 pp.
     Reproduced on microfilm in New Haven, Conn.: Research Publications, 1977 (History of Women #6558).

321. "This is the Year," Forerunner, 2 (Jan 1911), 7.
     1st line: "Forget all the Buried and welcome the Born!"
     Rpt. in Progressive Woman, 6 (June 1912), 15.

322. "Time," Forerunner, 2 (Jan 1911), 9.
     1st line: "'Time was!' said the Brazen Head--"

323. "The Back Way," Forerunner, 2 (Jan 1911), 10.
     1st line: "Along the same old garden path"

324. "B.C.," Forerunner, 2 (Jan 1911), 15.
     1st line: "Stood a man in History--"

325. "Wild Rivers," Forerunner, 2 (Jan 1911), 25.
     1st line: "Brown ragged rivers, straying wide"

326. "Five and Fifty," Girard, Kans., Coming Nation, 28 Jan 1911, p. 11.
     1st line: "If fifty men did all the work"
     Rpt. in Appeal to Reason, 11 April 1914, p. 3.
     Rpt. in Forerunner, 7 (April 1916), 92.
     Rpt. under title "The Foolish Fifty" in Public, 21 April 1916, p. 375.

327. "Individualism," Forerunner, 2 (Feb 1911), 38.
     1st line: "Said each leaf upon the tree"

328. "Bainville Effects," Forerunner, 2 (Feb 1911), 39.
     1st line: "Lockstep, handcuffs, ankle-ball-and-chain"

329. "Life and Death," Forerunner, 2 (Feb 1911), 49.
     1st line: "Life--life comes first; a movement, sense of joy"

330. "Our Pain," Forerunner, 2 (Feb 1911), 50.
     1st line: "My Pain is only one--"

331. "The Cattle Train," Forerunner, 2 (March 1911), 67.
     1st line: "Below my window goes the cattle train"

332. "The Outbreak," _Forerunner_, 2 (March 1911), 68.
    1st line: "There comes a time"

333. "Another Star (Suffrage Song for California),"
    Forerunner, 2 (March 1911), 77.
        1st line: "There are five a-light before us"
        Rpt. in _Suffrage Songs and Verses_, pp. 23-24.
        Rpt. in _Woman's Journal_, 11 March 1911, p. 80.
        Rpt. in _Woman's Journal_, 26 Aug 1911, p. 266.
        Rpt. in _Woman's Journal_, 9 Nov 1912, p. 354.

334. "How Worship We the Lord?" _Forerunner_, 2 (March 1911),
    78.
        1st line: "How worship ye the Lord?"

335. "The Slow People," _Forerunner_, 2 (March 1911), 84.
    1st line: "Slow to anger, the People--"

336. "Be Patient with Society," _Forerunner_, 2 (April 1911),
    95.
        1st line: "Be patient with Society! It is not very
        wise"

337. "The Hand of Man," _Forerunner_, 2 (April 1911), 98.
    1st line: "May our souls be cleanly shriven"
        Rpt. in _Reconstruction_, 1 (March 1919), 96.

338. "Transplanted," _Forerunner_, 2 (April 1911), 99.
    1st line: "Sometimes a plant in its own habitat"

339. "The Artist," _Forerunner_, 2 (May 1911), 126.
    1st line: "Here one of us is born, made as a lens"

340. "Contrasts," _Forerunner_, 2 (May 1911), 127.
    1st line: "Old England thinks our country"

341. "A Diet Undesired," _Forerunner_, 2 (June 1911), 153.
    1st line: "He was set to keep a flock of sheep"

342. "New Friends and Old," _Forerunner_, 2 (June 1911), 155.
    1st line: "There is hope till life is through, my
    dear!"

343. "Stones," _Forerunner_, 2 (June 1911), 160.
    1st line: "Let those cold stones that mark old bones"

344. "Idols," _Forerunner_, 2 (July 1911), 179.
    1st line: "King Olaf smote the Idols and tumbled them
    about"

345. "What Hope," Forerunner, 2 (July 1911), 183.
     1st line: "What hope may we feel for the slave of a
     slave?"

346. "Side Lights," Forerunner, 2 (July 1911), 184.
     1st line: "High shines the golden shield in front"

347. "Knowing Too Much," Forerunner, 2 (July 1911), 195.
     1st line: "For one who holds a righteous rage"

348. "Our Life," Forerunner, 2 (Aug 1911), 205.
     1st line: "A house of a thousand windows"

349. "A Mixture," Forerunner, 2 (Aug 1911), 211.
     1st line: "In poetry and painting and fiction we see"

350. "A Summer Sunday," Forerunner, 2 (Aug 1911), 218.
     1st line: "So still! So still! The breath of damask
     roses"

351. "Leaders," Forerunner, 2 (Aug 1911), 225.
     1st line: "Some leaders lead too far ahead"
     Rpt. in Woman's Journal, 7 Oct 1911, p. 320.

352. "Consequences," Forerunner, 2 (Sept 1911), 234.
     1st line: "You may have a fondness for grapes that
     are green"

353. "The Flag of Peace," Forerunner, 2 (Sept 1911), 234.
     1st line: "Men long have fought for their flying
     flags"
     Rpt. in 1000 Quotable Poems: An Anthology of Modern
     Verse, ed. Thomas Curtis Clark (Chicago: Willett,
     Clark & Co., 1937), vol. II, pp. 276-277.

354. "In the Street," Forerunner, 2 (Sept 1911), 246.
     1st line: "I heard strange music braying in the
     street"

355. "Begin Now," Forerunner, 2 (Oct 1911), 260.
     1st line: "O, never mind what the world has done"

356. "Mrs. Noah," Forerunner, 2 (Oct 1911), 263.
     1st line: "These ladies so slender and stark"

357. ["You may shut your eyes with a bandage,"] Forerunner, 2
     (Oct 1911), 264.

358. "To Choose," Forerunner, 2 (Oct 1911), 273.
     1st line: "In youth, hot youth of hungry heart"

359. "Happiness," Forerunner, 2 (Nov 1911), 287.
     1st line: "Happiness! Dancing Happiness!"

360. "Human Work," Forerunner, 2 (Nov 1911), 291.
     1st line: "Human work is a thing you do"

361. "Thereafter," Forerunner, 2 (Nov 1911), 292.
     1st line: "If I do right, though heavens fall"

362. "Recreation," Forerunner, 2 (Nov 1911), 301.
     1st line: "O hurry, People, hurry!"

363. "Climbing," Forerunner, 2 (Dec 1911), 317.
     1st line: "When you're climbing mountain ranges"

364. "More Females of the Species: After Kipling,"
     Forerunner, 2 (Dec 1911), 318.
     1st line: "When the traveler in the pasture meets the
     he-bull in his pride"
     Rpt. in Woman's Journal, 13 Jan 1912, p. 16.
     Rpt. in Out West, NS 5 (June 1913), 372.

365. "Achievements," Forerunner, 2 (Dec 1911), 319.
     1st line: "There are some folk born to beauty"

366. "Our Trespasses," Forerunner, 2 (Dec 1911), 329.
     1st line: "Forgive us, O forgive us, our trespasses,
     we cry"

1912

367. ["There was a young lady whose wish,"] Forerunner, 3
     (Jan 1912), 16.

368. "Pigs," Forerunner, 3 (Jan 1912), 21.
     1st line: "A Pig, his Piggess, and their Piglets lay"

369. "Plants," Forerunner, 3 (Feb 1912), 39.
     1st line: "Plants may grow in bud and leaf"

370. "Six and Eros," Forerunner, 3 (Feb 1912), 54.
     1st line: "There are six mighty loves, not counting
     Eros"

371. "Entailed," Forerunner, 3 (March 1912), 64.
     1st line: "There's an estate which we must needs
     inherit"

372. "The Educator," Forerunner, 3 (March 1912), 75.
     1st line: "I am a College President"

373. "The Rabbit, the Rhinoceros and I," Forerunner, 3 (March 1912), 83.
     1st line: "The Spirit of Philosophy descended"

374. "Thoughts and Facts," Forerunner, 3 (April 1912), 95.
     1st line: "Once we thought the world was flat"

375. "The Power," Forerunner, 3 (April 1912), 110.
     1st line: "The wide wind blew"

376. "Happy Day," Woman's Journal, 6 April 1912, p. 112.
     1st line: "We want to vote for a bright tomorrow"

377. "We Stand as One," Life and Labor, 2 (May 1912), 153.
     1st line: "Long have we lived apart"

378. "A Vandal," Forerunner, 3 (May 1912), 121.
     1st line: "'M. Lane. Brewster. New York.'"

379. "Idols," Forerunner, 3 (May 1912), 132.
     1st line: "When men made idols, carving the blank eyes"

380. "Sir Almroth Wright's Diagnosis," Forerunner, 3 (June 1912), 153.
     1st line: "'No doctor can ever lose sight'"

381. "The Ultra-Male," Forerunner, 3 (June 1912), 153.
     1st line: "Said the Stallion to the Mare"
     Rpt. in Robert E. Riegel, American Feminists (Lawrence: Univ. Press of Kansas, 1963), p. 169.

382. "'God with Us!'" Forerunner, 3 (July 1912), 173.
     1st line: "'God with us!' cried the men who fought"

383. "Ink Beggars," Forerunner, 3 (July 1912), 188-189.
     1st line: "Into the turbid, weary minds of people today"

384. "Shadows," Forerunner, 3 (Aug 1912), 201.
     1st line: "The shadow in her hair"

385. "The Human Law," Forerunner, 3 (Aug 1912), 214-215.
     1st line: "We watch the solemn courses of the stars"

386. "Moving," Forerunner, 3 (Sept 1912), 236-237.
     1st line: "We move; we must move--are we not alive?"

387. "Good Fighting," Forerunner, 3 (Oct 1912), 259.
     1st line: "When the old bull's power is waning"

388. "In Modern Verse," Forerunner, 3 (Nov 1912), 287.
    1st line: "In modern verse the poet is fain"

389. "You Have To," Forerunner, 3 (Nov 1912), 300.
    1st line: "You have to hold your head up"

390. "Oh, This Christmas," Forerunner, 3 (Dec 1912), 314.
    1st line: "Oh, this 'holy Christmas season'"

391. "As a Business," Forerunner, 3 (Dec 1912), 325.
    1st line: "Do men love the Painted Lady"

392. "How Long, Oh Grandpa," Forerunner, 3 (Dec 1912), 335.
    1st line: "How long, oh Grandpa, must a growing ape"
    Rpt. in Survey, 19 July 1913, p. 528.

1913

393. "Illiopolis," Forerunner, 4 (Jan 1913), 5.
    1st line: "There is a town in Illinois"

394. "Of All Large Lies," Forerunner, 4 (Jan 1913), 19.
    1st line: "Of all large lies wherewith the minds of
    men"

395. "Begin Again," Forerunner, 4 (Jan 1913), 27.
    1st line: "Begin again. The law is clear"

396. "The Year-Dawn," Forerunner, 4 (Jan 1913), 28.
    1st line: "When the sun comes back, when the night-
    clouds part"

397. "A Dream of Gold," Forerunner, 4 (Feb 1913), 45.
    1st line: "He sat alone, encumbered with his gold"
    [Written in collaboration with Martha A. Lane.]

398. "The Fountain of Youth," Forerunner, 4 (Feb 1913), 55.
    1st line: "When the children are grown up and
    married"

399. "Let Us Go Free," Forerunner, 4 (March 1913), 62.
    1st line: "To the Lords of Creation 'twas woman"

400. "Peace to the World," Forerunner, 4 (March 1913), 72.
    1st line: "Peace to the world! The hour is nigh"

401. "Perhaps," Forerunner, 4 (March 1913), 81.
    1st line: "We don't care much for heaven any more"

402. "What Do We Wish in Life?" Forerunner, 4 (April 1913),

90.
   1st line: "What do we wish in life?"

403. "The City of Death," <u>Forerunner</u>, 4 (April 1913), 104.
   1st line: "O city licked and nibbled night and day"
   Rpt. in <u>Survey</u>, 30 Aug 1913, p. 671.

404. "Little Gods," <u>Forerunner</u>, 4 (May 1913), 119.
   1st line: "When men believed in many gods"

405. "The Women are Coming!" <u>Forerunner</u>, 4 (May 1913), 123.
   1st line: "The women are coming to vote! to vote!"

406. ["The green slopes cream with 'innocents'' snow,"]
   <u>Forerunner</u>, 4 (June 1913), 143.

407. "O Heavenly World!" <u>Forerunner</u>, 4 (June 1913), 158.
   1st line: "O heavenly world, where folk may breathe"
   Rpt. in <u>Survey</u>, 22 Nov 1913, p. 202.

408. "Waiting for a Leader," <u>Forerunner</u>, 4 (June 1913), 167.
   1st line: "They were dwarfs and darkly blindfold"

409. ["Coming to England brings a sense,"] <u>Forerunner</u>, 4
   (July 1913), 173.

410. "The Woman in Prison," <u>Forerunner</u>, 4 (July 1913), 189.
   1st line: "'Open the door!' the woman cried"

411. "Twice Beautiful," <u>Forerunner</u>, 4 (Aug 1913), 206.
   1st line: "After long years of wandering in countries
   far and fair"

412. "A Little Garden in the Sea/Pantoum," <u>Forerunner</u>, 4 (Aug
   1913), 215.
   1st line: "My stateroom sings with ocean air"

413. "Food and Clothes," <u>Forerunner</u>, 4 (Sept 1913), 234.
   1st line: "There are such splendid things to do--"
   Rpt. in Hill, p. 276.

414. "A March for Women," <u>Forerunner</u>, 4 (Oct 1913), 258.
   1st line: "Long! Long! Long were the years of
   bondage"

415. "Three Little Antis," <u>Forerunner</u>, 4 (Nov 1913), 287.
   1st line: "Once upon a time there were three"

416. "The Head of the Board," <u>Forerunner</u>, 4 (Nov 1913), 307.
   1st line: "Abraham Stern, of the New York Schools"

417. "Feeding the Wolves," Forerunner, 4 (Dec 1913), 334.
     1st line: "The Russian mother, on her flying sledge"
     Rpt. in Woman's Journal, 10 Jan 1914, p. 11.
     Rpt. in Survey, 21 March 1914, p. 782.

1914

418. "Say It Again," Forerunner, 5 (Feb 1914), 44.
     1st line: "There came to me vision--the sight"

419. "Why Wait?" Forerunner, 5 (Feb 1914), 47.
     1st line: "Why wait? The earth is here"

420. "Now Comes Mary," Forerunner, 5 (March 1914), 63.
     1st line: "He has had Martha"

421. "Chivalry: Man Speaks," Forerunner, 5 (March 1914), 68.
     1st line: "Fighting is meat and drink to me--I am
     made so"

422. "A Prayer for All Speakers," Forerunner, 5 (March 1914),
     82.
     1st line: "Too often has the speaker bayed"

423. "This is a Lady's Hat: A Trio of Triolets," Forerunner,
     5 (April 1914), 92.
     1st line: "This is a lady's hat--"
     Rpt. in Public, 17 April 1914, p. 379.

424. "The Real Religion," Forerunner, 5 (May 1914), 121.
     1st line: "Man, the hunter, Man, the warrior"
     Rpt. in His Religion and Hers, pp. vii-viii.

425. "Life Everlasting," Forerunner, 5 (June 1914), 145.
     1st line: "Whoso standeth close to God"

426. "Crops," Forerunner, 5 (July 1914), 186.
     1st line: "If you are raising radishes"
     Rpt. in Amerikanische Turnzeitung, 10 Nov 1935, p.
     13.

427. "Faith and Knowledge," Forerunner, 5 (July 1914), 194.
     1st line: "Faith is but a little lantern"

428. "An Army with Banners," Forerunner, 5 (Aug 1914), 213.
     1st line: "Together men faced the mammoth"
     Rpt. in San Francisco Star, 18 Dec 1915, p. 9.

429. "Limiting Life," Forerunner, 5 (Aug 1914), 222.
     1st line: "'Life is too numerous!' said he"

430. "Santa Clara Hills," Forerunner, 5 (Sept 1914), 231.
1st line: "Oh bare, round-bosomed, dimpling hills!"

431. "Heights," Forerunner, 5 (Sept 1914), 249.
1st line: "The grasses run like sea-waves high"

432. "For Power," Forerunner, 5 (Oct 1914), 258.
1st line: "For power--we only have to hold"

433. "The Traitor," Forerunner, 5 (Oct 1914), 262.
1st line: "Because of us, our numbers and our growth"

434. "Matriatism," Forerunner, 5 (Nov 1914), 299.
1st line: "Small is the thought of 'Fatherland'"

435. "Womanhood," Delineator, 85 (Dec 1914), 5.
1st line: "We fear, while old walls break and old
bonds sever"

436. "Song for the World's Flag," Forerunner, 5 (Dec 1914),
321.
1st line: "As the green earth shines in the star-
filled sky"

437. "The Larger Love," Forerunner, 5 (Dec 1914), 325.
1st line: "Too strong and great for church or state"

438. "The Coming Light," Forerunner, 5 (Dec 1914), 332.
1st line: "And a light shall fly from mind to mind"

1915

439. "The Gunman," Forerunner, 6 (Jan 1915), 11.
1st line: "Prowling in the alley, loafing in the bar"

440. "Belgium and the World," Forerunner, 6 (Jan 1915), 19.
1st line: "There's a little land called Belgium"

441. "More Than Peace," Forerunner, 6 (Feb 1915), 37-38.
1st line: "We must have more than Peace"

442. "Since God Is So," Forerunner, 6 (Feb 1915), 44.
1st line: "Since God is true--a fact"

443. "The Larger Country," Forerunner, 6 (March 1915), 74.
1st line: "Shall we, who love our country"

444. "California Colors," Forerunner, 6 (April 1915), 93.
1st line: "Colors of a winter country"

445. "Campaign Song for Eastern States," Forerunner, 6 (April 1915), 100.
     1st line: "The Antis tell of Awful Things"
     Rpt. under title "Eastern States Campaign Song" in Woman's Journal, 17 April 1914, p. 120.

446. "The Ends of God," Forerunner, 6 (April 1915), 110.
     1st line: "God is a name man's growing mind"

447. "Our World," Forerunner, 6 (May 1915), 130-131.
     1st line: "Is it so hard, for us, whose minds have grown"

448. "'Special Dry Toast': Railroad Diner," Forerunner, 6 (June 1915), 149.
     1st line: "'Special dry toast'--at fifteen cents"

449. "The New Sovereignty," Forerunner, 6 (June 1915), 156-157.
     1st line: "There is no Sovereign State. The human race"

450. "The Daily Squid," Forerunner, 6 (Aug 1915), 206.
     1st line: "The Squid he has no implements"

451. "Summer Air," Forerunner, 6 (Aug 1915), 221.
     1st line: "As pleasant as the summer air"

452. "A Faith That Grows," Forerunner, 6 (Oct 1915), 258.
     1st line: "A faith that grows! We used to think"

453. "Full Motherhood: A Villanelle," Forerunner, 6 (Oct 1915), 272.
     1st line: "There are children many--this child of mine"

454. "Some Day," Forerunner, 6 (Nov 1915), 294.
     1st line: "Some day we shall be wise enough to know"

455. "Experts," Forerunner, 6 (Dec 1915), 313.
     1st line: "Professor Johnson bids us tax"

456. "Looking Across," Forerunner, 6 (Dec 1915), 315.
     1st line: "How can one write of love"

1916

457. "Why? To the United States of America 1915-1916," Forerunner, 7 (Jan 1916), 5.
     1st line: "Why does America sit so still"

458. "A Ruffle of Pantalette," Forerunner, 7 (Jan 1916), 11.
     1st line: "A ruffle of pantalette"

459. "Is It So?" Forerunner, 7 (Feb 1916), 37.
     1st line: "One vital point we have to ascertain"

460. "To One Who Suffers," Forerunner, 7 (Feb 1916), 44.
     1st line: "How can you, Soul, endure a life of pain"

461. "Wouldn't You Think," Star of Hope, ca. March 1916.
     1st line: "Wouldn't you think, if it is"
     Rpt. in Survey, 22 April 1916, p. 101.
     Rpt. in Public, 19 May 1916, p. 473.

462. "The Splendid Faith," Forerunner, 7 (May 1916), 129-130.
     1st line: "Such little faiths have served us in the
     past"

463. "The Power Called God," Forerunner, 7 (June 1916), 158-
     159.
     1st line: "God! Splendid God that works!"

464. "Their Answer," Forerunner, 7 (July 1916), 177.
     1st line: "What shall we do? The women prayed"

465. "Wives," Forerunner, 7 (Sept 1916), 234.
     1st line: "Man had a wife who had brawn and bone"

466. "With Fire and Sword," Forerunner, 7 (Sept 1916), 243.
     1st line: "With fire and sword the men of old"

467. "Two Ways to Govern," Forerunner, 7 (Sept 1916), 245.
     1st line: "By the process of commanding"

468. "The People," Forerunner, 7 (Sept 1916), 252.
     1st line: "The people is a beast of muddy brain"

469. "Santa Claus," Forerunner, 7 (Dec 1916), 325.
     1st line: "Isn't it time we stopped lying to
     children"

470. "Woman's Hour," Woman's Journal, 9 Dec 1916, p. 397.
     1st line: "Not for herself! Though sweet the air of
     freedom"

1920

471. "Pikers," New York Times, 31 Oct 1920, section 7, 1:1-2.
     1st line: "Sit in! Sit in! cry the Nations"
     Rpt. in Literary Digest, 27 Nov 1920, p. 42.

472. "To the Women of 1920," New York <u>World</u>, 2 Nov 1920,
14:3.
1st line: "On the women of 1920, so newly freed"

1923

473. "The Internationalist," <u>Life</u>, 15 March 1923, p. 13.
1st line: "He spoke with pride as a superior soul"

1924

474. "Twigs," <u>Life</u>, 21 Feb 1924, p. 4.
1st line: "'Tis an amusing thing to see"

1925

475. "The Oyster and the Starfish," <u>Forum</u>, 74 (Oct 1925),
629.
1st line: "Sat a fat and juicy Oyster in a large and
lumpy shell"

1927

476. "A Psalm of 'Lives,'" <u>Saturday Review of Literature</u>, 26
Nov 1927, p. 358.
1st line: "They tell us now in mystic numbers"
Excerpted in Halford E. Luccock, <u>Contemporary
American Literature and Religion</u> (Chicago and New
York: Willett, Clark & Co., 1934), p. 162.
Rpt. in Reed Smith, <u>The Teaching of Literature in
the High School</u> (New York: American Book Co.,
1935), pp. 365-366.

1931

477. "Two Hundred Words," in <u>A Purse of Gold</u> (New York:
privately printed, 1931), unnumbered page.
1st line: "Two hundred words--a scant array"
Copy extant in folder 271, CPG Papers.

1933

478. "The Front Wave," <u>Saturday Review of Literature</u>, 7 Jan
1933, p. 372.
1st line: "The little front wave ran up on the sand"
Rpt. in Halford E. Luccock, <u>Contemporary American
Literature and Religion</u> (Chicago and New York:
Willett, Clark & Co., 1934), p. 181.
Rpt. in Zona Gale, "Foreword" to <u>Living</u>, p. xxxii.

479. "Some Nordics," American Hebrew, 18 Aug 1933, p. 203.
     1st line: "Swelling with racial pride they stand"

1934

480. "A Hundred Years Hence," lyric published in broadside at
     the Ninth Conference on the Cause and Cure of War, 17
     Jan 1934.
     1st line: "A hundred years hence they'll be peace in
     the world"
     Copy extant in NAWSA Papers, Library of Congress.

1935

481. ["O rock and ice! I offered you my hand,"] in Living, p.
     55.

482. ["For this new year unknown whose steady wing,"] in
     Living, p. 135.

483. ["I wait the coming year too sad for fear,"] in Living,
     pp. 135-136.

484. "The Bad Little Coo-Bird," in Living, pp. 160-161.
     1st line: "In the morning, in the bed"
     According to CPS's diary (vol. 30, CPG Papers) and
     her autobiography, this poem may have been published
     as early as 1891, though I have been unable to
     locate an earlier printing.

485. "For 1899," in Living, p. 277.
     1st line: "For this New Year--and last"

486. "Blending," in Living, p. 296.
     1st line: "Sometimes that long, high-lying western
     wall"

487. ["So proud of our grandsires are we,"] in Living, p.
     325.

Undated

488. "Thankfulness."
     1st line: "Not one sorrow or distress"
     Unsigned clipping in folder 190, CPG Papers.

489. "Sophia and Amelia."
     1st line: "For four and forty varnished years"
     Unsigned clipping in folder 193, CPG Papers.

490. "The Crusade Hymn."
   1st line: "Our eyes have seen the glory of the coming
   of the day"
      Signed clipping in folder 256, CPG Papers.

FICTION

1886

491. "A Transparency," Alpha, 1 Dec 1886, pp. 6-7.

1890

492. "That Rare Jewel," Woman's Journal, 17 May 1890, p. 158.

493. "The Unexpected," Kate Field's Washington, 21 May 1890, pp. 335-336.
     Rpt. in Boston Budget, 29 June 1890, p. 10.
     Rpt. in Forerunner, 4 (Nov 1913), 281-284.

494. "Circumstances Alter Cases," Kate Field's Washington, 23 July 1890, pp. 55-56.
     Rpt. in Boston Budget, 17 Aug 1890, p. 10.
     Rpt. in Forerunner, 5 (April 1914), 85-88.

1891

495. "My Poor Aunt," Kate Field's Washington, 7 Jan 1891, pp. 9-11.
     Rpt. in Forerunner, 4 (Dec 1913), 309-313.

496. "Society and the Philosopher," Kate Field's Washington, 18 Feb 1891, p. 109.
     Rpt. in Forerunner, 5 (April 1914), 93-94.

497. "Society and the Baby," Kate Field's Washington, 18 March 1891, pp. 165-166.
     Rpt. in Woman Worker (London), 24 Nov 1909, p. 482.

498. "A Walk for Two," Pacific Monthly, 3 (May 1891), 194-198.

499. "The Giant Wistaria," New England Magazine, NS 4 (June 1891), 480-485.

500. "My Fellow Traveller," Pacific Rural Press, 27 June
     1891, p. 614.
        Rpt. in Pacific Monthly, 3 (June-July 1891), 237-241.

501. "Her Business," Wasp, 5 Sept 1891, p. [12].

502. "Go to the Sluggard, Thou Ant!" Wasp, 5 Sept 1891, p.
     [12].

503. "The Sole Use of Poetry," Wasp, 19 Sept 1891, p. 2.

504. "An Extinct Angel," Kate Field's Washington, 23 Sept
     1891, pp. 199-200.

1892

505. "The Yellow Wall-paper," New England Magazine, 5 (Jan
     1892), 647-656.
        Reviewed in Boston Transcript, 1 Jan 1892, 6:5.
        Reviewed in Boston Transcript, 8 April 1892, 6:2.
        Rpt. in The Great Modern American Stories, ed. W. D.
           Howells (New York: Boni and Liveright, 1920), pp.
           320-337.
        Rpt. in American Mystery Stories, ed. Carolyn Wells
           (New York: Oxford Univ. Press, 1927), pp. 177-197.
        Rpt. in Golden Book, 18 (Oct 1933), 363-373.
        Published in Finnish translation by Irene Tokoi under
           title "Keltainen Seinapaperi" in Nykyaika, 15 June
           1934, pp. 1-7.
        Rpt. in A Book of the Short Story, ed. E. A. Cross
           (New York: American Book Co., 1935), pp. 400-413.
        Rpt. in Psychopathology and Literature, ed. Leslie Y.
           Rabkin (San Francisco: Chandler Publishing Co.,
           1966), pp. 95-111.
        Rpt. in The Writer's Signature: Idea in Story and
           Essay, ed. Elaine Gottleib Hemley (Glenview, Ill.:
           Scott, Foresman and Co., 1972), pp. 87-99.
        Rpt. in The Oven Birds, ed. Gail Parker (New York:
           Doubleday, 1972), pp. 317-334.
        Rpt. in Fiction 100, 2nd ed. James H. Pickering (New
           York: Macmillan, 1978), pp. 363-371. 3rd ed., (New
           York: Macmillan, 1982), pp. 410-419.
        Adapted in "The Yellow Wall-paper" (Bloomington:
           Indiana University Audio-Visual Center, 1978).
           [Film and video recording.]
        Rpt. in Charlotte Perkins Gilman Reader, pp. 3-19.
        Adapted in "The Yellow Wall-paper" (Athens, Georgia:
           Peabody Recording Center, 1981). [Video recording.]
        See also items 529, 1556, 2418, 2433-2434, 2436-2437,
           2439, 2442, 2449, 2453.

1893

506. "The Rocking-Chair," Worthington's Illustrated, 1 (May 1893), 453-459.
Rpt. in Boston Budget, 25 June 1893, p. 10.

507. "Deserted," San Francisco Call, 10 July 1893, 9:1-2.

508. "An Elopement," San Francisco Call, 17 July 1893, 9:1.

509. "Through This," Kate Field's Washington, 13 Sept 1893, p. 166.

1894

510. "The Misleading of Pendleton Oaks," Impress, 6 Oct 1894, pp. 4-5. [Imitation of Rudyard Kipling.]
See also "Last Week's Story," Impress, 13 Oct 1894, p. 2; and "The Successful Guesser," Impress, 20 Oct 1894, p. 5.

511. "A Day's Berryin'," Impress, 13 Oct 1894, pp. 4-5. [Imitation of Mary E. Wilkins.]
See also "Story Studies II," Impress, 20 Oct 1894, p. 5.

512. "The Mother's Prayer," Impress, 20 Oct 1894, p. 4. [Imitation of Olive Schreiner.]
Rpt. in Forerunner, 4 (June 1913), 156-158.
See also "Story Studies III," Impress, 27 Oct 1894, p. 5; and "The Winner of the Story Prize," Impress, 3 Nov 1894, p. 2.

513. "Clifford's Tower," Impress, 27 Oct 1894, pp. 4-5. [Imitation of Nathaniel Hawthorne.]
See also "Story Studies IV," Impress, 3 Nov 1894, p. 4.

514. "Ad'line," Impress, 3 Nov 1894, pp. 4-5. [Imitation of Hamlin Garland.]
See also "Story Studies," Impress, 10 Nov 1894, p. 5; and "The Prize Winner," Impress, 17 Nov 1894, p. 5.

515. "Two Better Than One," Impress, 17 Nov 1894, pp. 4-5. [Imitation of Edward Everett Hale.]
See also "Story Studies," Impress, 24 Nov 1894, p. 5; and "The Prize Winners," Impress, 8 Dec 1894, p. 3.

516. "From 'Thurston Gower,'" Impress, 24 Nov 1894, pp. 4-5. [Imitation of George Eliot.]

See also "Story Studies," Impress, 1 Dec 1894, p. 5.

517. "Five Girls," Impress, 1 Dec 1894, pp. 4-5. [Imitation of Louisa May Alcott.]
See also "Story Studies," Impress, 8 Dec 1894, p. 5; and "Story Guesses," Impress, 15 Dec 1894, p. 5.

518. "The Unwatched Door," Impress, 8 Dec 1894, pp. 4-5. [Imitation of Edgar Allan Poe.]
See also "Story Studies," Impress, 15 Dec 1894, p. 5; and "Story Study Prize," Impress, 22 Dec 1894, p. 11.

519. "The Eating House," Impress, 15 Dec 1894, pp. 4-5. [Imitation of Charles Dickens.]
See also "Story Studies," Impress, 22 Dec 1894, p. 5; and "Prize Winner," Impress, 29 Dec 1894, p. 5.

520. "Entailed: A New Christmas Story," Impress, 22 Dec 1894, pp. 4-5.

521. "One Way Out," Impress, 29 Dec 1894, pp. 4-5. [Imitation of Henry James.]
See also "Story Studies," Impress, 5 Jan 1895, p. 5; and "The Story Study Prize," Impress, 12 Jan 1895, p. 5.

1895

522. "A Cabinet Meeting," Impress, 5 Jan 1895, pp. 4-5. [Imitation of Edward Bellamy.]
See also "Story Studies," Impress, 12 Jan 1895, p. 3; and "The Prize Winner," Impress, 19 Jan 1895, p. 5.

523. "An Unpatented Process," Impress, 12 Jan 1895, pp. 4-5. [Imitation of Mark Twain.]
See also "Story Studies," Impress, 26 Jan 1895, p. 3.

524. "My Landlady's Daughter," Impress, 19 Jan 1895, pp. 4-5. [Imitation of Washington Irving.]
See also "Story Studies," Impress, 2 Feb 1895, p. 3.

525. "The Ending of the First Lesson," Impress, 26 Jan 1895, pp. 4-5.

526. "My Cousin Mary," Impress, 9 Feb 1895, pp. 4-5.

527. "An Unnatural Mother," Impress, 16 Feb 1895, pp. 4-5.
Abridged in Forerunner, 4 (June 1913), 141-143.
Rpt. in full under title "The Unnatural Mother" in

Forerunner, 7 (Nov 1916), 281-285.
Rpt. in _Charlotte Perkins Gilman Reader_, pp. 57-65.

1898

528. "The Lake of Mrs. Johnworth," _Criterion_, 22 Oct 1898, pp. 3-4.

1899

529. _The Yellow Wall-paper_ (Boston: Small, Maynard & Co., 1899). 55 pp.
     Reproduced on microfilm in Wright's American Fiction series, series III, reel G12, no. 2177. Reproduced on microfilm Woodbridge, Conn.: Research Publications, 1970-78. Rpt. with an afterword by Elaine Hedges in Old Westbury, New York: Feminist Press, 1973. 63 pp.
     Reviewed by Anne Montgomerie in _Conservator_, 10 (June 1899), 60-61.
     Reviewed in Ruskin, Tenn., _Coming Nation_, 24 June 1899, p. 4.
     Reviewed by Henry B. Blackwell in _Woman's Journal_, 17 June 1899, p. 187.
     Reviewed in _Time and the Hour_, 17 June 1899, p. 9.
     Reviewed in _Literature_ (American edition), 14 July 1899, p. 18.
     Reviewed in Boston _Literary World_, 22 July 1899, p. 236.
     Reviewed in _Criterion_, 22 July 1899.

1904

530. "Their Dressmaker," _Woman's Journal_, 25 June 1904, p. 202.

1907

531. "A Woman's Utopia," _Times Magazine_, 1 (Jan 1907), 215-220; 1 (Feb 1907), 369-376; 1 (March 1907), 498-500. A fourth installment of this incomplete serial novel (pp. 591-597) is extant in page proofs in folder 260 of the Gilman Papers at Radcliffe College.

1908

532. "Aunt Mary's Pie Plant," _Woman's Home Companion_, 35 (June 1908), pp. 14, 18-19.

533. "Three Women," _Success_, 11 (Aug 1908), 490-491, 522-526.

See also item 681.

1909

534. "A Garden of Babies," Success, 12 (June 1909), 370-371, 410-411.

535. "Introducing the World, the Flesh, and the Devil," Forerunner, 1 (Nov 1909), 13.

536. "What Diantha Did," Forerunner, 1 (Nov 1909), 13-18; 1 (Dec 1909), 11-18; 1 (Jan 1910), 16-21; 1 (Feb 1910), 13-17; 1 (March 1910), 12-17; 1 (April 1910), 12-16; 1 (May 1910), 12-17; 1 (June 1910), 14-18; 1 (July 1910), 10-16; 1 (August 1910), 12-16; 1 (Sept 1910), 7-16; 1 (Oct 1910), 14-20; 1 (Nov 1910), 11-16; 1 (Dec 1910), 8-12.
    Reviewed in Woman's Journal, 28 May 1910, p. 88.
    Excerpted in Charlotte Perkins Gilman Reader, pp. 125-140.
    See also item 540.

537. "Three Thanksgivings," Forerunner, 1 (Nov 1909), 5-12.

538. "According to Solomon," Forerunner, 1 (Dec 1909), 1-5.

539. "The Poor Relation," Forerunner, 1 (Dec 1909), 18.

1910

540. What Diantha Did. New York: Charlton Co., 1910.
    Rpt. in London: T. Fisher Unwin, 1912. 262 pp.
    Reviewed in Womans Era, 1 (Jan 1911), 778-779.
    Reviewed in Bookman, 32 (Feb 1911), 578.
    Reviewed by Lillian Brandt in Survey, 11 Feb 1911, p. 808.
    Reviewed in A. L. A. Booklist, 7 (March 1911), 302.
    Reviewed in Independent, 16 March 1911, p. 571-572.
    Reviewed in London Academy, 31 Aug 1912, p. 272.
    Reviewed by Alice Stone Blackwell in Woman Citizen, 13 Sept 1919, pp. 366-367.
    See also item 536.

541. "Her Housekeeper," Forerunner, 1 (Jan 1910), 2-8.

542. "The Barrel," Forerunner, 1 (Jan 1910), 22.

543. "An Offender," Forerunner, 1 (Feb 1910), 1-6.

544. "Two Storks." Forerunner, 1 (Feb 1910), 12-13.

Rpt. in Woman's Journal, 26 Feb 1910, p. 33.
Rpt. in Public, 13 Jan 1911, pp. 38-39.
Rpt. in Life and Labor, 3 (March 1913), 76-77.
Rpt. in Woman's Voice: An Anthology, ed. Josephine
  Conger (Boston: Stratford Co., 1918), pp. 280-283.

545. "A Middlesized Artist," Forerunner, 1 (March 1910), 1-5.

546. "Naughty," Forerunner, 1 (March 1910), 10-11.

547. "Martha's Mother," Forerunner, 1 (April 1910), 1-6.

548. "A Village of Fools," Forerunner, 1 (April 1910), 11.

549. "When I Was a Witch," Forerunner, 1 (May 1910), 1-6.
  Rpt. in Charlotte Perkins Gilman Reader, pp. 21-31.

550. "The House of Apples," Forerunner, 1 (May 1910), 17-18.

551. "Making a Living," Forerunner, 1 (June 1910), 1-6.

552. "Prisoners," Forerunner, 1 (June 1910), 13.

553. "A Coincidence," Forerunner, 1 (July 1910), 1-4.

554. "Only an Hour," Forerunner, 1 (July 1910), 20.

555. "The Cottagette," Forerunner, 1 (Aug 1910), 1-5.
  Rpt. in Charlotte Perkins Gilman Reader, pp. 47-56.

556. "Her Pets," Forerunner, 1 (Aug 1910), 11.

557. "Mr. Robert Grey, Sr.," Forerunner, 1 (Sept 1910), 1-4.

558. "While the King Slept," Forerunner, 1 (Sept 1910), 17-18.

559. "The Boys and the Butter," Forerunner, 1 (Oct 1910), 1-5.

560. "The World and the Three Artists," Forerunner, 1 (Oct 1910), 8-9.

561. "My Astonishing Dodo," Forerunner, 1 (Nov 1910), 1-5.

562. "The Good Man," Forerunner, 1 (Nov 1910), 16.
  Rpt. in Public, 24 Feb 1911, p. 186.

563. "A Word in Season," Forerunner, 1 (Dec 1910), 1-5.

564. "The Permanent Child," Forerunner, 1 (Dec 1910), 15-17.
Rpt. in LaFollette's, 1 April 1911, p. 10.
Rpt. in Pasadena Star, 3 May 1911, p. 2.

1911

565. "The Crux," Forerunner, 2 (Jan 1911), 10-15; 2 (Feb
1911), 39-46; 2 (March 1911), 68-73; 2 (April 1911), 99-
103; 2 (May 1911), 127-132; 2 (June 1911), 155-160; 2
(July 1911), 184-189; 2 (Aug 1911), 211-218; 2 (Sept
1911), 234-240; 2 (Oct 1911), 264-270; 2 (Nov 1911),
292-298; 2 (Dec 1911), 319-325.
    Excerpted in Women in America: A History, ed. Carol
        Berkin and Mary Beth Norton (Boston: Houghton
        Mifflin, 1979), p. 176.
    Excerpted in Charlotte Perkins Gilman Reader, pp.
        118-122.
    See also item 566.

566. The Crux. New York: Charlton Co., 1911. 311 pp.
    Reviewed by Floyd Dell in Progressive Woman, 5 (Feb
        1912), 10.
    Reviewed in Independent, 21 March 1912, p. 629.
    See also item 565.

567. "Moving the Mountain," Forerunner, 2 (Jan 1911), 21-25;
2 (Feb 1911), 51-56; 2 (March 1911), 79-84; 2 (April
1911), 107-113; 2 (May 1911), 135-141; 2 (June 1911),
163-168; 2 (July 1911), 163-168; 2 (Aug 1911), 219-224;
2 (Sept 1911), 247-252; 2 (Oct 1911), 274-280; 2 (Nov
1911), 302-309; 2 (Dec 1911), 330-335.
    Excerpted in Charlotte Perkins Gilman Reader, pp.
        180-188.
    See also item 568.

568. Moving the Mountain. New York: Charlton Co., 1911.
290 pp.
    Reviewed in New York Times, 4 Feb 1912, section 6, p.
        52.
    Reviewed in Survey, 10 Feb 1912, p. 1745.
    Reviewed in Independent, 21 March 1912, pp. 629-630.
    See also item 567.

569. "The Widow's Might," Forerunner, 2 (Jan 1911), 3-7.
    Rpt. in Charlotte Perkins Gilman Reader, pp. 98-106.

570. "The Old Woman and the New Year," Forerunner, 2 (Jan
1911), 19-20.

571. "Mrs. Potter and the Clay Club," Forerunner, 2 (Feb

1911), 31-36.

572. "Some Sins are Worse Than Others," Forerunner, 2 (Feb 1911), 50.
    Rpt. in Public, 22 Nov 1912, pp. 1121-1122.

573. "Mrs. Beazley's Deeds," Woman's World, 27 (March 1911), 12-13, 58.
    Rpt. in Forerunner, 7 (Sept 1916), 225-232.

574. "An Honest Woman," Forerunner, 2 (March 1911), 59-65.
    Rpt. in Charlotte Perkins Gilman Reader, pp. 75-86.

575. "The Jumping-Off Place," Forerunner, 2 (April 1911), 87-93.

576. "The Sensible Dead Man," Forerunner, 2 (April 1911), 106-107.

577. "Lovely Pie," Forerunner, 2 (May 1911), 133.

578. "The Wild Oats of the Soul," Forerunner, 2 (June 1911), 161-162.

579. "In Two Houses," Forerunner, 2 (July 1911), 171-177.

580. "Her Doll," Forerunner, 2 (July 1911), 183.

581. "What Occupation?" Forerunner, 2 (Aug 1911), 199-204.

582. "The Only Hero," Forerunner, 2 (Aug 1911), 209-210.

583. "Turned," Forerunner, 2 (Sept 1911), 227-232.
    Rpt. in Charlotte Perkins Gilman Reader, pp. 87-97.

584. "Old Water," Forerunner, 2 (Oct 1911), 255-259.

585. "The Journey," Forerunner, 2 (Oct 1911), 270-271.

586. "Old Mrs. Crosley," Forerunner, 2 (Nov 1911), 283-287.

587. "Mother's Coming," Forerunner, 2 (Nov 1911), 300-301.
    Rpt. in Woman's Journal, 30 Dec 1911, p. 410.

588. "Making a Change," Forerunner, 2 (Dec 1911), 311-315.
    Rpt. in Charlotte Perkins Gilman Reader, pp. 66-74.

589. "The Pet of an Angel," Forerunner, 2 (Feb 1911), 328-329.

1912

590. "Mag-Marjorie," Forerunner, 3 (Jan 1912), 10-15; 3 (Feb 1912), 40-48; 3 (Mar 1912), 67-73; 3 (April 1912), 96-103; 3 (May 1912), 122-128; 3 (June 1912), 154-160; 3 (July 1912), 181-187; 3 (Aug 1912), 208-214; 3 (Sept 1912), 238-244; 3 (Oct 1912), 265-272; 3 (Nov 1912), 287-294; 3 (Dec 1912), 318-325.

591. "A Mischievous Rudiment," Forerunner, 3 (Jan 1912), 1-5.

592. "The Devout Farmers," Forerunner, 3 (Jan 1912), 20-21.

593. "Mrs. Elder's Idea," Forerunner, 3 (Feb 1912), 29-33.

594. "The Pious Engine," Forerunner, 3 (Feb 1912), 48.

595. "An Innocent Girl," Forerunner, 3 (March 1912), 57-61.

596. "Freed," Forerunner, 3 (March 1912), 65-66.

597. "An Unwilling Interview," Forerunner, 3 (April 1912), 85-89.
    Rpt. in Woman's Journal, 29 March 1913, pp. 98-99.

598. "Two Great Pleasures," Forerunner, 3 (April 1912), 103.

599. "A Strange Influence," Forerunner, 3 (May 1912), 113-116.

600. "The Lady Oyster," Forerunner, 3 (May 1912), 131-132.

601. "Baulked, or Ways a Little Harder," Forerunner, 3 (June 1912), 141-145.

602. "Mary Button's Principles," Forerunner, 3 (July 1912), 169-172.

603. "Improving on Nature," Forerunner, 3 (July 1912), 174-176.

604. "Her Memories," Forerunner, 3 (Aug 1912), 197-201.

605. "A Strange Land," Forerunner, 3 (Aug 1912), 207-208.
    Rpt. under title "A Certain Land" in Woman's Journal, 8 Feb 1913, p. 42.

606. "Maidstone Comfort," Forerunner, 3 (Sept 1912), 225-229.

607. "Morning Devotions," Forerunner, 3 (Sept 1912), 251.

608. "A Cleared Path," Forerunner, 3 (Oct 1912), 253-258.

609. "Lessons. I," Forerunner, 3 (Oct 1912), 263-264.

610. "Lost Women," Forerunner, 3 (Nov 1912), 281-284.

611. "The Sentence," Forerunner, 3 (Nov 1912), 295.

612. "Their House," Forerunner, 3 (Dec 1912), 309-314.

1913

613. "Won Over," Forerunner, 4 (Jan 1913), 10-15; 4 (Feb 1913), 38-43; 4 (March 1913), 64-70; 4 (April 1913), 93-98; 4 (May 1913), 124-130; 4 (June 1913), 150-156; 4 (July 1913), 179-185; 4 (Aug 1913), 207-213; 4 (Sept 1913), 235-241; 4 (Oct 1913), 263-268; 4 (Nov 1913), 290-295; 4 (Dec 1913), 318-323.

614. "Forsythe and Forsythe," Forerunner, 4 (Jan 1913), 1-5.

615. "Her Beauty," Forerunner, 4 (Feb 1913), 29-33.

616. "On a Branch," Forerunner, 4 (Feb 1913), 46-47.
     Rpt. in Public, 24 Oct 1914, pp. 1024-1025.

617. "The Chair of English," Forerunner, 4 (March 1913), 57-61.

618. "My Ancestors," Forerunner, 4 (March 1913), 73-75.

619. "Mrs. Hines' Money," Forerunner, 4 (April 1913), 85-89.

620. "The Fathers and the Mothers," Forerunner, 4 (April 1913), 103-104.

621. "A Personal Motive," Forerunner, 4 (May 1913), 113-118.
     Rpt. in Woman's Journal, 5 July 1913, pp. 210-211.

622. "Wild Oats and Tame Wheat," Forerunner, 4 (May 1913), 130-131.

623. "Bee Wise," Forerunner, 4 (July 1913), 169-173.

624. "'A City of Homes,'" Forerunner, 4 (July 1913), 177-178.

625. "A Council of War," Forerunner, 4 (Aug 1913), 197-201.

626. "The Same Field," Forerunner, 4 (Aug 1913), 217.

627. "The Lady and the Lodger," Forerunner, 4 (Sept 1913), 225-229.

628. "The Author's Strike," Forerunner, 4 (Sept 1913), 244-245.

629. "Mrs. Power's Duty," Forerunner, 4 (Oct 1913), 253-257.

630. "A Poor Joke," Forerunner, 4 (Oct 1913), 270-271.

631. "The Better Land," Forerunner, 4 (Dec 1913), 326-327.

1914

632. "Benigna Machiavelli," Forerunner, 5 (Jan 1914), 9-15; 5 (Feb 1914), 37-44; 5 (March 1914), 69-75; 5 (April 1914), 95-101; 5 (May 1914), 122-127; 5 (June 1914), 150-158; 5 (July 1914), 178-184; 5 (Aug 1914), 206-212; 5 (Sept 1914), 234-240; 5 (Oct 1914), 263-269; 5 (Nov 1914), 292-297; 5 (Dec 1914), 314-319.
    Excerpted in Charlotte Perkins Gilman Reader, pp. 143-168.

633. "Remarks from the Chair," Forerunner, 5 (Jan 1914), 1-4.

634. "This 'Shepherd' Imagery," Forerunner, 5 (Jan 1914), 8.

635. "Perspective," Forerunner, 5 (Jan 1914), 25.

636. "With a Difference," Forerunner, 5 (Feb 1914), 29-32.

637. "Fulfilment," Forerunner, 5 (March 1914), 57-61.

638. "Mrs. Mann's Clothes," Forerunner, 5 (May 1914), 113-117.

639. "Publicity," Forerunner, 5 (May 1914), 128-129.

640. "A Partnership," Forerunner, 5 (June 1914), 141-145.

641. "If I Were a Man," Physical Culture, 32 (July 1914), pp. 31-34.
    Rpt. in Charlotte Perkins Gilman Reader, pp. 32-38.

642. "His Mother," Forerunner, 5 (July 1914), 169-173.

643. "Boone Farm," Forerunner, 5 (Aug 1914), 197-201.

644. "If I Were a Woman," Physical Culture, 32 (Aug 1914), 152-156.

645. "A Side View," Forerunner, 5 (Aug 1914), 212-213.

646. "Mr. Peeble's Heart," Forerunner, 5 (Sept 1914), 225-229.
Rpt. in Charlotte Perkins Gilman Reader, pp. 107-115.

647. "The Incentive," Forerunner, 5 (Sept 1914), 242.

648. "The Hypnotizer," Forerunner, 5 (Oct 1914), 253-256.

649. "His Record," Forerunner, 5 (Nov 1914), 281-285.

650. "Anarchistic States," Forerunner, 5 (Dec 1914), 325-327.

1915

651. "Herland," Forerunner, 6 (Jan 1915), 12-17; 6 (Feb 1915), 38-44; 6 (March 1915), 65-72; 6 (April 1915), 94-100; 6 (May 1915), 123-129; 6 (June 1915), 150-155; 6 (July 1915), 181-187; 6 (Aug 207-213; 6 (Sept 1915), 237-243; 6 (Oct 1915), 165-270; 6 (Nov 1915), 287-293; 6 (Dec 1915), 319-325.
Excerpted in Charlotte Perkins Gilman Reader, pp. 191-199.
See also item 675.

652. "Mrs. Dwight's Future," Forerunner, 6 (Jan 1915), 1-5.

653. "Spoken To," Forerunner, 6 (Feb 1915), 29-33.

654. "Mrs. Merrill's Duties," Forerunner, 6 (March 1915), 57-61.

655. "A Gift for Needle Work," Forerunner, 6 (April 1915), 85-89.

656. "Girls and Land," Forerunner, 6 (May 1915), 113-117.

657. "Dr. Clair's Place," Forerunner, 6 (June 1915), 141-145.

658. "The Boarder Bit," Forerunner, 6 (July 1915), 169-173.

659. "Being Reasonable," Forerunner, 6 (Aug 1915), 197-201.

660. "The Pig of Gold," Forerunner, 6 (Sept 1915), 225-229.

661. "The Master of the Sunset," Forerunner, 6 (Oct 1915), 253-258.

662. "A Middle-Aged Charmer," Forerunner, 6 (Nov 1915), 281-

285.

663. "Encouraging Miss Miller," Forerunner, 6 (Dec 1915), 309-313.

1916

664. "With Her in Ourland," Forerunner, 7 (Jan 1916), 6-11; 7 (Feb 1916), 38-44; 7 (March 1916), 67-73; 7 (April 1916), 93-98; 7 (May 1916), 123-128; 7 (June 1916), 152-157; 7 (July 1916), 179-185; 7 (Aug 1916), 208-213; 7 (Sept 1916), 237-243; 7 (Oct 1916), 263-269; 7 (Nov 1916), 291-297; 7 (Dec 1916), 318-325.
     Excerpted in Charlotte Perkins Gilman Reader, pp. 201-208.

665. "Cleaning Up Elita," Forerunner, 7 (Jan 1916), 1-4.

666. "The Girl in the Pink Hat," Forerunner, 7 (Feb 1916), 29-33.
     Rpt. in Charlotte Perkins Gilman Reader, pp. 39-46.

667. "Her Overhearing," Forerunner, 7 (March 1916), 57-61.

668. "His Excuse," Forerunner, 7 (April 1916), 85-89.

669. "A Surplus Woman," Forerunner, 7 (May 1916), 113-118.

670. "Joan's Defender," Forerunner, 7 (June 1916), 141-145.

671. "The Artist," Forerunner, 7 (July 1916), 169-173.

672. "How They Were Denobled," Forerunner, 7 (Aug 1916), 197-202.

673. "The Vintage," Forerunner, 7 (Oct 1916), 253-257.

674. "A Growing Heart," Forerunner, 7 (Dec 1916), 309-313.

1979

675. Herland. With an introduction by Ann J. Lane. New York: Pantheon, 1979. xxiv + 146 pp.
     Reviewed by P. L. Adams in Atlantic, 243 (April 1979), 99.
     Reviewed by Louise Bernikow in the New York Times Book Review, 8 April 1979, p. 20.
     Reviewed in the New Yorker, 30 April 1979, p. 137.
     Reviewed by Carla Waldemar in the Christian Science Monitor, 7 June 1979, p. 19.

Reviewed in Ethics, 93 (Oct 1982), 110.
See also items 651 and 2445.

1980

676. Charlotte Perkins Gilman Reader. Ed. with introduction
   by Ann Lane. New York: Pantheon, 1980. xlii + 208 pp.
     Reviewed in Kirkus Reviews, 15 Aug 1980, p. 1101.
     Reviewed in Publishers Weekly, 29 Aug 1980, p. 356.
     Reviewed in Library Journal, 15 Sept 1980, p. 1878.
     Reviewed in Booklist, 1 Nov 1980, p. 394.
     Reviewed in Kliatt, 15 (Winter 1981), 19.
     Reviewed in Choice, 18 (Jan 1981), 659.
     Reviewed in New Boston Review, 6 (Jan 1981), 12.
     Reviewed in Progressive, 45 (Jan 1981), 56.
     Reviewed in Village Voice, 18 March 1981, p. 40.
     Reviewed in Times Literary Supplement, 1 May 1981, p.
     484.

677. "Unpunished," excerpt from hitherto unpublished novel,
   in Charlotte Perkins Gilman Reader, pp. 170-177.
     Complete typescript in folder 231, CPG Papers.

DRAMA AND DIALOGUES

1890

678. "The Ceaseless Struggle of Sex: A Dramatic View," Kate Field's Washington, 9 April 1890, pp. 239-240.

679. "Dame Nature Interviewed on the Woman Question as It Looks to Her," Kate Field's Washington, 27 Aug 1890, pp. 138-140.

1894

680. "The Twilight," Impress, 10 Nov 1894, pp. 4-5. [Imitation of Maurice Maeterlinck.]
     See also "Story Studies," Impress, 17 Nov 1894, p. 5; and "The Story Guessers," Impress, 24 Nov 1894, p. 5.
     Rpt. in Time and the Hour, 19 Feb 1898, pp. 7-9.

1911

681. "Three Women," Forerunner, 2 (May 1911), 115-123, 134.
     See also "About Dramatic Rights in 'Three Women' and 'Something to Vote For,'" Forerunner, 2 (July 1911), 179.
     See also item 533.

682. "Something to Vote For," Forerunner, 2 (June 1911), 143-153.
     See also "About Dramatic Rights in 'Three Women' and 'Something to Vote For,'" Forerunner, 2 (July 1911), 179.

NON-FICTION

1883

683. "The Providence Ladies Gymnasium," Providence Journal, 23 May 1883, 8:2.

1885

684. "The Sin of Sickness," Buffalo Christian Advocate, 5 Feb 1885, p. 4.

685. "On Advertising for Marriage," Alpha, 1 Sept 1885, p. 7.

1886

686. "Why Women Do Not Reform Their Dress," Woman's Journal, 9 Oct 1886, p. 338.
   See also Celia B. Whitehead, "Wanted, Martyrs," Woman's Journal, 6 Nov 1886, p. 359.

1887

687. "The Right to Earn Money," Woman's Journal, 8 Jan 1887, p. 12.

688. "A Protest Against Petticoats," Woman's Journal, 26 Feb 1887, p. 60.

689. "The Woman's Column/Women as Inventors," Providence People, 5 March 1887, 1:3.
   Attributed to CPS on basis of diary entries for 2 and 4 March 1887 (vol. 20, CPG Papers).

690. "Pungent Paragraphs," Woman's Journal, 12 March 1887, p. 88. [Re. suffrage.]

691. "The Woman's Column," Providence People, 19 March 1887, 4:4. [Re. suffrage.]
   Attributed to CPS on basis of diary entry for 12 March

1887 (vol. 20, CPG Papers).

692. "A Woman's Protest," Providence Journal, 23 March 1887,
8:6.
Signed "A Woman." Attributed to CPS on basis of diary
entry for 22 March 1887 (vol. 20) and clipping in
folder 263, CPG Papers.

693. "The Woman's Column," Providence People, 26 March 1887,
2:3. [Re. economic independence of women.]
Attributed to CPS on basis of diary entries for 20 and
21 March 1887 (vol. 20, CPG Papers).

694. "Woman," Providence People, 9 April 1887, 5:5. [Re.
local referendum on suffrage.]
Signed "A Workingman's Daughter." Attributed to CPS
on basis of diary entry for 1 April 1887 (vol. 20,
CPG Papers).

695. "Woman," Providence People, 16 April 1887, 5:5. [Re.
courtship and marriage.]
Attributed to CPS on basis of diary entry for 3 April
1887 (vol. 20, CPG Papers).

1888

696. Gems of Art for the Home and Fireside. Providence:
J. A. and R. A. Reid, [1888]. 102 pp.

1889

697. "Ivan Ilyitch and Other Stories," in Pacific Review, ca.
autumn 1889. [Review of stories by Tolstoy trans. by
Nathan Dole (New York: Crowell, 1887).]
Copy extant in folder 262, CPG Papers.

698. "How Much Must We Read?" Pacific Monthly, 1 (Oct 1889),
43-44.

1890

699. "Nationalism vs. Individualism," California Nationalist,
3 May 1890, p. 9.

700. "Altering Human Nature," California Nationalist, 10 May
1890, p. 10.

701. "An Unconscious Insult," Woman's Journal, 14 June 1890,
p. 190. [Review of play "Shenandoah" by Bronson Howard.]

702. "The Two Armies," Weekly Nationalist, 28 June 1890, p.
     6.

703. "Apropos of Literature," Pacific Monthly, 2 (July 1890),
     123.

704. "Human Nature," Weekly Nationalist, 26 July 1890, pp. 4-
     5.
         Rpt. as Nationalist tract, copies extant in the CPG
         Papers, folders 168 and 248.

705. "The Love Story," Pacific Monthly, 2 (Sept 1890), 176-
     177.

706. "Custom, and the Line of Modesty," Kate Field's
     Washington, 17 Sept 1890, pp. 182-183.

707. "Two Races in One," Kate Field's Washington, 5 Nov 1890,
     p. 69.

1891

708. "Are Women Better Than Men?" Pacific Monthly, 3 (Jan
     1891), 9-11.

709. "Living from Day to Day," Christian Register, 1 Jan
     1891, p. 4.

710. "Our Opportunity," Los Angeles Porcupine, 1 Jan 1891.

711. "The Maternal Instinct," Kate Field's Washington, 21 Jan
     1891, pp. 44-45.

712. "The Noble Animals," Kate Field's Washington, 28 Jan
     1891, pp. 54-55.

713. "The Bugaboo of Publicity," Kate Field's Washington, 25
     Feb 1891, p. 119.

714. "The Illogical Mind," Kate Field's Washington, 22 April
     1891, p. 252.
         Rpt. in Forerunner, 4 (Nov 1913), 288-289.

715. "A Lady on the Cap and Apron Question," Wasp, 6 June
     1891, p. 3.

716. "Scattering Touches," Wasp, 6 June 1891, p. 4.

717. "The Dress and the Body," Pacific Rural Press, 4 July
     1891, p. 6.

718. "The Body and the Dress," <u>Pacific</u> <u>Rural</u> <u>Press</u>, 11 July 1891, p. 26.

719. "The Divine Right of Mothers," <u>Christian</u> <u>Register</u>, 30 July 1891, p. 488.

720. "Time to Read for the Housekeeper," <u>Pacific</u> <u>Rural</u> <u>Press</u>, 1 Aug 1891, pp. 90-91.
    Rpt. in <u>Woman's</u> <u>Journal</u>, 9 July 1904, p. 218.

721. "'Ought a Woman to Earn Her Living?'" <u>Kate</u> <u>Field's</u> <u>Washington</u>, 26 Aug 1891, pp. 136-137.
    See also Alice M. Whitlock, "Ought a Woman to Earn Her Living?" <u>Kate</u> <u>Field's</u> <u>Washington</u>, 5 Aug 1891, pp. 89-90; and Whitlock's reply to CPS in <u>Kate</u> <u>Field's</u> <u>Washington</u>, 9 Sept 1891, pp. 169-170.

722. "The Budget's Phonograph/Charlotte Perkins Stetson Discusses Earning a Living--and Living," <u>Boston</u> <u>Budget</u>, 6 Sept 1891, p. 2.

723. "Our Most Valuable Livestock," <u>Pacific</u> <u>Rural</u> <u>Press</u>, 17 Oct 1891, p. 330.

724. "Papers for the Women/Charlotte Perkins Stetson's Opinion of Them," <u>Oakland</u> <u>Times</u>, 19 Oct 1891, 2:1-2.

725. "More Dressmaker Philosophy," <u>Kate</u> <u>Field's</u> <u>Washington</u>, 21 Oct 1891, pp. 266-267.

726. "Garden or Museum," <u>Pacific</u> <u>Rural</u> <u>Press</u>, 14 Nov 1891, p. 414.

727. "Cows, Hens, and Women," <u>Kate</u> <u>Field's</u> <u>Washington</u>, 16 Dec 1891, pp. 408-409.
    Rpt. in <u>Woman's</u> <u>Journal</u>, 16 Jan 1892, p. 18.

1892

728. "A Matter of Figure/The Dressmaker's Dummy is Fearfully and Wonderfully Made," column syndicated for release through the American Press Association on 14 May 1892.
    Copy extant in CPG Papers, oversize vol. 1.

729. "The Shape of Her Dress," <u>Pacific</u> <u>Rural</u> <u>Press</u>, 2 Jan 1892, p. 6.
    Rpt. in <u>Woman's</u> <u>Journal</u>, 16 July 1904, p. 226.

730. "How to Receive Gossip," <u>Kate</u> <u>Field's</u> <u>Washington</u>, 3 Feb 1892, pp. 68-69.

Rpt. in Forerunner, 4 (Dec 1913), 324-326.

731. "The Sense of Duty in Women," Christian Register, 10 March 1892, p. 152.

732. "The Reactive Lies of Gallantry," Belford's, NS 2 (April 1892), 205-208.

733. "Masculine, Feminine, and Human," Kate Field's Washington, 6 July 1892, pp. 6-7.
Rpt. in Woman's Journal, 9 July 1892, p. 220.

734. "A Snare for the Philanthropic," Kate Field's Washington, 5 Oct 1892, p. 214.

735. "Another Reply," Oakland Enquirer, 7 Oct 1892, 4:2-3. [Re. People's Party.]

736. "The Woman of John Smith," Kate Field's Washington, 2 Nov 1892, p. 277.

737. "The Child--A Forecast," Union Signal, 10 Nov 1892, p. 7.

738. "Have We a Right to Our Own Opinions?" Kate Field's Washington, 23 Nov 1892, p. 327.

1893

739. The Labor Movement. A Prize Essay Read Before the Trades and Labor Unions of Alameda County, California, 5 September 1892. Oakland: Alameda County Federation of Trades, 1893. 19 pp.
Excerpted in Boston New Nation, 24 June 1893, p. 315. Reproduced on microfilm New Haven, Conn.: Research Publications, 1977 (History of Women 8563).

740. "The Domestic Cookshop," Worthington's Illustrated, 1 (Jan 1893), 65-67.

741. "Seen Through Feminine Spectacles: State Woman's Alliance," Stockton Mail, 7 Jan 1893, 3:1-2.

742. "A Paper Conscience," Stockton Mail, 7 Jan 1893, 3:2-3. Attributed to CPS on basis of entry in folder 16, CPG Papers.

743. "What is Success in Life?" San Francisco Call, 8 Jan 1893, p. 6.

744. "The Social Clearing House," Kate Field's Washington, 11 Jan 1893, pp. 20-21.

745. "A Woman's View/What She Thinks on Various Topics," Stockton Mail, 21 Jan 1893, 3:1-2.

746. "Seven Best Books by California Authors," San Francisco Call, 27 Jan 1893, p. 7.

747. "Climax of Folly/Charlotte Perkins Stetson on Crinoline," San Francisco Call, 4 Feb 1893, p. 3.

748. "Grasshopper Conversation," Kate Field's Washington, 22 March 1893, pp. 182-183.

749. "Seen in Proverbs," Worthington's Illustrated, 1 (April 1893), 361-363.

750. "The Owl, the Snake, and the Prairie Dog," Kate Field's Washington, 26 April 1893, p. 260.

751. "She Who is to Come/Charlotte P. Stetson on the Twentieth Century Woman," San Francisco Call, 28 May 1893, p. 11.

752. "The Recurrent Crinoline," Worthington's Illustrated, 1 (June 1893), 578-583.

753. "The Vegetable Chinaman," Housekeeper's Weekly, 24 June 1893, p. 3.

754. "Women Who Drink," Stockton Mail, 12 July 1893, 4:3-4.

755. "The Scapegoats of Society," Stockton Mail, 13 July 1893, 4:4.

756. "What Might Be Done," Stockton Mail, 14 July 1893, 4:4.

757. "The Poor Young Man," Kate Field's Washington, 19 July 1893, pp. 37-38.

758. "The Saloon and Its Annex," Stockton Mail, 21 July 1893, 4:3-4.

759. "Dirt and Patience," Stockton Mail, 26 July 1893, 4:3.

760. "The Tramp Phenomena," Stockton Mail, 27 July 1893, 4:3-4.

761. "Sentiments of Elopers," Stockton Mail, 1 Aug 1893, 4:4

762. "The California Servant Question," <u>Stockton</u> <u>Mail</u>, 3 Aug 1893, 4:2.

763. "House Service," <u>Stockton</u> <u>Mail</u>, 4 Aug 1893, 4:2-3.

764. "Bicycle Roads," <u>Stockton</u> <u>Mail</u>, 7 Aug 1893, 4:3.

765. "Women and Money," <u>Stockton</u> <u>Mail</u>, 8 Aug 1893, 4:3.

766. "What 'World Expositions' Mean," <u>Stockton</u> <u>Mail</u>, 9 Aug 1893, 4:3.

767. "A Time for Honor," <u>Oakland</u> <u>Enquirer</u>, 10 Aug 1893, 5:4. [Re. Southern Pacific railroad.]

768. "The Entering Wedge," <u>Stockton</u> <u>Mail</u>, 10 Aug 1893, 4:3.

769. "New York's Great Parade," <u>Stockton</u> <u>Mail</u>, 11 Aug 1893, 4:3.

770. "The Lady Managers and a Fool," <u>Stockton</u> <u>Mail</u>, 12 Aug 1893, 4:4.
    Reply to verses signed "The Wanderer" and entitled "The Lady Managers," <u>Stockton</u> <u>Mail</u>, 8 Aug 1893, 4:2. See also reply by "The <u>Wanderer</u>" in "Concerning a Fool," <u>Stockton</u> <u>Mail</u>, 19 Aug 1893, 5:1. See also reply by <u>CPS</u>, "'The Wanderer's' Return," <u>Stockton</u> <u>Mail</u>, 24 Aug 1893, 4:4. See also reply "A Woman," <u>Stockton</u> <u>Mail</u>, 28 Aug 1893, 4:4.

771. "As Good as Gold," <u>Stockton</u> <u>Mail</u>, 18 Aug 1893, 4:3.

772. "Women and the Fair," <u>Stockton</u> <u>Mail</u>, 19 Aug 1893, 4:3.

773. "We and Our Railroad," <u>Oakland</u> <u>Enquirer</u>, 31 Aug 1893, 6:1. [Re. Southern Pacific railroad.]

774. "Matters of Opinion," <u>Worthington's</u> <u>Illustrated</u>, 2 (Sept 1893), 272-273.

775. "Education," Pacific Coast Women's Press Association <u>Bulletin</u>, 1 (Sept 1893), 2. [Comments re. kindergarten and manual training in the schools.]

776. "Our Exchanges," Pacific Coast Women's Press Association <u>Bulletin</u>, 1 (Sept 1893), 2. [Reviews of current issues of such magazines as <u>Overland</u>, <u>Century</u>, <u>Review of Reviews</u>, <u>Popular Science Monthly</u>, <u>McClures</u>, <u>Demorest's</u>.]

777. "Reforms," Pacific Coast Women's Press Association
Bulletin, 1 (Sept 1893), 3.

778. "Among Our Members," Pacific Coast Women's Press
Association Bulletin, 1 (Sept 1893), 5. See also
Impress, 1 (Nov 1893), 6; 1 (Dec 1893), 6; 1 (Jan 1894),
6; 1 (Feb 1894), 7; 1 (April 1894), 3; 1 (May 1894), 5;
1 (June 1894), 6; 1 (Aug 1894), 2; 1 (Sept 1894), 2.

779. Boston New Nation, 23 Sept 1893, p. 435. [Apothegm.]

780. "Likes and Dislikes," Worthington's Illustrated, 2 (Oct
1893), 392-394.

781. "The Right People," Kate Field's Washington, 11 Oct
1893, pp. 228-229.

782. "The Women's Press Reform Movement," Impress, 1 (Nov
1893), 1-2.

783. "From Our Exchange and Others," Impress, 1 (Nov 1893),
2. [Reviews of current magazines, with particular
reference to W. D. Howells' "The Man of Letters as a Man
of Business" in Scribner's, Howells' "Letters of an
Altrurian Traveler" in Cosmopolitan, Hamlin Garland on
western American literature in Forum, and Grace Ellery
Channing's "Unconsidered Wisdom" in Kate Field's
Washington.]

784. "Our Midwinter Congresses," Impress, 1 (Nov 1893), 4.

785. "Actions Louder Than Words," Impress, 1 (Nov 1893), 5.
[Re. Emma Seiler.]

786. "The Pacific Coast Federation of Clubs," Impress, 1 (Nov
1893), 5. [Comment re. program, with particular
reference to forthcoming address on "Newspapers" by
Frederick Beecher Perkins. See also "Editorial Notes,"
Impress, 1 (Dec 1893), 1; and "The Social Meeting,"
Impress, 1 (Dec 1893), 4.]

787. "Books Received," Impress, 1 (Nov 1893), 6. [Review of
Richard T. Ely, Outlines of Economics (New York:
Macmillan, 1893).]

788. "Our Youngest Writers," Impress, 1 (Nov 1893), 6. [Re.
local story competition.]

789. "An Ideal Press/Chat with Charlotte Perkins Stetson,"
San Francisco Call, 12 Nov 1893, p. 3.

790. "The Modern Conscience," Worthington's Illustrated, 2 (Dec 1893), 617-621.

791. "Editorial Notes," Impress, 1 (Dec 1893), 1. [Comments re. John Davis on "fiat money" in Arena, Dec 1893; Olive Schreiner, Dream Life and Real Life (Boston: Roberts Bros., 1893); W. D. Howells' serialized "Letters of an Altrurian Traveler" in Cosmopolitan.]

792. "Exchanges and Others," Impress, 1 (Dec 1893), 2. [Reviews of such current magazines as Dial, Century, Current Topics, The Writer.]

793. "Book Reviews," Impress, 1 (Dec 1893), 3. [Reviews of Sarah Grand, The Heavenly Twins (New York: Cassell, 1893); Emily M. Bishop, Americanized Delsarte Culture (Washington, D.C.: E. M. Bishop, 1893).]

794. "Our Paper," Impress, 1 (Dec 1893), 4.

795. "The Woman's Congress and the General Congresses," Impress, 1 (Dec 1893), 5.

796. "The Fox Who Had Not Lost His Tail," Kate Field's Washington, 27 Dec 1893, p. 406.

1894

797. "Editorial Notes," Impress, 1 (Jan 1894), 1. [Comments re. Rudyard Kipling's The Rhyme of the Three Sealer and forthcoming Woman's Congress.]

798. "Exchanges and Others," Impress, 1 (Jan 1894), 2. [Reviews of current magazines, with particular reference to Edith Wharton's "The Fullness of Life" in Scribner's, Brander Matthews' sketch of Andrew Lang and James Russell Lowell's "The Function of the Poet" in Century.]

799. "Book Reviews," Impress, 1 (Jan 1894), 3. [Reviews of Frances Hodgson Burnett, The One I Knew Best of All (New York: Scribner's 1893); and Frances M. Milne, For To-Day (Boston: Arena Pub. Co., 1893).]

800. "Unemployed Women," Impress, 1 (Jan 1894), 4.

801. "Our New Headquarters," Impress, 1 (Jan 1894), 4-5. [Re. Pacific Coast Women's Press Assn. offices.]

802. Impress, 1 (Jan 1894), 6. [Review of The Ladies' Friend (Philadelphia: Press of Mathew Carey, 1793).]

803. "Editorial Notes," Impress, 1 (Feb 1894), 1. [Comments re. advertising, Jane Addams, Woman's Congress.]

804. "Los Angeles Public Library," Impress, 1 (Feb 1894), 2.

805. "Benefit for the Unemployed Women," Impress, 1 (Feb 1894), 2.

806. "The College Settlement," Impress, 1 (Feb 1894), 2.

807. "The Unveiling of Isabella," Impress, 1 (Feb 1894), 2. [Re. Harriet Hosmer statue.]

808. "The Business League for Women," Impress, 1 (Feb 1894), 3.

809. "Arthur McEwen's Letter," Impress, 1 (Feb 1894), 3. [Re. local muckraker.]

810. Impress, 1 (Feb 1894), 4-6. [Re. Pacific Coast Women's Press Association business.]

811. "Our Exchanges and Others," Impress, 1 (Feb 1894), 6. [Reviews of current magazines, with particular reference to Walter Blackburn Harte, "The Reform Spirit in Literature," Worthington's Illustrated, Jan 1894; C. B. Ashley, "Evolution in Relation to Popular Economy," Popular Science Monthly, Feb 1894; "In Re Walt Whitman and Other Books on Whitman" and John Burroughs, "Walt Whitman and His Art," Poet-lore, Feb 1893.]

812. "Miss Addams' Address to the [Woman's Congress Association]," Impress, 1 (Feb 1894), 6.

813. "A New Basis for the Servant Question," Worthington's Illustrated, 3 (March 1894), 304-309.

814. "Bring Up the Rear," Kate Field's Washington, 14 March 1894, pp. 163-164.

815. "Editorial Notes," Impress, 1 (April 1894), 1. [Re. Industrial Army, Arthur McEwen, forthcoming Woman's Congress.]

816. "Our Paper," Impress, 1 (April 1894), 2.

817. "'For the Good of the Order,'" Impress, 1 (April 1894), 2.

818. "Meadow Larks," Impress, 1 (April 1894), 2.

819. "The Ideal Wife," Impress, 1 (April 1894), 3.

820. "Pacific Coast Women's Press Association," Impress, 1 (April 1894), 4. [News and reports.]

821. "Book Review," Impress, 1 (April 1894), 5. [Re. Stanley J. Weyman, A Gentleman of Finance (New York: Longman, Green & Co., 1893; and Ambrose Bierce, Can Such Things Be? (New York: Cassell Pub. Co., 1893).]

822. "Exchanges and Others," Impress, 1 (April 1894), 5-6. [Re. current issues of New Cycle, Overland Monthly, Poet-lore on the verse of Hamlin Garland, works in McClure's by Andrew Carnegie and Emile Zola, the suspension of the Boston New Nation.]

823. "Editorial Notes," Impress, 1 (May 1894), 1. [Re. Woman's Congress, suspension of Arthur McEwen's Letter, critique of literary realism.]

824. "The Woman's Congress Auxiliary: To the California Exposition," Impress, 1 (May 1894), 2-3. [Report and program.]

825. "Pacific Coast Woman's Press Association," Impress, 1 (May 1894), 4-5. [News and reports.]

826. Impress, 1 (May 1894), 5. [Re. Lester Ward and Maurice Maeterlinck.]

827. "Congress Notes," Impress, 1 (May 1894), 6.

828. "Editorial Notes," Impress, 1 (June 1894), 1. [Re. suffrage, E. L. Godkin's essay on socialism in Forum, Helen Campbell, Lester Ward on the transmission of acquired traits.]

829. Impress, 1 (June 1894), 2. [Review of Rudyard Kipling, "Kaa's Hunting!" McClure's, June 1894.]

830. "Official Report of Woman's Congress," Impress, 1 (June 1894), 3.

831. "Our Day at the Fair," Impress, 1 (June 1894), 3.

832. "Pacific Coast Women's Press Association," Impress, 1 (June 1894), 4. [News and reports.]

833. "The Lurline Baths," Impress, 1 (June 1894), 6.
    See also "Watching the Swimmers," Impress, 1 (July

1894), 6.

834. "Book Review," Impress, 1 (June 1894), 6. [Re. Richard T. Ely, Socialism (New York: Crowell, 1894).]

835. "Our Exchanges and Others," Impress, 1 (June 1894), 7. [Re. articles by Edward Carpenter and Richard Maurice Bucke in Conservator for May 1894; W. D. Howells' "Dinner, Very Informally" in Cosmopolitan for June 1894; final installment of Mark Twain's Pudd'nhead Wilson in Century for June 1894.]

836. "Editorial Notes," Impress, 1 (July 1894), 1. [Re. Helen Campbell, Hamlin Garland's essay on Homestead strike in McClure's for June 1894.]

837. "She Didn't Care," Impress, 1 (July 1894), 2.

838. "Our Exchanges and Others," Impress, 1 (July 1894), 3. [Includes reference to Ambrose Bierce.]

839. "Pacific Coast Women's Press Association," Impress, 1 (July 1894), 4-5. [News and reports.]

840. "Book Reviews," Impress, 1 (July 1894), 6. [Re. Mrs. Humphry Ward, Marcella (New York and London: Macmillan, 1894); Rufus C. Hopkins, Roses and Thistles (San Francisco: Doxey, 1894).]

841. "From Santa Barbara," Impress, 1 (July 1894), 7.

842. "Editorial Notes," Impress, 1 (Aug 1894), 1. [Re. forthcoming convention of the PCWPA, defense of the populist tint of the magazine.]

843. "The Special Meeting," Impress, 1 (Aug 1894), 2.

844. "Our Exchanges and Others," Impress, 1 (Aug 1894), 2-3. [Includes review of John Dewey's essay "The Chaos in Moral Training" in current Popular Science Monthly.]

845. "Pacific Coast Women's Press Association," Impress, 1 (Aug 1894), 4-5. [News and reports.]

846. "The Book Party," Impress, 1 (Aug 1894), 5.

847. "Book Reviews," Impress, 1 (Aug 1894), 6. [Re. Virna Woods, A Modern Magdalene (Boston: Lee & Shepard, 1894); and an essay by Washington Gladden in McClure's for Aug 1894.]

848. "Realistic Fiction," Impress, 1 (Aug 1894), 7.

849. "What Our Papers Might Be," Impress, 1 (Aug 1894), 7.

850. "Editorial Notes," Impress, 1 (Sept 1894), 1. [Re. Ambrose Bierce, planning meeting for next Woman's Congress.]

851. "A Card of Thanks," Impress, 1 (Sept 1894), 2.

852. "Announcement: 'The Impress,'" Impress, 1 (Sept 1894), 3. [Re. conversion to sixteen-page weekly paper with next issue.]

853. "A Request," Impress, 1 (Sept 1894), 3. [Appeal for subscribers.]

854. "Pacific Coast Women's Press Association," Impress, 1 (Sept 1894), 4-5. [News and reports.]

855. "Book Reviews," Impress, 1 (Sept 1894), 6. [Includes comment re. Charles Bellamy, An Experiment in Marriage (Albany: Albany Book Co., 1894); and Kathleen M. Caffyn, A Yellow Aster (London: Hutchinson, 1894).]

856. "The Other Clubs," Impress, 1 (Sept 1894), 7.

857. "The Year's Work," Impress, 1 (Sept 1894), 7. [Review of magazine for the past year.]

858. "Work of Women and Children," Impress, 1 (Sept 1894), 7.

859. "Land Must Be Free That We May Live," Arena, 10 (Oct 1894), 640-642.

860. "What We Are Doing," Impress, 6 Oct 1894, pp. 1-2. [Re. anarchism, railroad regulation, Sino-Japanese war.]

861. "Mrs. [Alice Kingsbury-]Cooley's New Play," Impress, 6 Oct 1894, p. 2. [Re. work of local playwright.]

862. "End of the Century," Impress, 6 Oct 1894, p. 2.

863. "Bits of Criticism," Impress, 6 Oct 1894, pp. 2-3. [Explication of poem by Joaquin Miller.]

864. "Every-Day Ethical Problems," Impress, 6 Oct 1894, pp. 3-4; 13 Oct 1894, p. 5; 20 Oct 1894, p. 3; 27 Oct 1894, p. 3; 3 Nov 1894, p. 5; 10 Nov 1894, p. 3; 17 Nov 1894, p. 3; 24 Nov 1894, p. 3; 1 Dec 1894, p. 3; 8 Dec 1894,

p. 3; 15 Dec 1894, p. 3; 22 Dec 1894, p. 3; 29 Dec 1894, pp. 3, 5; 12 Jan 1895, p. 3; 19 Jan 1895, p. 3; 26 Jan 1895, p. 3; 2 Feb 1895, p. 3; 9 Feb 1895, p. 3; 16 Feb 1895, p. 3.
See also CPS, "What Our Ethical Answers Show," Impress, 29 Dec 1894, p. 3.

865. "The Woman's Exchange," Impress, 6 Oct 1894, p. 4.

866. "Pacific Coast Women's Press Association," Impress, 6 Oct 1894, pp. 6-7. [News of fourth convention of PCWPA.]

867. "The Woman's Congress," Impress, 6 Oct 1894, p. 7. [Report on the forthcoming congress.]

868. "Literature," Impress, 6 Oct 1894, p. 10. [Re. Susan Blow, Symbolic Education (New York: Appleton, 1894); and R. Anna Morris, Physical Education in the Public Schools (New York: American Book Co., 1892).]

869. "Magazines of the Month," Impress, 6 Oct 1894, p. 11. [Re. current issues of such magazines as Review of Reviews, Current Literature, Quarterly Illustrator, Century, Overland, with especial comment on essay about Maeterlinck in Poet-lore.]

870. "Art in Photography," Impress, 6 Oct 1894, p. 11.

871. "Art, Music and the Drama," Impress, 6 Oct 1894, p. 13. [Re. local crafts and performances.]

872. "Mrs. Cooper in St. Louis," Impress, 6 Oct 1894, p. 13.

873. "What We Are Doing," Impress, 13 Oct 1894, pp. 1-2. [Re. irrigation, Arthur McEwen's Letter, obituary of Oliver Wendell Holmes, New York state elections.]

874. "A Word to a Woman," Impress, 13 Oct 1894, p. 2. [Review of woman's magazine.]

875. "Pacific Coast Women's Press Association," Impress, 13 Oct 1894, p. 6. [News and reports.]

876. "Women's Clubs," Impress, 13 Oct 1894, p. 7.

877. "The Channing Auxiliary," Impress, 13 Oct 1894, p. 7.

878. "Our Premium to Women's Clubs," Impress, 13 Oct 1894, p. 7.

879. "Magazines of the Month," Impress, 13 Oct 1894, p. 11.
[Re. current issues of McClure's, Popular Science
Monthly, Cosmopolitan, essay about Henry D. Lloyd in
Arena.]

880. "Art, Music and Drama," Impress, 13 Oct 1894, p. 12.
[Re. local arts and crafts.]

881. "What We Are Doing," Impress, 20 Oct 1894, pp. 1-2.
[Re. public education, racial discrimination, women's
fashions and dress reform.]

882. "Do We Get 'The News?'" Impress, 20 Oct 1894, pp. 2-3.

883. "The Decadence is Upon Us," Impress, 20 Oct 1894, p. 3.

884. "Pacific Coast Women's Press Association," Impress, 20
Oct 1894, p. 6. [News and reports re. the Equal Rights
League and Laurel Hall Club.]

885. "Literature," Impress, 20 Oct 1894, p. 10. [Re. Yellow
Book.]

886. "Magazines of the Month," Impress, 20 Oct 1894, p. 11.
[Re. current issues of Cosmopolitan, Atlantic Monthly,
Scribner's, McClure's.]

887. "The Crisis of American Democracy," Impress, 20 Oct
1894, p. 11.

888. "Art, Music and the Drama," Impress, 20 Oct 1894, p. 12.
[Re. Aubrey Beardsley and a local production of Arthur
Wing Pinero's "The Second Mrs. Tanqueray."]
    See also "Mrs. Kendal's 'Paula,'" Impress, 27 Oct
    1894, pp. 12-13.

889. "What We Are Doing," Impress, 27 Oct 1894, pp. 1-2.
[Re. tax evasion by Pullman Car Co., dishonesty of
railroad monopoly, dress reform, Czar Alexander III.]
    Section on dress reform reprinted in Woman's Journal,
    29 Dec 1894, p. 409.

890. "The Texas Woman's Congress," Impress, 27 Oct 1894, pp.
2-3.

891. "Pacific Coast Women's Press Association," Impress, 27
Oct 1894, pp. 6-7. [News and reports.]

892. "Literature," Impress, 27 Oct 1894, p. 10. [Re.
Ballades and Rondeaus, ed. Gleeson White (New York:

Appleton, 1888).]

893. "Reform Literature," Impress, 27 Oct 1894, p. 10.

894. "Among the Magazines," Impress, 27 Oct 1894, p. 11.
[Re. current issues of such magazines as Out of Doors
for Women and Poet-lore.]

895. "What We Are Doing," Impress, 3 Nov 1894, pp. 1-2. [Re.
increasing unemployment, local municipal sanitation,
death of Alexander III, speech by Lyman Trumbull.]

896. "Women in City Government," Impress, 3 Nov 1894, p. 2.

897. "Pacific Coast Women's Press Association," Impress, 3
Nov 1894, p. 6. [News of a reception to Helen Campbell
and other reports.]

898. "Equal Rights Women Indorse [sic] Candidates," Impress,
3 Nov 1894, p. 7.

899. "Ohio Federation of Women's Clubs," Impress, 3 Nov 1894,
p. 7.

900. "Magazines of the Month," Impress, 3 Nov 1894, p. 11.
[Re. current issues of Land of Sunshine, New Cycle,
essays on Napoleon and Lincoln in McClure's for Nov
1894.]

901. "Music and the Drama," Impress, 3 Nov 1894, p. 12. [Re.
local performances.]

902. "What We Are Doing," Impress, 10 Nov 1894, pp. 1-2.
[Re. local political corruption, juvenile delinquency,
municipal management of street railways.]

903. "Political Ethics," Impress, 10 Nov 1894, p. 2.

904. "Boys in Our Prisons," Impress, 10 Nov 1894, p. 2.

905. "Pacific Coast Women's Press Association," Impress, 10
Nov 1894, p. 6. [News and reports.]

906. "The Ebell Society," Impress, 10 Nov 1894, p. 7.

907. "The Union for Practical Progress," Impress, 10 Nov
1894, p. 7.

908. "Literature," Impress, 10 Nov 1894, p. 10. [Re. Charles
A. Keeler, A Light Through the Storm (San Francisco:

Doxey, 1894).]

909. "Magazines of the Month," Impress, 10 Nov 1894, p. 11.
[Re. such articles in current magazines as Sylvester
Baxter, "Public Control of Urban Transit," and Albion
Tourgee, "The Story of a Thousand, Cosmopolitan;
"Motherhood as a Grand Profession," Current Topics;
story by Grace Ellery Channing in Outing.]

910. "What We Are Doing," Impress, 17 Nov 1894, pp. 1-2.
[Re. college hazings, dress reform, Grover Cleveland's
economic policies.]

911. "Women as a Class," Impress, 17 Nov 1894, pp. 2-3.

912. "The Ethical Association," Impress, 17 Nov 1894, p. 3.

913. "Women as Jurors," Impress, 17 Nov 1894, p. 3.

914. "Pacific Coast Women's Press Association," Impress, 17
Nov 1894, p. 6. [News and reports.]

915. "Literature," Impress, 17 Nov 1894, p. 10. [Re. Mary E.
Wilkins, A Humble Romance and Other Stories (New York:
Harper, 1887).]

916. "Magazines of the Month," Impress, 17 Nov 1894, p. 11.
[Re. current issues of such magazines as New England
Magazine, Poet-lore, Popular Science Monthly.]

917. "The Art of Dressmaking," Impress, 17 Nov 1894, p. 11.

918. "Art, Music and the Drama," Impress, 17 Nov 1894, p. 12.
[Re. local performances.]

919. "What We Are Doing," Impress, 24 Nov 1894, pp. 1-2.
[Re. strikes, WCTU convention, local canal.]

920. "Thinking as an Exercise," Impress, 24 Nov 1894, p. 2.

921. "The Horse Show," Impress, 24 Nov 1894, pp. 2-3.

922. "The Ethical Association Lecture," Impress, 24 Nov 1894,
p. 3.

923. "Pacific Coast Women's Press Association," Impress, 24
Nov 1894, p. 6. [News and reports.]

924. "Woman's Congress Association of the Pacific Coast,"
Impress, 24 Nov 1894, p. 7. [News and reports.]

925. "Literature," Impress, 24 Nov 1894, pp. 10-11. [Omnibus review of new releases on child culture.]

926. "Magazines of the Month," Impress, 24 Nov 1894, p. 11. [Re. current issues of such magazines as New Science Review and Review of Reviews.]

927. "California Architecture," Impress, 24 Nov 1894, p. 12.

928. "Mr. [John] Bonner's Talk," Impress, 24 Nov 1894, p. 12. [Lecture on Napoleon.]
    See also CPS, "Literary Notes," Impress, 1 Dec 1894,
       p. 11; and CPS, "Word Pictures of Women," Impress,
       16 Feb 1895, p. 11.

929. "What We Are Doing," Impress, 1 Dec 1894, p. 1. [Re. food distribution, woman voters in Colorado, women's clubs, federal banking policy.]

930. "Who Massacred the Armenians?" Impress, 1 Dec 1894, p. 2.

931. "Prof. Anderson and San Francisco," Impress, 1 Dec 1894, p. 3.

932. "Pacific Coast Women's Press Association," Impress, 1 Dec 1894, p. 6. [News of equal rights meeting and reports.]

933. "Woman's Congress Association of the Pacific Coast," Impress, 1 Dec 1894, p. 7. [News and report of a W.C.T.U. convention.]

934. "Among the Magazines," Impress, 1 Dec 1894, p. 11. [Re. Edward Everett Hale's memoir of Oliver Wendell Holmes in Review of Reviews for Nov 1894; interview of Arthur Conan Doyle in McClure's for Nov 1894; essay by Jacob Riis in Century for Nov 1894.]

935. "Mrs. [Emma Frances] Dawson Honored," Impress, 1 Dec 1894, p. 12. [Re. local poet.]

936. "Conventionalized Dress," Impress, 1 Dec 1894, p. 12.

937. "What We Are Doing," Impress, 8 Dec 1894, pp. 1-2. [Re. wheat crop, suicide, People's Party, socialism.]

938. "The Glory That Was Greece," Impress, 8 Dec 1894, pp. 2-3.

939. "A City's Loss," Impress, 8 Dec 1894, p. 3.

940. "Pacific Coast Women's Press Association," Impress, 8 Dec 1894, p. 6. [News and reports.]

941. "Woman's Congress Association of the Pacific Coast," Impress, 8 Dec 1894, p. 7. [News and reports.]

942. "Literature," Impress, 8 Dec 1894, p. 10. [Re. of Ida Coolbrith et al., A Collection of Wildflowers of California (San Francisco: Popular Bookstore, 1894); William Ordway Partridge, Art for America (Boston: Roberts Bros., 1894).]

943. "Magazines of the Month," Impress, 8 Dec 1894, p. 11. [Re. current issues of Overland Monthly and Review of Reviews.]

944. "Literary Notes," Impress, 8 Dec 1894, p. 11. [Includes review of Lilian Whiting, The World Beautiful (Boston: Roberts Bros., 1894).]

945. "Argument for the Appellant," Impress, 8 Dec 1894, p. 11. [Re. legal brief of Horace W. Philbrook in local trial.]

946. "The Theaters," Impress, 8 Dec 1894, p. 12. [Re. local productions, including a performance of Richard III with Thomas W. Keene.]
    See also "The Theaters," Impress, 15 Dec 1894, p. 12.

947. "What We Are Doing," Impress, 15 Dec 1894, p. 1. [Re. solitary confinement, municipal corruption.]

948. "'The Times Are Hard,'" Impress, 15 Dec 1894, p. 2.

949. "Pacific Coast Women's Press Association," Impress, 15 Dec 1894, p. 6. [News and reports.]

950. "Woman's Congress Association of the Pacific Coast," Impress, 15 Dec 1894, p. 7. [News and reports.]

951. "Magazines of the Month," Impress, 15 Dec 1894, p. 11. [Re. Kipling's "The Walking Delegate" in Century for Dec 1894; Edward Everett Hale's "If Jesus Came to Boston" in New England Magazine for Dec 1894.]

952. "Color," Impress, 15 Dec 1894, p. 12.

953. "A Want 'The Impress' Fills," Impress, 15 Dec 1894, p.

12.

954. "The Review," Impress, 22 Dec 1894, pp. 1-2. [Re. farm income, tax-ememption for church property, prison conditions, unemployment, death of prize-fighter, exploitation of child and woman labor.]

955. "Organized Love," Impress, 22 Dec 1894, p. 3.

956. "The Santa Claus Story," Impress, 22 Dec 1894, p. 3.

957. "Pacific Coast Women's Press Association," Impress, 22 Dec 1894, p. 6. [News and reports.]

958. "Woman's Congress Association of the Pacific Coast," Impress, 22 Dec 1894, p. 7. [News and reports.]

959. "Books," Impress, 22 Dec 1894, pp. 10-11. [Re. Edward Cary, George William Curtis (Boston: Houghton Mifflin, 1894); Oliver Wendell Holmes, The Last Leaf (Boston: Houghton Mifflin, 1894); Aubrey Beardsley in The Yellow Book.]

960. "Magazines of the Month," Impress, 22 Dec 1894, p. 11. [Re. current magazines, with especial comment about Thorstein Veblen's "Economic Theory of Woman's Dress" in Popular Science Monthly for Dec 1894.]

961. "Art, Music, Drama," Impress, 22 Dec 1894, p. 12. [Re. "pictures in the home" and local performances.]

962. "The Review," Impress, 29 Dec 1894, pp. 1-2. [Re. death of Robert Louis Stevenson, rural poverty, Henry D. Lloyd's address before the American Federation of Labor, bank embezzlements.]

963. "On Good Resolutions," Impress, 29 Dec 1894, pp. 2-3.

964. "A Woman-at-Large," Impress, 29 Dec 1894, p. 3.

965. "Pacific Coast Women's Press Association," Impress, 29 Dec 1894, p. 6. [News and reports.]

966. "Woman's Congress Association of the Pacific Coast," Impress, 29 Dec 1894, p. 7. [News and reports.]

967. "Magazines of the Month," Impress, 29 Dec 1894, p. 11. [Re. current magazines, with especial comment about Unity, ed. by Jenkin Lloyd Jones, and Horace E. Scudder's memoir of Oliver Wendell Holmes in the

Atlantic Monthly.]

968. "Art, Music, Drama," Impress, 29 Dec 1894, p. 12. [Re. "Beauty and Motion" and local performances.]

1895

969. "The Review," Impress, 5 Jan 1895, pp. 1-2. [Re. free kindergartens and municipal corruption.]

970. "Goat Island's Future," Impress, 5 Jan 1895, p. 2.

971. "Pacific Coast Women's Press Association," Impress, 5 Jan 1895, p. 6. [News and report on "how to make publishers pay" for contributions.]

972. "Woman's Congress Association of the Pacific Coast," Impress, 5 Jan 1895, p. 7. [News and reports.]

973. "Among the Magazines," Impress, 5 Jan 1895, p. 11. [Re. current magazines, with especial comment about Joaquin Miller's "Song of the Balboa Sea" in Overland Monthly for Jan 1895.]

974. "Art, Music, Drama," Impress, 5 Jan 1895, p. 12. [Re. "the harm of ugliness" and local performances.]

975. "Literary Notes," Impress, 5 Jan 1895, p. 12. [Includes review of Kate Douglas Wiggin, "The Kindergarten as a School of Life for Women" in Table Talk for Dec 1894.]

976. "The Review," Impress, 12 Jan 1895, pp. 1-2. [Re. lynching, treatment of diptheria, persecution of Armenians, critique of contempt of court proceedings against Eugene V. Debs and others.]

977. "John Smith and Armenia," Impress, 12 Jan 1895, pp. 2-3.

978. "Pacific Coast Women's Press Association," Impress, 12 Jan 1895, p. 6. [News and reports.]

979. "Woman's Congress Association," Impress, 12 Jan 1895, p. 7. [News and reports.]

980. "The Pure Food Exposition," Impress, 12 Jan 1895, p. 7.

981. "Magazines of the Month," Impress, 12 Jan 1895, p. 11. [Re. current magazines, with especial comment about Havelock Ellis' essay "The Genius of France" in Atlantic Monthly for Jan 1895; and an essay by Robert Grant and

"The Amazing Marriage" by George Meredith in
Scribner's.]

982. "Literary Art," Impress, 12 Jan 1895, p. 12.

983. "At the Theaters," Impress, 12 Jan 1895, p. 12. [Re.
local performances.]

984. "The Review," Impress, 19 Jan 1895, pp. 1-2. [Re. urban
sanitation and overcrowding, People's Party, forthcoming
lecture by Laurence Gronlund.]

985. "Good Government as an Investment," Impress, 19 Jan
1895, pp. 2-3.

986. "Pure Food is Fashionable," Impress, 19 Jan 1895, p. 3.

987. "Pacific Coast Women's Press Association," Impress, 19
Jan 1895, p. 6. [News and reports.]

988. "Woman's Congress Association," Impress, 19 Jan 1895, p.
7. [News and reports.]

989. Impress, 19 Jan 1895, p. 10. [Review of Gertrude G. de
Aguirre, Women in the Business World; or Hints and Helps
to Prosperity (Boston: Arena Pub. Co., 1894).]

990. "Magazines of the Month," Impress, 19 Jan 1895, p. 11.
[Re. current magazines, including Cosmopolitan, Arena,
and New England Kitchen.]

991. "To Remember Robert Louis Stevenson," Impress, 19 Jan
1895, p. 12.

992. "The Yale Lecture," Impress, 19 Jan 1895, p. 12.

993. "At the Theaters," Impress, 19 Jan 1895, p. 12. [Re.
local performances.]

994. "The Review," Impress, 26 Jan 1895, pp. 1-2. [Re. San
Francisco city charter, urban violence, woman
architects, Nicaragua Canal bill in Congress.]

995. "City Government as a Home Influence," Impress, 26 Jan
1895, p. 3.

996. "A Pleasant Reception," Impress, 26 Jan 1895, p. 3.

997. "Pacific Coast Women's Press Association," Impress, 26
Jan 1895, p. 6. [News and reports.]

998. "Woman's Congress Association," _Impress_, 26 Jan 1895, p. 7. [News and reports.]

999. "Magazines of the Month," _Impress_, 26 Jan 1895, p. 11. [Re. current magazines, including _Popular Science Monthly_, _Century_, _Education_.]

1000. "The City Hall Facade," _Impress_, 26 Jan 1895, p. 12.

1001. "Mr. Gronlund's Lecture," _Impress_, 26 Jan 1895, p. 12.

1002. "The Review," _Impress_, 2 Feb 1895, pp. 1-2. [Re. status of women among the poor in San Francisco, railroad monopoly on the west coast.]

1003. "Newspaper Work," _Impress_, 2 Feb 1895, p. 2.

1004. "A Bank Officer's Fall," _Impress_, 2 Feb 1895, pp. 2-3.

1005. "The Pure Food Exposition," _Impress_, 2 Feb 1895, p. 3.

1006. "Pacific Coast Women's Press Association," _Impress_, 2 Feb 1895, p. 6. [News and reports.]

1007. "Woman's Congress Association," _Impress_, 2 Feb 1895, p. 7. [News and reports.]

1008. "Books," _Impress_, 2 Feb 1895, p. 10. [Re. Susie Lee Bacon, _A Siren's Song_ (Chicago: C. H. Kerr & Co., 1895); and Jerome A. Anderson, _Driftings in Dreamland_ (San Francisco: Lotus Pub. Co., 1894).]

1009. "Magazines of the Month," _Impress_, 2 Feb 1895, p. 11. [Re. current magazines, such as _Overland Monthly_, _Metaphysical Magazine_, _Journal of Household Economics_.]

1010. "This is Too Much," _Impress_, 2 Feb 1895, p. 11. [Reply to criticisms leveled by another local magazine.]

1011. "The Review," _Impress_, 9 Feb 1895, pp. 1-2. [Re. railroad monopoly, initiative and referendum, mob violence.]

1012. "Hair Cloth and Public Morals," _Impress_, 9 Feb 1895, p. 3.

1013. "Pacific Coast Women's Press Association," _Impress_, 9 Feb 1895, p. 6. [News and reports.]

1014. "Woman's Congress Association," _Impress_, 9 Feb 1895, p.

7. [News and reports.]

1015. "Magazines of the Month," _Impress_, 9 Feb 1895, p. 11.
[Re. current magazines, with especial comment about
Theodore Roosevelt's "The Present Status of Civil
Service Reform" in _Atlantic Monthly_, Feb 1895.]

1016. "Seeing Beauty," _Impress_, 9 Feb 1895, p. 12.

1017. "At the Theaters," _Impress_, 9 Feb 1895, p. 12. [Re.
local performances.]

1018. "The Review," _Impress_, 16 Feb 1895, pp. 1-2. [Re.
woman suffrage, child labor.]

1019. "Child Labor," _Impress_, 16 Feb 1895, p. 2.

1020. "Consumers," _Impress_, 16 Feb 1895, p. 3.

1021. "Pacific Coast Women's Press Association," _Impress_, 16
Feb 1895, p. 6. [News and reports.]

1022. "Woman's Congress Association," _Impress_, 16 Feb 1895,
p. 7. [News and reports.]

1023. "Mind Your Own Business," _Impress_, 16 Feb 1895, p. 7.

1024. "Magazines of the Month," _Impress_, 16 Feb 1895, p. 11.
[Re. such current magazines as _Century_, _New England
Kitchen Magazine_, _Pacific Unitarian_.]

1025. "Literary Notes," _Impress_, 16 Feb 1895, p. 11. [Brief
reports.]

1026. "How to Enjoy Art," _Impress_, 16 Feb 1895, p. 12.

1027. "Mrs. Charlotte Stetson Perkins" [sic], San Francisco
Call, 22 May 1895, 9:3. [Letter to editor re. Woman's
Congress.]

1028. "The Woman's Congress," ca. late May 1895.
Undated copy extant in folder 248, CPG Papers.

1029. "Beauty as an Educator," _Land of Sunshine_, 3 (Sept
1895), 193-194.

1030. "The Solution to the Labor Problem," _Arena_, 14 (Oct
1895), 272-274.

1031. "The Superior Northerner," _Land of Sunshine_, 3 (Oct

1895), 209-211.

1896

1032. "The Voting Mother," Political Equality Series, 1 (June 1896), 1-4. [NAWSA brochure.]
Rpt. in Woman's Journal, 20 June 1896, p. 195.

1033. "The American Government," Woman's Column, 6 June 1896, p. 3.
See also item 2200.

1897

1034. "First Class in Sociology," American Fabian, 3 (Jan 1897), 9-11.

1035. "First Class in Sociology. Second Lesson," American Fabian, 3 (March 1897), 11-13.

1036. "First Class in Sociology. Third Lesson," American Fabian, 3 (May 1897), 7-9.

1037. "First Class in Sociology. Fourth Lesson," American Fabian, 3 (June 1897), 2-3.

1038. "Woman Suffrage and the West," Kansas Suffrage Reveille, 2 (June 1897), 2.

1039. "From a Business Point of View," American Fabian, 3 (Sept 1897), 3.

1040. "First Class in Sociology. Fifth Lesson," American Fabian, 3 (Sept 1897), 6-7.

1041. "In Future Summers," American Fabian, 3 (Sept 1897), 9.

1042. "Inequality," American Fabian, 3 (Oct 1897), 1-2.

1043. "When Socialism Began," American Fabian, 3 (Nov 1897), 1-2.

1044. "Working Love," American Fabian, 3 (Dec 1897), 1-2.

1898

1045. Women and Economics: A Study of the Economic Relation Between Men and Women as a Factor in Social Evolution. Boston: Small, Maynard & Co., 1898. 340 pp.
2nd printing (358 pp. with index) issued in 1899 by

Small & Maynard; 3rd in 1900; 4th in 1905 by Small &
Maynard in Boston and G. P. Putnam's Sons in London;
5th jointly issued in 1908; 6th jointly issued in 1910;
7th issued by G. P. Putnam's Sons of New York and
London in 1912; 8th by Putnam's in 1915; 9th edition
with new introduction by CPG (item 2061) issued by
Putnam's in 1920.
  Rpt. of 2nd printing with an introduction by Carl N.
Degler (New York: Harper & Row, 1966). Reviewed in
Choice, 4 (June 1967), 452. Rpt. of 9th printing (New
York: Gordon Press, 1975). Also rpt. in Magnolia,
Mass.: Peter Smith, 1970; New York: Source Book
Press, 1970. Reproduced on microfiche in Washington:
NCR Microcard Editions, 1970.
    Reviewed by Henry B. Blackwell in Woman's Journal, 25
      June 1898, p. 204.
    Reviewed by Helena Born in Conservator, 9 (July
      1898), 76-77.
    Reviewed in Time and the Hour, 16 July 1898, pp. 10-
      11.
    Reviewed in American Fabian, 4 (Nov 1898), 9-10.
    Reviewed in New York Times Saturday Review of Books,
      5 Nov 1898, p. 738.
    Reviewed in Boston Advertiser, 5 Nov 1898, 8:1-3.
    Reviewed in Outlook, 10 Dec 1898, p. 923.
    Reviewed in Boston Literary World, 24 Dec 1898, p.
      451.
    Reviewed by Helen A. Clarke in Poet-lore, 11 (Jan
      1899), 124-128.
    Reviewed in Sewanee Review, 7 (Jan 1899), 121-122.
    Reviewed in Book Notes, NS 2 (Jan 1899), 11-12.
    Reviewed in Literature (American edition), 17 Jan
      1899, p. 43.
    Reviewed in Independent, 26 Jan 1899, p. 283.
    Reviewed in Dial, 1 Feb 1899, pp. 85-86.
    Reviewed in Southern Educational Journal, 12 (March
      1899), 191-193.
    Reviewed in Brooklyn Eagle, 11 March 1899, 6:5.
    Reviewed in Ruskin, Tenn., Coming Nation, 8 April
      1899, p. 4.
    Reviewed by Emma N. Ireland in Nation, 8 June 1899,
      p. 443.
    Reviewed by Charles F. Lummis in Land of Sunshine, 11
      (July 1899), 118.
    Reviewed by Annie L. Muzzey in Arena, 22 (Aug 1899),
      264-272.
    Reviewed in London Bookman, 16 (Sept 1899), 163-164.
    Reviewed by Jeanette Harbour Perry in Critic, 35 (Oct
      1899), 890-893.
    Reviewed by Winifred Black in Denver Post. Rpt. in

Deseret Evening News, 25 Nov 1899, 19:1-5.
Reviewed by Mabel Hurd in Political Science
    Quarterly, 14 (Dec 1899), 712-713.
Reviewed in Humanitarian, 15 (Dec 1899), 449-452.
Published in Dutch translation by Aletta H. Jacobs
    under title De economische toestand der vrouw: een
    studie over de economische verhouding tusschen
    mannen en vrouwen als een factor in de sociale
    evolutie (Haarlem: H. D. Tjeeak Willink & Zoon,
    1900). 291 pp.
Published in part in Danish translation under title
    "Kvinden og Erhvervslivet" in Kvinden og Samfundet
    (Copenhagen), 11 Sept 1900, pp. 1-2; 18 Sept 1900,
    pp. 1-2; 25 Sept 1900, pp. 1-2.
Published in Italian translation by Carolina Pirouti
    under title La Donna e l'Economia Sociale
    (Florence: Barbera, 1902). Reviewed in Il
    Bollettino Bibliografico, 48 (January 1902), 1-2.
Published in German translation by Marie Stritt under
    title Mann und Frau (Dresden and Leipzig: Heinrich
    Minden, 1902). 286 pp.
Reviewed by "Vernon Lee" [Violet Paget] in North
    American Review, 175 (July 1902), 71-90. Rpt.
    under title "The Economic Parasitism of Women" in
    Gospels of Anarchy and Other Contemporary Studies
    (New York: Bretano's, 1909), pp. 263-297.
Published in Russian translation by Izdanie M.
    Mamurovskavo under title Ekonomicheskoe Rabstvo
    Zhenshchinii (Moscow: 1903). xiii + 265 pp.
Reviewed by Harry Thurston Peck in Bookman, 23 (June
    1906), 404-405.
Excerpted in The Cry for Justice, ed. Upton Sinclair.
    (Philadelphia: John C. Winston Co., 1915), pp.
    209-210.
Excerpted in The American Woman: Who Was She? ed.
    Anne Firor Scott (Englewood Cliffs: Prentice-Hall,
    1971), pp. 45-49, 137-138.
Excerpted in Roots of Bitterness: Documents of the
    Social History of American Women, ed. Nancy F.
    Cott. (New York: E. P. Dutton, 1972), pp. 366-
    370.
Excerpted in Feminism: The Essential Historical
    Writing, ed. Mirian Schneir (New York: Random
    House, 1972), pp. 231-246.
Excerpted in The Feminist Papers: From Adams to de
    Beauvoir, ed. Alice S. Rossi (New York and London:
    Columbia Univ. Press, 1973), pp. 572-598.
Excerpted in The Roots of American Feminist Thought,
    ed. James L. Cooper and Sheila McIsaac Cooper
    (Boston: Allyn and Bacon, 1973), pp. 193-217.

Excerpted in Women's Liberation in the Twentieth Century, ed. Mary C. Lynn (New York: John Wiley & Sons, 1975), pp. 22-28.
Excerpted in The Awakening by Kate Chopin, ed. by Margaret Culley (New York: W. W. Norton and Co., 1976), pp. 134-138.

1046. "What Makes for Encouragement," American Fabian, 4 (Jan 1898), 2-3.

1047. "First Class in Sociology. Sixth Lesson," American Fabian, 4 (Feb 1898), 6-8.

1048. "First Class in Sociology. VII Lesson," American Fabian, 4 (March 1898), 6-7.

1049. "Selfishness and Socialism," American Fabian, 4 (April 1898), 1-2.

1050. "Myopic Vanity," Criterion, 23 April 1898, p. 14.

1051. "The Artist's Appetite," Criterion, 30 April 1898, p. 20.

1052. "Socialism and Patriotism," American Fabian, 4 (May 1898), 5-6.

1053. "The Plague of Inefficiency," Scribner's, 23 (May 1898), 635-636.
Published anonymously. Attributed to CPG on the basis of the entry in her diary for 29 March 1898 (vol. 38, CPG Papers).

1054. "War as a Socializer," American Fabian, 4 (June 1898), 5-6.

1055. "The Dead Hand," Denver New Nation, 2 June 1898, p. 11.

1056. "The Working Principles of Socialism," Denver New Nation, 11 June 1898, pp. 3-4.
Rpt. in Ruskin, Tenn., Coming Nation, 2 July 1898, p. 3.

1057. "Who Will Do the Dirty Work?" Denver New Nation, 18 June 1898, p. 5.

1058. "Egoism, Altruism and Socialism," American Fabian, 4 (Aug 1898), 1-2.
See also F. H. M., "Egoists and Altruists," American Fabian, 4 (Sept 1898), 5. Rpt. in Ruskin, Tenn.,

Coming Nation, 27 Aug 1898, p. 1.

1059. "Does the War Postpone Social Reforms?" American Fabian, 4 (Aug 1898), 6.

1060. "Household Cooking and Intemperance," Union Signal, 10 Aug 1898, p. 4.

1061. "Economic Basis of the Woman Question," Woman's Journal, 1 Oct 1898, pp. 313-314.
    Rpt. in Up from the Pedestal, ed. Aileen S. Kraditor (New York: Quadrangle, 1968), pp. 175-178.

1062. "Causes and Uses of the Subjection of Women," Woman's Journal, 24 Dec 1898, p. 410.

1899

1063. "Socialism and Women," Ruskin, Tenn., Coming Nation, 11 Feb 1899, p. 1.

1064. "A Discrimination," Ruskin, Tenn., Coming Nation, 15 April 1899, p. 2.

1065. "What One Teacher is Doing," Southern Educational Journal, 12 (May 1899), 246-247.

1066. "The Great Meeting of Women in London," Saturday Evening Post, 27 May 1899, p. 758.

1067. "The Working Few," Club Woman, 4 (June 1899), 84.

1068. "The Automobile as a Reformer," Saturday Evening Post, 3 June 1899, p. 778.

1069. "Woman's Economic Place," Cosmopolitan, 27 (July 1899), 309-313. [Reply to Harry Thurston Peck, "The Woman of To-day and of Tomorrow," Cosmopolitan, 27 (June 1899), 149-162.]
    See also Alice S. Blackwell, "Medieval Professor Peck," Woman's Journal, 17 June 1899, p. 188; 24 June 1899, p. 196. Excerpted in Woman's Column, 1 July 1899, p. 2.

1070. "The Fear of Want," Saturday Evening Post, 8 July 1899, p. 26.
    Rpt. in Current Literature, 26 (Sept 1899), 223.

1071. "The Flagstone Method," Saturday Evening Post, 15 July 1899, p. 42.

1072. "Children That Make Good Citizens," Saturday Evening Post, 22 July 1899, p. 58.

1073. "The Woman's Congress of 1899," Arena, 22 (Sept 1899), 342-350.

1074. "The International Congress of Women," Ainslee's, 4 (Sept 1899), 145-151.

1075. "What Work Is," Cosmopolitan, 27 (Oct 1899), 678-682. Reviewed in Literary Digest, 21 Oct 1899, p. 486.

1076. "Why Not Nursery Suites?" Saturday Evening Post, 11 Nov 1899, p. 382.

1077. "The Home Without a Kitchen," Puritan, 7 (Dec 1899), 417-422.

1078. "To Exterminate the Criminal," Saturday Evening Post, 2 Dec 1899, p. 462.

1079. "Good Conduct and School Study," Saturday Evening Post, 16 Dec 1899, p. 510.

1080. "The 'Right People,'" Independent, 28 Dec 1899, pp. 3489-3490.

1900

1081. "Equal Pay for Equal Work," in Women in Industrial Life, vol. 6 of International Congress of Women of 1899, ed. Countess of Aberdeen (London: T. Unwin Fisher, 1900), pp. 198-202.

1082. "'Superfluous Women,'" Woman's Journal, 7 April 1900, p. 105.

1083. "Mending Morals by Making Muscle," Saturday Evening Post, 19 May 1900, p. 1078.

1084. "Misspelling and Other Unpunished Crimes," Saturday Evening Post, 2 June 1900, p. 1134.

1085. "Six Mothers," Harper's Bazar, 2 June 1900, pp. 282-284.
        Rpt. in Concerning Children, pp. 200-211.

1086. "Our Uneasy Consciences," Saturday Evening Post, 16 June 1900, p. 1182.

1087. "Esthetic Dyspepsia," Saturday Evening Post, 4 Aug 1900, p. 12.

1088. Concerning Children. Boston: Small, Maynard & Co., 1900. 298 pp.
    2nd printing issued in Feb 1901. 1st British edition London: G. P. Putnams's Sons, 1900. Rpt. by the Rational Press Association by arrangement (London: Watts & Co., 1907). 95 pp. Reproduced on microfilm New Haven, Conn.: Research Publications, 1976 (History of Women 5217.1).
      Reviewed in New York Times Saturday Review of Books, 5 Jan 1901, p. 4.
      Reviewed in Dial, 16 Jan 1901, p. 49.
      Chapter 10 excerpted under title "The Respect Due to Youth" in Littell's Living Age, 2 March 1901, pp. 594-597.
      Reviewed by Oscar Lovell Triggs in Unity, 9 May 1901, p. 155.
      Reviewed in Athenaeum, 18 May 1901, pp. 628-629.
      Reviewed by Florence Hull Winterburn in Charities, 1 Feb 1902, pp. 120-121.
      Published in Dutch translation by Martina G. Kramers under title Over Kinderen (Haarlem: H.D. Tjeenk Willink & Zoon, 1904). 223 pp.
      Published in German translation by Helene Riesz under title Kinder-Kultur (Berlin: Kulturverlag, 1906). 195 pp.
      Chapter 6 excerpted under title "'Naughtiness' in Our Children" in Ladies' Home Journal, 26 (May 1909), 64.

1901

1089. "Woman, the Discovery of the Century," Success, 4 (Jan 1901), 554, 584.

1090. "Ideals of Child Culture," in Child Study for Mothers and Teachers, ed. Margaret Sangster (Philadelphia: Booklovers Library, 1901), pp. 93-101.

1902

1091. "Get Thee to a Nunnery, Go?" Truth, 21 (May 1902), 107.

1092. "Things We Are Told," Truth, 21 (June 1902?), 139.
    Copy extant in folder 250, CPG Papers.

1093. "Should Wives Work?" Success, 5 (Sept 1902), 501-502.
    Reviewed in Literary Digest, 13 Sept 1902, p. 310.

See also Effie S. Black, "Should Wives Work?"
     <u>Success</u>, 5 (Nov 1902), 686-687.

1094. "Social Parentage and the Child," Ruskin, Tenn., <u>Coming</u>
      <u>Nation</u>, 20 Dec 1902, p. 2.

<u>1903</u>

1095. <u>The Home: Its Work and Influence</u>. New York: McClure,
      <u>Phillips & Co., 1903. 347 pp.</u>
      1st British edition issued London: Heinemann, 1904.
      2nd American printing New York: Charlton, 1910. Also
      rpt. New York: Source Book Press, 1970; Washington:
      NCR Microcard Editions; with an introduction by William
      L. O'Neill, Urbana: Univ. of Illinois Press, 1972; and
      reproduced on microfilm New Haven, Conn.: Research
      Publications, 1976 (History of Women 5218).
         Reviewed in San Francisco <u>Chronicle</u>, 8 Nov 1903,
            supplement, 8:5.
         Reviewed in <u>Boston</u> <u>Transcript</u>, 11 Nov 1903, 19:4.
         Reviewed in <u>Public Opinion</u>, 12 Nov 1903, p. 632.
         Reviewed by <u>Henry B. Blackwell</u> in <u>Woman's</u> <u>Journal</u>, 14
            Nov 1903, p. 363.
         Reviewed in San Francisco <u>Bulletin</u>, 15 Nov 1903,
            magazine section, 8:1-3.
         Reviewed in <u>Boston Herald</u>, 21 Nov 1903, 11:6.
         Reviewed by <u>Harry Thurston</u> Peck in <u>New</u> <u>York</u> <u>American</u>,
            21 Nov 1903, 10:1-3.
         Reviewed in <u>Chicago</u> <u>Tribune</u>, 28 Nov 1903, p. 15.
         Reviewed by <u>Olivia H.</u> Dunbar in <u>Critic</u>, 43 (Dec
            1903), 568-570.
         Reviewed in <u>New</u> <u>York</u> <u>Commercial</u> <u>Advertiser</u>, 7 Dec
            1903, 5:5-6.
         Reviewed in <u>Outlook</u>, 19 Dec 1903, pp. 961-962.
         Reviewed in <u>Detroit</u> Free Press, 19 Dec 1903, 11:2-3.
         Reviewed in <u>New York Times Saturday</u> <u>Review</u> of <u>Books</u>,
            26 Dec 1903, p. 983.
         Reviewed in <u>Independent</u>, 7 Jan 1904, pp. 39-41.
         Reviewed by <u>La Salle A.</u> Maynard in <u>Frank Leslie's</u>
            <u>Illustrated Newspaper</u>, 7 Jan 1904, p. 16.
         Reviewed in <u>New</u> <u>York</u> Tribune, 10 Jan 1904, sec. II,
            4:3.
         Reviewed in <u>Literary</u> <u>Digest</u>, 16 Jan 1904, p. 91.
         Reviewed by <u>Bailey Millard</u> in San Francisco <u>Examiner</u>,
            17 Jan 1904, 45:1-2.
         Excerpted in <u>Chicago</u> <u>Tribune</u>, 31 Jan 1904, p. 55.
         Reviewed by <u>Edith Granger in</u> <u>Dial</u>, 16 April 1904, pp.
            260-261.
         Reviewed in <u>Club Woman</u>, 11 (March 1904), 92.
         Reviewed in <u>Centralblatt</u> des <u>Bundes</u> <u>deutscher</u>

Frauenvereine, 1 June 1904, pp. 35-36.
Reviewed by Mary K. Ford in Current Literature, 37
(July 1904), 41-43.
Reviewed by Charles F. Lummis in Out West, 21 (Sept
1904), 299-301.
Published in Swedish translation by Frigga Carlberg
under title Hemmet, dess verksamhet och inflytande
(Stockholm: Wahlström & Widstrand, 1907). 203 pp.
Published in German translation by Marie Stritt under
title Unser Heim, sein Einfluss und seine Wirkung
(Dresden and Leipzig: Heinrich Minden, 1913). 296
pp.
Reviewed in Literary Digest, 1 April 1911, pp. 634-
635.
Reviewed by C.W. in Woman's Journal, 22 April 1911,
p. 127.
Reviewed in A.L.A. Booklist, 8 (Dec 1911), 186.
Excerpted in The Oven Birds, ed. Gail Parker (New
York: Doubleday, 1972), pp. 339-351.
Reviewed in Publishers' Weekly, 16 Oct 1972, p. 52.
Reviewed in Psychology Today, 7 (June 1973), 102.
Excerpted in Women's Liberation in the Twentieth
Century, ed. Mary C. Lynn (New York: John Wiley &
Sons, 1975), pp. 15-22.

1096. "The Advance of Working Woman," Century Club Advance, 1
(Jan-March 1903), 65-67.

1097. "Fortschritte der Frauen in Amerika," Neues Frauenleben
(Vienna), 1, no. 1 (1903), 2-5.

1098. "The Home as a Food Purveyor," Success, 6 (April 1903),
219-220.
Excerpted in New York Tribune, 7 April 1903, 7:4.

1099. "The Home as an Environment for Women," Success, 6
(July 1903), 411-412.

1100. "All the World to Her," Independent, 9 July 1903, pp.
1613-1616.
Rpt. in Woman's Journal, 1 Aug 1903, p. 242.
Reviewed in Literary Digest, 1 Aug 1903, pp. 128-129.

1101. "The Home as a Place for Children," Success, 6 (Sept
1903), 504-505.

1102. "The Home as a Social Medium," Success, 6 (Oct 1903),
558-559.

1103. "Does the Higher Education of Women Tend to Happiness

in Marriage?" <u>Success</u>, 6 (Dec 1903), 722.

1904

1104. <u>Human Work</u>. New York: McClure, Phillips & Co., 1904.
     389 pp.
          Reproduced on microfilm New Haven, Conn.: Research
     Publications, 1976 (History of Women 5219).
          Reviewed in <u>Brooklyn Eagle</u>, 13 May 1904, 7:6.
          Reviewed in <u>Outlook</u>, 28 May 1904, p. 240.
          Reviewed by <u>Henry B</u>. Blackwell in <u>Woman's Journal</u>, 4
          June 1904, p. 179.
          Reviewed in <u>New York Times Saturday Review of Books</u>,
          11 June 1904, p. 387.
          Reviewed in Boston <u>Literary World</u>, 35 (July 1904),
          196.
          Reviewed in Boston <u>Transcript</u>, 20 July 1904, 16:1-2.
          Reviewed by <u>H. W.</u> Boynton in <u>Atlantic Monthly</u>, 94
          (Aug 1904), 274-275.
          Reviewed by Charles F. Lummis in <u>Out West</u>, 21 (Sept
          1904), 299-301.
          Reviewed by Mary K. Ford in <u>Current Literature</u>, 37
          (Oct 1904), 373-375.
          Reviewed in <u>Literary Digest</u>, 1 Oct 1904, p. 430.
          Reviewed by <u>Charles R. Henderson</u> in <u>Dial</u>, 16 Oct
          1904, pp. 239-240.
          Reviewed in <u>Independent</u>, 3 Nov 1904, pp. 1034-1035.
          Reviewed in <u>Seattle Post-Intelligencer</u>, 24 July 1905,
          6:6.

1105. "Should a Girl Work Who Does Not Have To?" <u>Success</u>, 7
     (Jan 1904), 20-21.

1106. "A New Year's Letter," <u>Woman's Journal</u>, 2 Jan 1904, p.
     2.

1107. "Vital Issues," <u>Woman's Journal</u>, 2 Jan 1904, p. 2.
          Reviewed in <u>Woman's Tribune</u>, 16 Jan 1904, p. 19.

1108. "Five Million Men," <u>Woman's Journal</u>, 2 Jan 1904, p. 2.

1109. "The World's Mother," <u>Woman's Journal</u>, 2 Jan 1904, p.
     2.

1110. "From Now On," <u>Woman's Journal</u>, 2 Jan 1904, p. 2.

1111. "The Home of Tomorrow," <u>Woman's Journal</u>, 9 Jan 1904, p.
     10.
          Rpt. in <u>Woman's Column</u>, 9 Jan 1904, p. 2.

1112. "Girls' Wild Oats," Woman's Journal, 9 Jan 1904, p. 10.
Rpt. in Woman's Column, 9 Jan 1904, p. 3.
Rpt. in Forerunner, 5 (March 1914), 67-68.

1113. "Women's Work in Bermuda," Woman's Journal, 9 Jan 1904,
p. 10.

1114. "A Platform for the Woman's Movement," Woman's Journal,
16 Jan 1904, p. 18.

1115. "Masculine, Feminine and Human," Woman's Journal, 16
Jan 1904, p. 18.

1116. "Present Obstacles," Woman's Journal, 16 Jan 1904, p.
18.

1117. "'Successful Women of America,'" Woman's Journal, 16
Jan 1904, p. 18.

1118. "Speaking of Skirts," Woman's Journal, 16 Jan 1904, p.
18.

1119. "Progress in New Jersey," Woman's Journal, 16 Jan 1904,
p. 18.

1120. "Ministers' Wives," Woman's Journal, 16 Jan 1904, p.
18.

1121. "Wholesale Drugs and Foods," Woman's Journal, 16 Jan
1904, p. 18.

1122. "Two Kinds of Prevention, Woman's Journal, 16 Jan 1904,
pp. 18-19.

1123. "'Dance for Miss Twombly,'" Woman's Journal, 16 Jan
1904, p. 19.

1124. "'Supporting the Family,'" Woman's Journal, 23 Jan
1904, p. 26.

1125. "Wife-Desertion," Woman's Journal, 23 Jan 1904, p. 26.

1126. "The Increase in Suicide," Woman's Journal, 23 Jan
1904, p. 26.

1127. "Shall Suffrage Clubs Work for Anything Besides
Suffrage?" Woman's Journal, 30 Jan 1904, p. 34.

1128. "The Ethical Training of Children?" Woman's Journal, 30
Jan 1904, p. 34.

1129. "Schools and Mothers," Woman's Journal, 30 Jan 1904, p. 34.

1130. "Woman's Industrial Progress," Woman's Journal, 30 Jan 1904, p. 34.

1131. "What We Like," Woman's Journal, 30 Jan 1904, p. 34.

1132. "Domestic Art," Craftsman, 5 (Feb 1904), 512.

1133. "Competing with Men," Woman's Journal, 6 Feb 1904, p. 42.
    Rpt. in Woman's Column, 6 Feb 1904, p. 4.

1134. "Tuberculosis and New York," Woman's Journal, 6 Feb 1904, p. 42.

1135. "The Home and the Orphan Asylum," Woman's Journal, 6 Feb 1904, p. 42.

1136. "The British Mother," Woman's Journal, 6 Feb 1904, p. 42.

1137. "Woman's Sphere," Woman's Journal, 13 Feb 1904, p. 50.

1138. "Country Women's Clubs," Woman's Journal, 13 Feb 1904, p. 50.

1139. "Reporters' Ridicule," Woman's Journal, 13 Feb 1904, p. 50.

1140. "A Girl of Spirit," Woman's Journal, 13 Feb 1904, p. 50.

1141. "Why Great Women are Few," Woman's Journal, 20 Feb 1904, p. 58.

1142. "Why We Ignore Reason," Woman's Journal, 20 Feb 1904, p. 58.
    Rpt. in Forerunner, 5 (April 1914), 109.

1143. "Not a Woman's Candidate," Woman's Journal, 20 Feb 1904, p. 58. [Re. William Randolph Hearst.]
    See also "Hearst's 'Examiner,'" Woman's Journal, 9 April 1904, p. 1144 and CPG's rejoinder "A Gentle Defender," Woman's Journal, 16 April 1904, p. 122.

1144. "At the Convention," Woman's Journal, 20 Feb 1904, p. 58. [Re. National American Woman Suffrage Association annual convention in Washington, D.C.]

1145. "The Last Ditch," Woman's Journal, 27 Feb 1904, p. 66.

1146. "Answer to an Inquirer," Woman's Journal, 27 Feb 1904, p. 66.

1147. "Cooking as a Marital Duty," Woman's Journal, 27 Feb 1904, p. 66.
   See also reply by L.N., "Housework Defended," Woman's Journal, 26 March 1904, p. 98.
   Reply by CPG, "As to Housework," Woman's Journal, 2 April 1904, p. 106.
   See also Bertha S. Papazian, "Concerning Housekeeping," Woman's Journal, 23 April 1904, p. 130.

1148. Woman's Journal, 27 Feb 1904, p. 66. [Re. two items about suffrage in the New York Times for 20 Feb 1904.]

1149. "Suffrage Work," Woman's Journal, 5 March 1904, p. 74.

1150. "The New Woman in China," Woman's Journal, 5 March 1904, p. 74.

1151. "The New York Women's Club House," Woman's Journal, 5 March 1904, p. 74.

1152. "Housework and Athletics," Woman's Journal, 5 March 1904, p. 74.

1153. "Opposing Currents," Woman's Journal, 12 March 1904, p. 82.

1154. "The Memorial to Miss Porter," Woman's Journal, 12 March 1904, p. 82.

1155. "The 'Double Standard,'" Woman's Journal, 12 March 1904, p. 82.

1156. "'Wanted--Young Girl to Mind Baby and Do Light Housework,'" Woman's Journal, 12 March 1904, p. 82.
   Rpt. in Forerunner, 5 (April 1914), 88-89.

1157. "'Women in Panic in Blazing Car,'" Woman's Journal, 12 March 1904, p. 82.
   Rpt. in Forerunner, 5 (Oct 1914), 262.

1158. "Our Attitude Toward Russia," Woman's Journal, 19 March 1904, p. 90.

1159. "A Piece of the Millennium," Woman's Journal, 19 March

1904, p. 90.

1160. "The Girls' Share," Woman's Journal, 19 March 1904, p. 90.

1161. "Carnegie's 'City Beautiful,'" Woman's Journal, 19 March 1904, p. 90.

1162. "What Shall the Suffrage Clubs Do?" Woman's Journal, 19 March 1904, p. 90.

1163. "What are Vital Issues?" Woman's Journal, 26 March 1904, p. 98.

1164. "Marrying and Money," Woman's Journal, 26 March 1904, p. 98.

1165. "A Child's Vocabulary," Woman's Journal, 26 March 1904, p. 98.

1166. "Married Teachers," Woman's Journal, 26 March 1904, p. 98.

1167. "An Advancing Cause," Current Literature, 36 (April 1904), 388-389. [Re. National American Woman Suffrage Association annual convention in Washington, D.C.]

1168. "The Educated Women," Twentieth Century Home, 1 (April 1904), 65-67.

1169. "The Model Home," Woman's Journal, 2 April 1904, p. 106.
  Rpt. in Forerunner, 4 (Dec 1913), 314-315.

1170. "Women's Names," Woman's Journal, 9 April 1904, p. 114.

1171. "'Woman's Welfare,'" Woman's Journal, 9 April 1904, p. 114. [Rev. of magazine Woman's Welfare.]

1172. "Property in Children," Woman's Journal, 9 April 1904, p. 114.

1173. "'Naughty Baby,' 'Good Baby,'" Woman's Journal, 9 April 1904, p. 114.

1174. "Old Greece in Young America," Woman's Journal, 16 April 1904, p. 122.

1175. "Apropos of Prof. Ward's Theory," Woman's Journal, 16 April 1904, p. 122.

1176. "What is Practical?" Woman's Journal, 23 April 1904, p. 130.

1177. "Those Fingers and Teacups," Woman's Journal, 23 April 1904, p. 130.

1178. "A Conservative to the Front," Woman's Journal, 23 April 1904, p. 130. [Re. the New York Evening Post.]

1179. "Women and French Literature," Woman's Journal, 23 April 1904, p. 130.

1180. "[Frank] Wedekind's 'Erdgeist,'" Woman's Journal, 30 April 1904, p. 138.

1181. "Scientific Sweeping," Woman's Journal, 30 April 1904, p. 138.

1182. "An Industrial Sanitarium," Woman's Journal, 30 April 1904, p. 138.

1183. "The Needy Schoolma'am," Success, 7 (May 1904), 370.

1184. "Love Stories and Life Stories," Woman's Journal, 7 May 1904, p. 146.

1185. "The Married Teacher," Woman's Journal, 7 May 1904, p. 146.

1186. "'The Truth (?) About Women in Industry,'" Woman's Journal, 14 May 1904, p. 154.

1187. "The Ivy and the Oak," Woman's Journal, 14 May 1904, p. 154.

1188. "A Theatre Fire and No Panic," Woman's Journal, 14 May 1904, p. 154.

1189. "A Blue Baby," Woman's Journal, 14 May 1904, p. 154.

1190. "Hazing and Child Culture," Woman's Journal, 21 May 1904, p. 162.

1191. "The Day-unto-Dooryard Theory," Woman's Journal, 21 May 1904, p. 162.

1192. "With or Without Calling," Woman's Journal, 28 May 1904, p. 170.

1193. "Dirt and Patience," Woman's Journal, 28 May 1904, p.

170.

1194. Current Literature, 36 (June 1904), 624-625. [Review of D. Ely van de Warker, Woman's Unfitness for the Higher Co-education (New York: Grafton Press, 1904).]

1195. "'Mrs. Wiggs' and a Dangerous Morality," Critic, 44 (June 1904), 508-510. [Review of Alice Caldwell Rice, Mrs. Wiggs of the Cabbage Patch (New York: Century, 1901).]

1196. "Woman's 'Manifest Destiny,'" Woman's Journal, 4 June 1904, p. 178.
    Rpt. in Forerunner, 4 (Dec 1913), 335.

1197. "Educated Bodies," Woman's Journal, 4 June 1904, p. 178.
    Rpt. in Forerunner, 5 (March 1914), 75.

1198. "Interesting People," Woman's Journal, 11 June 1904, p. 186.

1199. "Why 'Dual,'" Woman's Journal, 11 June 1904, p. 186.
    Rpt. in Woman's Column, 11 June 1904, p. 1.

1200. "A Wreath of Corpses," Woman's Journal, 11 June 1904, p. 186.
    Rpt. in Forerunner, 5 (April 1914), 94-95.

1201. "Burglars, Thieves, or Servants," Woman's Journal, 11 June 1904, p. 186.

1202. "Domestic Economy," Independent, 16 June 1904, pp. 1359-1363.
    Reviewed in New York Times, 19 June 1904, 6:4-5.

1203. "A Steamer Letter," Woman's Journal, 18 June 1904, p. 194. [Travel letter dated 27 May 1904, written en route to Europe and the International Congress of Women in Berlin.]

1204. "Another 'Woman's Paper,'" Woman's Journal, 18 June 1904, p. 194.

1205. "From Germany," Woman's Journal, 25 June 1904, p. 202.

1206. "Letter from Berlin," Woman's Journal, 2 July 1904, p. 210.

1207. "The Beauty of a Block," Independent, 14 July 1904, pp.

67-72.

1208. "Homeward Bound," Woman's Journal, 23 July 1904, p. 234. [Travel letter dated 6 July 1904, en route to New York.]
  Excerpted under title "A Splendid Picture" in Woman's Column, 23 July 1904, p. 1.

1209. "Stealing a Servant," Woman's Journal, 23 July 1904, p. 234.
  See also L.F.C., "'Stealing a Servant,'" Woman's Journal, 3 Dec 1904, p. 386.

1210. "Woman's Alleged Inhumanity to Woman," Woman's Journal, 23 July 1904, p. 234.

1211. "Is the Woman's Movement Slow?" Woman's Journal, 30 July 1904, p. 242.
  See also CPG, "A Correction," Woman's Journal, 10 Sept 1904, p. 290.

1212. "Feminine Occupations," Woman's Journal, 30 July 1904, p. 242.

1213. "Natural Feelings," Woman's Journal, 30 July 1904, p. 242.

1214. "Village Improvement," Woman's Journal, 30 July 1904, p. 242.

1215. "Homes for Working Women," Twentieth Century Home, 1 (Aug 1904), 18-21.

1216. "A Children's Car," Woman's Journal, 6 Aug 1904, p. 250.
  Rpt. in Woman's Column, 6 Aug 1904, p. 2.

1217. "Prospects," Woman's Journal, 13 Aug 1904, p. 258.

1218. "What Can the Present Woman Do?" Woman's Journal, 13 Aug 1904, p. 258.

1219. "The Making of Americans," Woman's Journal, 13 Aug 1904, p. 258.

1220. "The Bachelor Maid's Objections to Marriage," Woman's Journal, 20 Aug 1904, p. 266.

1221. "A Certain Attitude Toward Maternity," Woman's Journal, 20 Aug 1904, p. 266.

1222. "Social Heredity," Woman's Journal, 20 Aug 1904, p. 266.

1223. "Nature of Humanity," Chautauqua Assembly Herald, 24 Aug 1904, pp. 1, 5, 8.

1224. "Housing for Children," Independent, 25 Aug 1904, pp. 434-438.

1225. "Woman's Place," Chautauqua Assembly Herald, 25 Aug 1904, pp. 1, 6-8.

1226. "Society and the Baby," Chautauqua Assembly Herald, 26 Aug 1904, pp. 1, 5, 8.

1227. "Home and the World," Chautauqua Assembly Herald, 27 Aug 1904, pp. 1-3.

1228. "Today's Lecture/Mrs. Charlotte P. Gilman Speaks on What We Do or How We Might Live," Chautauqua Assembly Herald, 27 Aug 1904, p. 8.

1229. "Woman's Day," Woman's Journal, 27 Aug 1904, p. 274.

1230. "Why Graves?" Woman's Journal, 27 Aug 1904, p. 274.

1231. "The Growing Power of Woman: Impressions of the Congress in Berlin," Booklovers, NS 4 (Sept 1904), 385-390.

1232. "Malthusianism and Race Suicide," Woman's Journal, 3 Sept 1904, p. 282.

1233. "From Chautauqua," Woman's Journal, 3 Sept 1904, p. 282.
    Rpt. in Woman's Column, 3 Sept 1904, p. 2.

1234. "Alone in the World," Woman's Journal, 10 Sept 1904, p. 290.

1235. "Another of President [David Starr] Jordan's Views," Woman's Journal, 10 Sept 1904, p. 290.

1236. "The Refusal to Marry," Woman's Journal, 17 Sept 1904, p. 298.
    Rpt. in Woman's Column, 17 Sept 1904, p. 2.

1237. "A Limit to Newspaper License," Woman's Journal, 17 Sept 1904, p. 298.

1238. "A Life-Saver," Woman's Journal, 17 Sept 1904, p. 298.

1239. "Public Sins and Private Indifference," Woman's Journal, 24 Sept 1904, p. 306.

1240. "Why This Insistence?" Woman's Journal, 24 Sept 1904, p. 306.
Reviewed by Alice Stone Blackwell in "Mrs. Gilman on Strawberry Jam," Woman's Journal, 24 Sept 1904, p. 308.
Rpt. in Forerunner, 6 (March 1915), 81-82.

1241. "International Duties," Armenia, 1 (Oct 1904), 10-14.
Rpt. in Woman's Journal, 15 Oct 1904, pp. 330-331.
See also CPG's letter to editor of Armenia, 1 (Oct 1904), 7-8.

1242. "'Over-Marriage,'" Woman's Journal, 1 Oct 1904, p. 314.

1243. "School for Wives," Woman's Journal, 1 Oct 1904, p. 314.

1244. "Impure Food," Woman's Journal, 1 Oct 1904, p. 314.

1245. "World Peace and Sex Combat," Woman's Journal, 8 Oct 1904, p. 322.

1246. "Women and World Organization," Woman's Journal, 8 Oct 1904, p. 322.

1247. "The Mother Heart," Woman's Journal, 15 Oct 1904, p. 330.

1248. "An Englishman on American Women," Woman's Journal, 15 Oct 1904, p. 330. [Re. H. B. Mariott-Watson]

1249. "The Clothing of Children," Woman's Journal, 22 Oct 1904, p. 338.

1250. "The Living-Room," Woman's Journal, 29 Oct 1904, p. 346.
See also "Two Views of Mrs. Gilman," Woman's Journal, 26 Nov 1904, p. 381.

1251. "Two 'Natural Protectors,'" Woman's Journal, 29 Oct 1904, p. 346.

1252. Woman's Journal, 29 Oct 1904, p. 346. [Re. sex bias of an item in the New York Times for 23 Oct 1904.]
See reply in "Topics of the Times," New York Times, 1

Nov 1904, 8:4-5.

1253. "Changes in Food," Woman's Journal, 5 Nov 1904, p. 354.

1254. "Brain Growth," Woman's Journal, 12 Nov 1904, p. 362.

1255. "The Hotel and the Home," Woman's Journal, 12 Nov 1904, p. 362.
    Rpt. in Woman's Column, 12 Nov 1904, p. 2.

1256. "Japan's Reserve," Woman's Journal, 19 Nov 1904, p. 370.
    See also "Two Views of Mrs. Gilman," Woman's Journal, 26 Nov 1904, p. 381.

1257. "'Society and Clubs,'" Woman's Journal, 26 Nov 1904, p. 378.

1258. "The Office of the Mother," Success, 7 (Dec 1904), 802.

1259. "The Passing of the Home in Great American Cities," Cosmopolitan, 38 (Dec 1904), 137-147.

1260. "To My Readers in Especial," Woman's Journal, 3 Dec 1904, p. 386.

1261. "Kitchen Dirt and Civic Health," Independent, 8 Dec 1904, pp. 1296-1299.
    Reviewed in Independent, 5 Jan 1905, p. 6.
    Excerpted in Woman's Journal, 7 Jan 1905, pp. 2-3.

1262. "These 'Muncipal Nurseries,'" Woman's Journal, 10 Dec 1904, p. 394.
    Rpt. in Woman's Column, 10 Dec 1904, pp. 2-3.

1263. "The 'Craving for Notoriety,'" Woman's Journal, 17 Dec 1904, p. 402.
    Reviewed by Alice Stone Blackwell in Woman's Journal, 24 Dec 1904, p. 412.

1264. "'Even Mother,'" Woman's Journal, 24 Dec 1904, p. 410.

1265. "Santa Claus," Woman's Journal, 24 Dec 1904, p. 410.

1266. "A Valedictory," Woman's Journal, 31 Dec 1904, p. 418.

1905

1267. "Sermons Out of Church: The Faith of Our Fathers, The Heavenly Sabbath, The Congratulations of Religion, The

Devil, Sacrifice, On Sanctity, A United Church."
Columns for syndicated publication (New York:
Charlton, 1905). Broadside copy extant in CPG Papers,
oversize vol. 1.

1268. "Duty of Surplus Women," Independent, 19 Jan 1905, pp.
126-130.
Excerpted in Woman's Journal, 4 Feb 1905, p. 18.
Excerpted under title "One of the Best Things" in
Woman's Voice: An Anthology, ed. Josephine Conger-
Kaneko (Boston: Stratford Co., 1918), p. 142.

1269. "The Home and the Hospital," Good Housekeeping, 40 (Feb
1905), 192-194.
Excerpted in Woman's Journal, 21 Jan 1905, p. 9.

1270. "Why These Clothes?" Independent, 2 March 1905, pp.
466-469.
Excerpted in Woman's Journal, 11 March 1905, p. 38.

1271. "Man is More Beautiful," Grand Magazine, 1 (April
1905), 467-471.

1272. "An Excuse for Existence," Woman's Journal, 29 April
1905, p. 65.

1273. "Symbolism in Dress," Independent, 8 June 1905, pp.
1294-1297.

1274. "Modesty: Feminine and Other," Independent, 29 June
1905, pp. 1447-1450.

1275. "False Idols!" Grand Magazine, 1 (July 1905), 920-925.

1276. "Are Women Morally Superior to Men?" Grand Magazine, 2
(Aug 1905).
Reviewed in Current Literature, 39 (Sept 1905), 288-
289.

1277. "Foreign Critics and American Women," Success, 8 (Sept
1905), 614-616. [Reply to Emil Reich, "The Future
Influence of American Women," Success, 8 (Jan 1905),
19-20.]

1278. "Housing for the Poor," New York Evening Post, 18 Nov
1905, p. 4.
Rpt. in Woman's Journal, 16 Dec 1905, pp. 199, 201.

1906

1279. "What He Craved," Critic, 48 (Feb 1906), 186-188.
      [Review of story "A Young Wife's Confession" in Good
      Housekeeping, 40 (Feb 1905), 164-166.]

1280. "Good Tidings of Women--the World's Best Hope," Woman's
      Home Companion, 33 (Feb 1906), 5, 47.

1281. "Dr. Weininger's 'Sex and Character,'" Critic, 48 (May
      1906), 414-417. [Review of Otto Weininger, Sex and
      Character (New York: Putnam, 1906).]

1282. "Passing of Matrimony," Harper's Bazar, 40 (June 1906),
      495-498.

1283. "Sensible Vacation," Independent, 7 June 1906, pp.
      1337-1344.

1284. "Has the Club-Woman Supplanted the Church Woman?"
      Woman's Home Companion, 33 (July 1906), 18.
      Reviewed in Literary Digest, 14 July 1906, p. 57.

1285. "The Untrained Mother," National Home Journal, 21 (July
      1906), 18.

1286. "Some Light on the [Single Woman's] 'Problem,'"
      American Magazine, 62 (Aug 1906), 427-428.

1287. "Home-Worship," Independent, 4 Oct 1906, pp. 788-792.
      See also Mrs. L. H. Harris, "The Monstrous Altruism,"
          Independent, 4 Oct 1906, pp. 792-797; CPG, "Why
          Monstrous?" Independent, 4 Oct 1906, p. 798; and "A
          Father's View of the Home," Independent, 18 Oct
          1906, pp. 911-914.
      Reviewed in New York Tribune, 6 Oct 1906, 11:5.
      Reviewed in Boston Herald, 8 Oct 1906, 6:1-2.
      Reviewed in Harper's Weekly, 27 Oct 1906, pp. 1522-
          1523.

1907

1288. The Punishment That Educates. Motherhood Leaflets No.
      38. Cooperstown, N.Y.: Crist, Scott, and Parshall,
      1907.

1289. "Paid Motherhood," Independent, 10 Jan 1907, pp. 75-78.

1290. "Social Consciousness," American Journal of Sociology,
      12 (March 1907), 690-691.

1291. "Social Darwinism," American Journal of Sociology, 12 (March 1907), 713-714.

1292. "Homes Without Housekeeping: A Present Demand," Delineator, 69 (May 1907), 875-876, 955.

1293. "The Progress of Women in the Last 50 Years," Woman's Home Companion, 34 (May 1907), 20.

1294. "The Home of Today and Tomorrow," Good Housekeeping, 45 (July 1907), 22-26.
      See also Ella Morris Kretschmar, "Her Mess of Pottage," Good Housekeeping, 45 (July 1907), 26-30.

1295. "Why Cooperative Housekeeping Fails," Harper's Bazar, 41 (July 1907), 625-629.

1296. "How Old is She?" Harper's Bazar, 41 (Aug 1907), 810-811.
      Published anonymously. Attributed to CPG on the basis of internal evidence and a copy in folder 263, CPG Papers.

1297. "Is Cupid a Convention?" Independent, 15 Aug 1907, pp. 373-375.
      Reviewed by Henry B. Blackwell in Woman's Journal, 24 Aug 1907, p. 134.
      Reviewed in Seattle Post-Intelligencer, 22 Sept 1907, magazine section, p. 2.

1298. "A Girl's Right to an Education/A Plea for the Proper Training of the Future Mothers of the Race," New York Times, 7 Sept 1907, 10:1-2.

1299. "The Diversity of Divorce," National Home Journal, 1 (Oct 1907), 15.

1300. "When We Fly," Harper's Weekly, 9 Nov 1907, pp. 1650, 1664.

1301. Women and Social Service. An address delivered before the Boston Equal Suffrage Association for Good Government on 14 Nov 1907. Warren, Ohio: National American Woman Suffrage Association, 1907. 12 pp.
      Reproduced on microfilm New Haven, Conn.: Research Publications, 1977 (History of Women 7959).

1302. "In What Fields of Employment Do Women Excel?" Boston Globe, 24 Nov 1907, 36:3-4.

1303. "Modern Beatitudes--The Joys of the Commonplace,"
      Circle, 1 (Dec 1907), 368.

1304. "Better Than Santa Claus," Christian Register, 12 Dec
      1907, pp. 1402-1403.

1908

1305. "How Home Conditions React Upon the Family," Papers and
      Proceedings of the American Sociological Society, 3
      (1908), 16-29.
         Rpt. in American Journal of Sociology, 14 (March
            1909), 592-605.
         Rpt. in Readings in Social Problems, ed. Albert B.
            Wolfe (Boston and New York: Ginn and Co., 1916),
            pp. 521-534.
         See also item 2228.

1306. "Five Kinds of Love," Harper's Bazar, 42 (Jan 1908),
      63-65.

1307. "Some Thoughts on General Beauty and Local Pride,"
      Circle, 2 (March 1908).

1308. "Child Labor in the Schools," Independent, 21 May 1908,
      pp. 1135-1139.

1309. "Pets and Children," Independent, 13 Aug 1908, pp. 365-
      367.

1310. "A Suggestion on the Negro Problem," American Journal
      of Sociology, 14 (July 1908), 78-85.
         Reviewed in Literary Digest, 10 Oct 1908, pp. 499-
            500.

1311. "The Woman of Fifty," Success, 11 (Oct 1908), 622-623,
      644.

1312. "Woman and the Ballot," Marsh's Magazine, 1 (Oct 1908),
      5, 12.

1313. "Private Homes and Common Kitchens," New Idea Woman's
      Magazine, 18 (Nov 1908), 8.

1314. "Have You Paid Your Board?" Independent, 26 Nov 1908,
      pp. 1221-1223.
         Rpt. in New York Daily People, 2 Dec 1908, 4:4-5; and
            6 Dec 1908, 3:1-2.
         Excerpted in New York Weekly People, 12 Dec 1908,
            2:3-4.

1315. "Woman, the Enigma," Harper's Bazar, 42 (Dec 1908),
1193-1197.
      Reviewed in Springfield Republican, 20 Dec 1908,
         30:1-2.

1909

1316. "Why Are There No Women on the President's Commission?"
Good Housekeeping, 48 (Jan 1909), 120-122.

1317. "Mothering the World," Woman Worker (London), 27 Jan
1909, p. 75.

1318. "The Irresponsible Nursemaid," Harper's Bazar, 43
(March 1909), 282-283.

1319. "How to Make Better Men," Woman Worker (London), 3
March 1909, p. 205.

1320. "Race Improvement," Independent, 25 March 1909, pp.
629-632.
      Excerpted in New York Daily People, 31 March 1909,
         2:7.

1321. "Unnecessary Fears," Appleton's, 13 (April 1909), 385-
389.
      Published anonymously. Attributed to CPG on basis of
         letter from Ripley Hitchcock to CPG dated 7 May
         1909 (folder 126, CPG Papers).

1322. "Masculine, Feminine, and Human," Appleton's, 13 (May
1909), 513-517.
      Published anonymously. Attributed to CPG on the
         basis of internal evidence and a copy in folder
         250, CPG Papers.

1323. "The Money Value of Women's Work," New Idea Woman's
Magazine, 19 (May 1909), 6, 46.

1324. "When She Feels She's Falling in Love," New York Sunday
American, 9 May 1909.

1325. "Why Walk Backward?" Appleton's, 13 (June 1909), 666-
669.

1326. "What Are Women Anyway?" Collier's, 5 June 1909, p. 19.

1327. "What I'd Like to Tell Every Mother," New Idea Woman's
Magazine, 20 (Sept 1909), 4, 52.

1328. "A Square Deal for the Divorced Woman," Pictorial
Review, 11 (Nov 1909), 13, 75.

1329. "A Small God and a Large Goddess," Forerunner, 1 (Nov
1909), 1-4.

1330. "Where the Heart Is," Forerunner, 1 (Nov 1909), 18-19.

1331. "Our Androcentric Culture, or The Man-Made World,"
Forerunner, 1 (Nov 1909), 20-24; 1 (Dec 1909), 19-23; 1
(Jan 1910), 23-27; 1 (Feb 1910), 19-22; 1 (March 1910),
18-22; 1 (April 1910), 17-21; 1 (May 1910), 19-22; 1
(June 1910), 19-23; 1 (July 1910), 17-20; 1 (Aug 1910),
17-20; 1 (Sept 1910), 18-22; 1 (Oct 1910), 21-25; 1
(Nov 1910), 17-21; 1 (Dec 1910), 20-24.
See also item 1381.

1332. "Comment and Review," Forerunner, 1 (Nov 1909), 24-26.
[Review of American Magazine, Aug 1909.]

1333. "Personal Problems," Forerunner, 1 (Nov 1909), 26-27.
[CPG addresses readers' questions. See also
Forerunner, 1 (Dec 1909), 29; 1 (Jan 1910), 30; 1 (Feb
1910), 25; 1 (March 1910), 24-25; 1 (April 1910), 24; 1
(May 1910), 24; 1 (June 1910), 25; 1 (July 1910), 22-
24; 1 (Aug 1910), 23-24; 1 (Sept 1910), 25-26; 1 (Oct
1910), 28-29; 1 (Nov 1910), 24.]

1334. "An Obvious Blessing," Forerunner, 1 (Dec 1909), 5-6.

1335. "Why We Honestly Fear Socialism," Forerunner, 1 (Dec
1909), 7-10.
Rpt. in Political Action, n.d. Copy extant in folder
250, CPG Papers.

1336. "Comment and Review," Forerunner, 1 (Dec 1909), 23-28.
[Comment on childbearing; review of Sarah Harvey
Porter, The Life and Times of Anne Royall (Cedar
Rapids: Torch Press, 1908); comments on Christmas.]

1910

1337. "Children's Clothing," Harper's Bazar, 44 (Jan 1910),
24.

1338. "Reasonable Resolutions," Forerunner, 1 (Jan 1910), 1.

1339. "Private Morality and Public Immorality," Forerunner, 1
(Jan 1910), 9-11.

1340. "The Humanness of Women," Forerunner, 1 (Jan 1910), 12-14.

1341. "Comment and Review," Forerunner, 1 (Jan 1910), 28-30. [Review of H. G. Wells, Ann Veronica (New York: Harper, 1909); comment re. Woman's Journal; review of Jessie D. Childs, The Sea of Matrimony (New York and Baltimore: Broadway Pub. Co., 1909).]

1342. "The Shopper's Defense," Pictorial Review, 11 (Feb 1910), 26.

1343. "Kitchen-Mindedness," Forerunner, 1 (Feb 1910), 7-11.

1344. "Comment and Review," Forerunner, 1 (Feb 1910), 23-24. [Discussion of literary purposes.]

1345. Womans Era, 1 (March 1910), 152. [Apothegm.]

1346. "Parlor-Mindedness," Forerunner, 1 (March 1910), 6-10.

1347. "Comment and Review," Forerunner, 1 (March 1910), 24. [Review of Meredith Nicholson, The Lords of High Decision (New York: Doubleday, Page, 1909).]

1348. "Nursery-Mindedness," Forerunner, 1 (April 1910), 7-10.

1349. "Comment and Review," Forerunner, 1 (April 1910), 22-23. [Review of William J. Robinson, Never Told Tales (New York: Altrurians, 1909).]

1350. "Economic Waste in the Home," Womans Era, 1 (April 1910), 157-161.

1351. "Believing and Knowing," Forerunner, 1 (May 1910), 7-8.

1352. "Prize Children," Forerunner, 1 (May 1910), 10-11.

1353. "Comment and Review," Forerunner, 1 (May 1910), 23. [Review of Gerald Stanley Lee, Inspired Millionaires (New York: Kennerley, 1908).]

1354. "Suffrage," Forerunner, 1 (May 1910), 24.

1355. "Ten Suggestions," Forerunner, 1 (June 1910), 6-9.

1356. "Genius, Domestic and Maternal," Forerunner, 1 (June 1910), 10-12; and 1 (July 1910), 5-7.

1357. "Comment and Review," Forerunner, 1 (June 1910), 24-25.

[Review of Ida Tarbell, "The American Woman," _American Magazine_, May 1910.]

1358. "Improved Methods of Habit Culture," _Forerunner_, 1 (July 1910), 7-9.

1359. "Comment and Review," _Forerunner_, 1 (July 1910), 21. [Reviews of Nancy Musselman Schoonmaker, _The Eternal Fires_ (New York: Broadway Pub. Co., 1910); Stanton Coit, _Women in Church and State_ (Bayswater, England: West End London Ethical Society, 1910); Stanton Coit, "The Group Spirit," _Ethical World_, 15 March 1910.]

1360. "Wholesale Hypnotism," _Forerunner_, 1 (Aug 1910), 6-7.

1361. "The Kitchen Fly," _Forerunner_, 1 (Aug 1910), 8-10.

1362. "Comment and Review," _Forerunner_, 1 (Aug 1910), 20-22. [Review of "Two Preventable Causes of Insanity" in _Popular Science Monthly_, June 1910; comment re. sex bias in _New York Times_; review of magazine _The Englishwoman_; comment re. _Woman's Journal_.]

1363. "The Editor's Problem," _Forerunner_, 1 (Aug 1910), 24; and 1 (Sept 1910), 26. [Plea for subscribers.]

1364. "What Virtues Are Made Of," _Forerunner_, 1 (Sept 1910), 5-6.

1365. "Animals in Cities," _Forerunner_, 1 (Sept 1910), 6.

1366. "The Beauty Women Have Lost," _Forerunner_, 1 (Sept 1910), 22-23.

1367. "Comment and Review," _Forerunner_, 1 (Sept 1910), 24. [Review of Alexander Irvine, _From the Bottom Up_ (New York: Doubleday, 1910); and comments on feminist papers.]

1368. "Is It Wrong to Take Life?" _Forerunner_, 1 (Oct 1910), 6-8.

1369. "Woman and the State," _Forerunner_, 1 (Oct 1910), 10-14.

1370. "Comment and Review," _Forerunner_, 1 (Oct 1910), 26-27. [Review of Lester Ward, _Pure Sociology_ (New York: Macmillan, 1909); comment re. _Pure Food Magazine_; review of Hervey White, _A Ship of Souls_ (New York: Maverick Press, 1910).]

1371. "Why Texts?" Forerunner, 1 (Nov 1910), 6.

1372. "Women Teachers, Married and Unmarried," Forerunner, 1 (Nov 1910), 8-10.

1373. "A Frequent Question," Forerunner, 1 (Nov 1910), 21.

1374. "Comment and Review," Forerunner, 1 (Nov 1910), 24. [Reviews of Lavinia L. Dock, Hygiene and Morality (New York: Putnam's, 1910); Cicely Hamilton, Marriage as a Trade (New York: Moffat, Yard, & Co., 1909); Mary Johnston, "To Have and Hold," Woman's Journal, 8 Oct 1910).]

1375. "Christmas Love," Forerunner, 1 (Dec 1910), 5-7.

1376. "Our Overworked Instincts," Forerunner, 1 (Dec 1910), 12-13.

1377. "The New Motherhood," Forerunner, 1 (Dec 1910), 17-18.

1378. "How We Waste Three-Fourths of Our Money," Forerunner, 1 (Dec 1910), 18-19.

1379. "The Nun in the Kitchen," Forerunner, 1 (Dec 1910), 24.

1380. "Comment and Review," Forerunner, 1 (Dec 1910), 25-26. [Reviews of Ellen Key, The Century of the Child (New York: Putnam's, 1909); and Molly Elliot Sewell, "The Ladies' Battle," Atlantic Monthly, Sept 1910).]

1911

1381. The Man-Made World or Our Androcentric Culture. New York: Charlton Co., 1911. 260 pp.
    Rpt. in London: T. Fisher Unwin, 1911. 3rd ed. New York: Charlton 1914. Also rpt. in New York: Source Book Press, 1970; New York: Johnson Reprint Co., 1971; and reproduced on microform in Washington: NCR Microcard Editions, 1971; Chicago: Library Resources, 1971; and New Haven, Conn.: Research Publications, 1976 (History of Women #6557).
    Reviewed in New York Times Magazine, 15 Jan 1911, p. 14.
    Reviewed in New York Times Review of Books, 26 Feb 1911, p. 111.
    Reviewed in A.L.A. Booklist, 7 (April 1911), 330.
    Reviewed in Independent, 13 April 1911, p. 793.
    Reviewed in Literary Digest, 22 April 1911, p. 796.
    Reviewed in Current Literature, 50 (May 1911), 548-

550.
Reviewed by T. D. A. Cockerell in Dial, 16 June 1911,
pp. 471-472.
Reviewed by Lilian Brandt in Survey, 12 Aug 1911, p.
696.
Reviewed in American Journal of Sociology, 17 (Nov
1911), 417.
Reviewed in Woman's Journal, 16 Dec 1911, p. 398.
Published in Swedish translation by Alma Faustman
under the title Den av mannen skapade världen
(Stockholm: P. A. Norstedt & Sons, 1912). 170 pp.
Excerpted in The Writer's Signature: Idea in Story
and Essay, ed. Elaine Gottlieb Hemley (Glenview,
Ill.: Scott, Foresman and Co., 1972), pp. 99-105.

1382. "Hope," Forerunner, 2 (Jan 1911), 8-9.

1383. "Past, Present and Future," Forerunner, 2 (Jan 1911),
16-18.

1384. "Comment and Review," Forerunner, 2 (Jan 1911), 26-28.
[Reviews of Prince A. Morrow, Social Diseases and
Marriage (New York and Philadelphia: Lea Bros. & Co.,
1910); Marion Talbot, The Education of Women (Chicago:
Univ. of Chicago Press, 1910); Edith B. Lowry,
Confidences: Talks with a Young Girl Concerning
Herself (Chicago: M. D. Forbes & Co., 1910); Hervey
White, In an Old Man's Garden (Woodstock, N.Y.:
Maverick Press, 1910).]

1385. "For 1911," Forerunner, 2 (Jan 1911), 28-29.
Excerpted in Women in America: A History, ed. Carol
Berkin and Mary Beth Norton (Boston: Houghton
Mifflin, 1979), pp. 175-176.

1386. "Self Control," Forerunner, 2 (Feb 1911), 36-38.

1387. "Living and the Social Leader," Forerunner, 2 (Feb
1911), 46-49.

1388. "A Request from Your Grandchildren," Forerunner, 2 (Feb
1911), 56.

1389. "Comment and Review," Forerunner, 2 (Feb 1911), 57-58.
[Reviews of H. G. Wells, The History of Mr. Polly (New
York: Duffield & Co., 1910); Edgar Chambliss, Roadtown
(New York: Roadtown Press, 1910); Emma Goldman,
Anarchism and Other Essays (New York: Mother Earth
Pub. Assn., 1910).]

1390. "Anger and the Enemy," Forerunner, 2 (March 1911), 65-66.

1391. "The Argument of Legs," Forerunner, 2 (March 1911), 67.

1392. "Answers to 'Antis,'" Forerunner, 2 (March 1911), 73-77.

1393. "Comment and Review," Forerunner, 2 (March 1911), 85-86. [Reviews of Elizabeth Hamilton-Muncie, Four Epochs of Life (New York: privately printed, 1910); Eugene A. Hecker, A Short History of Woman's Rights (New York: Putnam's, 1910); Thereas Serber Malkiel, The Diary of a Shirtwaist Striker (New York: Co-operative Press, 1910).]

1394. "Immortal Life," Forerunner, 2 (April 1911), 93-95.

1395. "The Woman of Fifty," Forerunner, 2 (April 1911), 96-98.

1396. "Comment and Review," Forerunner, 2 (April 1911), 114. [Review of magazine The Teacher; comment re. socialism.]

1397. "A Socialist Prayer," Forerunner, 2 (May 1911), 124.

1398. "A Word from the Great Auk," Forerunner, 2 (May 1911), 125.

1399. "This Superiority," Forerunner, 2 (May 1911), 126.

1400. "The 'Article of Fact,'" Forerunner, 2 (May 1911), 134.

1401. "Comment and Review," Forerunner, 2 (May 1911), 141-142. [Review of Henry C. Rowland's story "Her Masterpiece" in recent issue of Ainslee's; comments on poison in food, androcentric patterns of thought, and the home of Louisa May Alcott.]

1402. "Happiness and Religion," Forerunner, 2 (June 1911), 154.

1403. "That Obvious Purpose," Forerunner, 2 (June 1911), 162.

1404. "N.G.," Forerunner, 2 (June 1911), 168.

1405. "Comment and Review," Forerunner, 2 (June 1911), 169-170. [Review of H. G. Wells, The New Machiavelli (New York: Duffield & Co., 1910); David Graham Phillips' story "The Grain of Dust"; Louise Beecher Chancellor, The Players of London (New York: B. W. Dodge Co., 1909).]

1406. "What Do You Believe?" Forerunner, 2 (July 1911), 178-179.

1407. "On Dogs," Forerunner, 2 (July 1911), 180-182; and 2 (Aug 1911), 206-209.

1408. "Comment and Review," Forerunner, 2 (July 1911), 196-198. [Reviews of Newton Mann, The Import and Outlook of Socialism (Boston: James H. West & Co., 1910); Charles Edward Stowe and Lyman Beecher Stowe, The Life of Harriet Beecher Stowe (Boston and New York: Houghton Mifflin, 1889); Olive Schreiner, Woman and Labour (New York: Frederick A. Stokes, 1911); comment on Walt Whitman.]

1409. "Personality and God," Forerunner, 2 (Aug 1911), 204-205.

1410. "Comment and Review," Forerunner, 2 (Aug 1911), 225-226. [Review of William J. Locke's story "The Glory of Clementina" in a recent Saturday Evening Post.]

1411. "When We Know God," Forerunner, 2 (Sept 1911), 232-233.

1412. "'Does a Man Support His Wife?" Forerunner, 2 (Sept 1911), 240-246.
        Rpt. in Does a Man Support His Wife? (New York:
        Charlton, 1911), pp. 9-20. Reproduced on microfilm
        in New Haven, Conn.: Research Publications, 1977
        (History of Women #7972).

1413. "Comment and Review," Forerunner, 2 (Sept 1911), 253-254. [Comment re. recruitment of National Guard.]

1414. "A Modern Woman on the Modern Girl," Pictorial Review, 13 (Oct 1911), 10.

1415. "Happiness," Forerunner, 2 (Oct 1911), 259-260.

1416. "Names--Especially Women's," Forerunner, 2 (Oct 1911), 261-263.

1417. "An Unsavory Subject," Forerunner, 2 (Oct 1911), 272-273.

1418. "Comment and Review," Forerunner, 2 (Oct 1911), 280-

282. [Review of Ellen Key, Love and Marriage (New York and London: Putnam's, 1911).]

1419. "The Woman's Party," Forerunner, 2 (Nov 1911), 288-291.

1420. "The Instinct of Worship," Forerunner, 2 (Nov 1911), 298-300.

1421. "Comment and Review," Forerunner, 2 (Nov 1911), 309-310. [Comments re. voting; on women's courage; on pain; review of Literary Digest, 7 Oct 1911.]

1422. "Play Supervisors," Forerunner, 2 (Dec 1911), 315.

1423. "Giving," Forerunner, 2 (Dec 1911), 316-317.

1424. "Gratitude as a Virtue," Forerunner, 2 (Dec 1911), 326-328.

1425. "Looking and Seeing," Forerunner, 2 (Dec 1911), 328.

1426. "Comment and Review," Forerunner, 2 (Dec 1911), 336-338. [Review of Rudyard Kipling's "Study in Natural History" in Ladies' Home Journal, Nov 1911; comment on human work.]

1912

1427. "Our Brains and What Ails Them," Forerunner, 3 (Jan 1912), 22-26; 3 (Feb 1912), 49-54; 3 (March 1912), 77-82; 3 (April 1912), 104-109; 3 (May 1912), 133-139; 3 (June 1912), 161-167; 3 (July 1912), 189-195; 3 (Aug 1912), 215-221; 3 (Sept 1912), 245-251; 3 (Oct 1912), 273-279; 3 (Nov 1912), 301-307; 3 (Dec 1912), 328-334.

1428. "Mind Cleaning," Forerunner, 3 (Jan 1912), 5-6.

1429. "The Work Before Us," Forerunner, 3 (Jan 1912), 6-9.

1430. "What Do Men Think of Women?" Forerunner, 3 (Jan 1912), 15-16.

1431. "In the Near Future," Forerunner, 3 (Jan 1912), 18.

1432. "What Young People Are For," Forerunner, 3 (Jan 1912), 19-20.

1433. "Comment and Review," Forerunner, 3 (Jan 1912), 27-28. [Reviews of magazine The Altrurian; Percival Gibbon, "The Adventures of Miss Gregory," serial in McClure's,

Sept 1910-Feb 1912; The Poems of Max Ehrmann (New York: Dodge Pub. Co., 1910).]

1434. "Women and Democracy," Forerunner, 3 (Feb 1912), 33-37.

1435. "Miss Ida Tarbell's 'Uneasy Woman,'" Forerunner, 3 (Feb 1912), 37-39. [Review of essay in American Magazine, Jan 1912.]

1436. "Comment and Review," Forerunner, 3 (Feb 1912), 55-56. [Comment on policy of New York School Board of firing teachers who marry; reviews of Edward A. Ross, The Changing Chinese (New York: Century, 1911); magazine The American Teacher; Edwin Björkman, Is There Anything New Under the Sun? (New York: Kennerley, 1911).]

1437. "Her Own Money: Is a Wife Entitled to the Money She Earns?" Mother's Magazine, 7 (Feb 1912), 5-7.

1438. "New Ideals of Love and Marriage," Pictorial Review, 13 (Feb 1912), 6, 70.

1439. "Why Make Dust?" Forerunner, 3 (March 1912), 61.

1440. "The New Immorality," Forerunner, 3 (March 1912), 62-64.

1441. "Teaching the Mothers," Forerunner, 3 (March 1912), 73-75.

1442. "By One's Bootstraps," Forerunner, 3 (March 1912), 76.

1443. "Two Rooms and a Bath," Forerunner, 3 (March 1912), 76.

1444. "Alimony," Forerunner, 3 (March 1912), 82.
          Rpt. in Living, pp. 307-308.

1445. "Comment and Review," Forerunner, 3 (March 1912), 84. [Comments on book review policy, on Ida Tarbell's serial-essay "The Uneasy Woman" in American Magazine; comment re. woman's business.]

1446. "What 'Authorities' May Do in America," Forerunner, 3 (April 1912), 89.

1447. "The New Faith," Forerunner, 3 (April 1912), 90-91.

1448. "Miss Tarbell's Third Paper," Forerunner, 3 (April 1912), 92-95. [Review of Ida Tarbell's serial-essay "The Uneasy Woman" in American Magazine.]

See reply by Josephine Conger-Kaneko in <u>Progressive Woman</u>, 5 (May 1912), 11-12.

1449. "An Argument Against Women Jurors," <u>Forerunner</u>, 3 (April 1912), 110.

1450. "Comment and Review," <u>Forerunner</u>, 3 (April 1912), 110-112. [Comment re. <u>Woman's Journal</u>, the <u>Progressive Woman</u>, and the New York State Association Opposed to Woman Suffrage.]

1451. "The Real Truth in Christianity," <u>Forerunner</u>, 3 (May 1912), 117-119.

1452. "Miss Tarbell's 'The Homeless Daughter,'" <u>Forerunner</u>, 3 (May 1912), 120-121.

1453. "How Much is a Dollar?" <u>Forerunner</u>, 3 (May 1912), 119.

1454. "The Beast Prison," <u>Forerunner</u>, 3 (May 1912), 128-130.

1455. "Good and Bad Taste in Suicide," <u>Forerunner</u>, 3 (May 1912), 130.

1456. "Comment and Review," <u>Forerunner</u>, 3 (May 1912), 139-140. [Reviews of Leroy Scott, <u>The Counsel for the Defense</u> (Garden City: Doubleday, 1912); G. K. Chesterton, <u>The Innocence of Father Brown</u> (New York: John Lane Co., 1911); and the magazine <u>The Quest</u>; comments re. the power of the press, a peace statue for Panama, the decision of a Denver judge, "a school of matrimony," and "the saving of women in disaster."]

1457. Review of Otis Tufton Mason, <u>Woman's Share in Primitive Culture</u> (New York: Appleton's, ca. 1904) in <u>Truth</u>, May 1912, pp. 109-110.
Copy extant in folder 262, CPG Papers.

1458. "Are Women Human Beings?" <u>Harper's Weekly</u>, 25 May 1912, p. 11.
Excerpted in <u>Up the Pedestal</u>, ed. Aileen S. Kraditor (New York: Quadrangle, 1968), pp. 325-331.
Excerpted in <u>Woman and Womanhood in America</u>, ed. Ronald W. Hogeland (Lexington, Mass.: D. C. Heath & Co., 1973), pp. 133-135.

1459. "Instincts, Morals and Ethics," <u>Forerunner</u>, 3 (June 1912), 145-147.

1460. "Sloyd and Cooking," <u>Forerunner</u>, 3 (June 1912), 147.

1461. "Woman Suffrage and the Average Mind," Forerunner, 3 (June 1912), 148-153.

1462. "Comment and Review," Forerunner, 3 (June 1912), 167-168. [Reviews of Caroline Lloyd, Henry Demarest Lloyd: A Biography (New York and London: Putnam's, 1912); Walter E. Weyl, The New Democracy (New York: Macmillan, 1912); William English Walling, Socialism As It Is (New York: Macmillan, 1912); Marie Jennie Howe, An Anti-Suffrage Monologue (New York: NAWSA, n.d.); comment re. Lewis Carroll's "Alice in Wonderland."]

1463. "The Divine Right of Judges," Forerunner, 3 (July 1912), 172-173.

1464. "The Order of Duties," Forerunner, 3 (July 1912), 176-177.

1465. "Price Tyranny," Forerunner, 3 (July 1912), 177-181.

1466. "Art in the Schools," Forerunner, 3 (July 1912), 187-188.

1467. "Comment and Review," Forerunner, 3 (July 1912), 195-196. [Reviews of Samuel Merwin, The Citadel (New York: Century, 1912); Zona Gale, Mothers to Men (New York: Macmillan, 1912); the magazine The Wild Hawk, edited by Hervey White.]

1468. "The Need of Prayer," Forerunner, 3 (Aug 1912), 202-204.

1469. "Is Health Worth Having?" Forerunner, 3 (Aug 1912), 204-206.

1470. "Monarchy and Democracy," Forerunner, 3 (Aug 1912), 222.

1471. "Comment and Review," Forerunner, 3 (Aug 1912), 222-224. [Reviews of Rudyard Kipling, "Warning to Labor," American Magazine, July 1912; magazine The Woman Voter, organ of the Woman Suffrage Party.]

1472. "The Stretching Limit of Honesty," Forerunner, 3 (Sept 1912), 230-231.

1473. "Ideas That Hinder Socialism," Forerunner, 3 (Sept 1912), 232-236.

1474. "Imprisonment for Life," Forerunner, 3 (Sept 1912),

237.

1475. "Interstate Sanitation," Forerunner, 3 (Sept 1912), 237.

1476. "The New Party," Forerunner, 3 (Sept 1912), 252. [Re. the Progressive Party.]

1477. "A Moving Faith," Forerunner, 3 (Sept 1912), 258-259.

1478. "Class Consciousness, World Consciousness and Socialism," Forerunner, 3 (Oct 1912), 260-262.

1479. "Euthanasia Again," Forerunner, 3 (Oct 1912), 262-263.

1480. "Comment and Review," Forerunner, 3 (Oct 1912), 279-280. [Reviews of Mary Austin, A Woman of Genius (Garden City: Doubleday, 1912); and Edna Ferber's "Emma McChesney" stories.]

1481. "Should Wives Have Wages?" Pictorial Review, 14 (Oct 1912), 9, 80.

1482. "The New Vision," Forerunner, 3 (Nov 1912), 285-287.

1483. "His Share," Forerunner, 3 (Nov 1912), 294-295.

1484. "Summer Work," Forerunner, 3 (Nov 1912), 296-297.

1485. "Is There a Double Standard in Filial Duty?" Forerunner, 3 (Nov 1912), 297-298.

1486. "Birth and Death," Forerunner, 3 (Nov 1912), 299-300.

1487. "Comment and Review," Forerunner, 3 (Nov 1912), 307-308. [Reviews of the magazine Life and Labor, organ of the National Woman's Trade Union League; Henry Adams, Democracy (New York: Henry Holt & Co., 1880); G. K. Chesterton's poem "Lepanto."]

1488. "Should Women Use Violence?" Pictorial Review, 14 (Nov 1912), 11, 78-79.

1489. "The Pillory," Forerunner, 3 (Dec 1912), 315-317.

1490. "This Bitterness," Forerunner, 3 (Dec 1912), 317.

1491. "The Happiness That Belongs to Us," Forerunner, 3 (Dec 1912), 326-327.

1492. "The End of the Advertising Nuisance," Forerunner, 3 (Dec 1912), 327-328.

1493. "Comment and Review," Forerunner, 3 (Dec 1912), 335-336. [Reviews of Maria Thompson Daviess, The Elected Mother (Indianapolis: Bobbs-Merrill, 1912); essay "Where Are the Old Ladies?" in Century, Oct 1912; comment re. states that have approved woman suffrage.]

1494. "How to Lighten the Labor of Women," McCalls, 40 (Dec 1912), 14-15, 77.

1495. "Education and Social Progress," American Teacher, 1 (Dec 1912), 134-135.
    Rpt. in Forerunner, 4 (March 1913), 71-72.

1496. "The Woman of Fifty," Pictorial Review, 14 (Dec 1912), 11.

1913

1497. "Humanness," Forerunner, 4 (Jan 1913), 20-25; 4 (Feb 1913), 48-54; 4 (March 1913), 76-81; 4 (April 1913), 105-110; 4 (May 1913), 132-138; 4 (June 1913), 160-165; 4 (July 1913), 190-196; 4 (Aug 1913), 218-223; 4 (Sept 1913), 246-251; 4 (Oct 1913), 272-277; 4 (Nov 1913), 298-303; 4 (Dec 1913), 328-334.

1498. "A Platform for Women," Forerunner, 4 (Jan 1913), 6-7.

1499. "Morals and Politics," Forerunner, 4 (Jan 1913), 7.

1500. "The Court of Infant Relations," Forerunner, 4 (Jan 1913), 8-9.

1501. "Fighting, Growing and Making," Forerunner, 4 (Jan 1913), 16-18.

1502. "The Cost and the Price of Living," Forerunner, 4 (Jan 1913), 25-26.

1503. "The Smoke Evil," Forerunner, 4 (Jan 1913), 27.

1504. "Comment and Review," Forerunner, 4 (Jan 1913), 28. [Review of N. J. Locke, Stella Maris (New York: Grosset & Dunlap, 1913).]

1505. "Some Domestic Myths," Pictorial Review, 14 (Jan 1913), 7, 53.

1506. "Our Changing Virtues," Forerunner, 4 (Feb 1913), 33-35.

1507. "On Ellen Key and the Woman Movement," Forerunner, 4 (Feb 1913), 35-38.
    Reviewed in Current Opinion, 54 (March 1913), 220-221.

1508. "A Crime Beyond Excuse," Forerunner, 4 (Feb 1913), 44.

1509. "Noise as an Offense," Forerunner, 4 (Feb 1913), 47.

1510. "The Women Selling Eggs," Forerunner, 4 (Feb 1913), 54.

1511. "An Amusing Editorial," Forerunner, 4 (Feb 1913), 55-56.

1512. "The Comfort of God," Forerunner, 4 (March 1913), 61-62.

1513. "The Oldest Profession in the World," Forerunner, 4 (March 1913), 63-64.

1514. "'Hysterically Worded,'" Forerunner, 4 (March 1913), 75.

1515. "Comment and Review," Forerunner, 4 (March 1913), 82-84. [Review of Warren Fite, "The Feminist Mind," Nation, 6 Feb 1913; comment re. equal suffrage in Washington and Budapest.]

1516. "Race Pride," Forerunner, 4 (April 1913), 89-90.

1517. "Prisons, Convicts and Women Voters," Forerunner, 4 (April 1913), 91-92.

1518. "Are We Quangle-Wangles?" Forerunner, 4 (April 1913), 92.

1519. "Milk, Motherhood and Morality," Forerunner, 4 (April 1913), 99-102.

1520. "Comment and Review," Forerunner, 4 (April 1913), 111-112. [Reviews of the Armory Exhibition; Eugène Brieux' play "Damaged Goods"; the magazine The American Teacher.]

1521. "Our Hurrying Heretics," Forerunner, 4 (May 1913), 118-119.

1522. "A Thousand Farmers' Wives," Forerunner, 4 (May 1913), 120-121.

1523. "A Minimum Wage and Other Things," Forerunner, 4 (May 1913), 121-123.

1524. "Birds, Bugs and Women," Forerunner, 4 (May 1913), 131-132.

1525. "More Social Uses of Schoolhouses," Forerunner, 4 (May 1913), 138.

1526. "The Cream of the World," Forerunner, 4 (May 1913), 138.

1527. "Comment and Review," Forerunner, 4 (May 1913), 139-140. [Comments re. the International Society for the Creation of a World Center; sex bias in the New York Times; reviews of the magazine The Survey; Martha Bensley Bruere and Robert Bruere, Increasing Home Efficiency (New York: Macmillan, 1912); Harriet Howe, Along the Way (Woodstock, N.Y.: Maverick Press, 1913); Margaret Ladd Franklin, The Case for Women Suffrage: A Bibliography (New York: National College Equal Suffrage League, 1913).]

1528. "English and American Women," London Daily News and Leader, 20 May 1913.
    Excerpted in New York Times, 20 May 1913, 4:3.

1529. "The New Mothers of a New World," Forerunner, 4 (June 1913), 145-149.

1530. "A Religion of Growth and Happiness," Forerunner, 4 (June 1913), 159.

1531. "Comment and Review," Forerunner, 4 (June 1913), 165-167. [Obituary of Lester F. Ward; editorial on bill in Illinois legislature legitimizing children born to unmarried parents.]

1532. "The Normal Social Group To-Day," Forerunner, 4 (July 1913), 174-176.

1533. "Paws and Hoofs," Forerunner, 4 (July 1913), 178.

1534. "Without Votes," Forerunner, 4 (July 1913), 178.

1535. "Our Ugliness," Forerunner, 4 (July 1913), 187.

1536. "The Hope of Heaven," Forerunner, 4 (July 1913), 188-189.

1537. "Comment and Review," Forerunner, 4 (July 1913), 196. [Comments re. militant workers, the church leagues.]

1538. "The Waste of Private Housekeeping," Annals of the American Academy, 48 (July 1913), 91-95.
Rpt. in The New Feminism in Twentieth-Century America, ed. June Sochen (Lexington, Mass.: D. C. Heath and Co., 1971), pp. 36-41.

1539. "Faith in Humanity," Forerunner, 4 (Aug 1913), 202-203.

1540. "The Woman Suffrage Congress in Buda-Pest," Forerunner, 4 (Aug 1913), 204-206.

1541. "The Balkan War and Universal Peace," Forerunner, 4 (Aug 1913), 213-214.

1542. "Plagarism," Forerunner, 4 (Aug 1913), 216-217.

1543. "Comment and Review," Forerunner, 4 (Aug 1913), 223-224. [Review of Josephine Dasecam Bacon, "The Mortgage," Saturday Evening Post, 19 July 1913.]

1544. "Pain Measure," Forerunner, 4 (Sept 1913), 229.

1545. "The Finger of God," Forerunner, 4 (Sept 1913), 230-231.

1546. "Our Sleeping Cars," Forerunner, 4 (Sept 1913), 231-232.

1547. "Our First Necessity," Forerunner, 4 (Sept 1913), 233-234.

1548. "The Drama We Might Have," Forerunner, 4 (Sept 1913), 242-243.

1549. "'The Great Adventure,'" Forerunner, 4 (Sept 1913), 251.

1550. "Comment and Review," Forerunner, 4 (Sept 1913), 252. [Comment re. the detective story formula.]

1551. "What 'Love' Really Is," Pictorial Review, 14 (Sept 1913), 11, 57.

1552. "Justice Instead of Sacrifice," Forerunner, 4 (Oct

1913), 257-258.

1554. "Education for Motherhood," Forerunner, 4 (Oct 1913), 259-262. [Review of Ellen Key, "Education for Motherhood," Atlantic Monthly, July and Aug 1913.]

1555. "Minimum Wage and Maximum Price," Forerunner, 4 (Oct 1913), 269-270.

1556. "Why I Wrote 'The Yellow Wallpaper'?" Forerunner, 4 (Oct 1913), 271.
Rpt. in Charlotte Perkins Gilman Reader, pp. 19-20.

1557. "The Theory of the Upper Dog," Forerunner, 4 (Oct 1913), 277.

1558. "Comment and Review," Forerunner, 4 (Oct 1913), 278-280. [Review of Illiteracy in the United States, and an Experiment for its Elimination (Washington, D.C.: Government Printing Office, 1913).]

1559. "Motherhood and the Modern Woman," Physical Culture, 30 (Oct 1913), 382-385.

1560. "Property Rights and Wrongs," Forerunner, 4 (Nov 1913), 285-287.

1561. "Illegitimate Children," Forerunner, 4 (Nov 1913), 295-297.

1562. "Comment and Review," Forerunner, 4 (Nov 1913), 303-308. [Review of Sir Almroth Wright, The Unexpurgated Case Against Woman Suffrage (New York: Hoeber, 1913); comment re. "the single moral standard."]

1563. "The Forerunner for 1914," Forerunner, 4 (Nov 1913), 308.

1564. "Our Wickedest Waste," Pictorial Review, 15 (Nov 1913), 18, 72.

1565. "Unhappy Marriages: The Cause and the Remedy," Physical Culture, 30 (Nov 1913), 503-505.

1566. "'The Brute in Man,'" Forerunner, 4 (Dec 1913), 316-317.

1567. "Comment and Review," Forerunner, 4 (Dec 1913), 336. [Review of John D. Barry, Intimations (San Francisco: Paul Elder, 1913).]

1914

1568. "Social Ethics," Forerunner, 5 (Jan 1914), 20-25; 5
(Feb 1914), 48-53; 5 (March 1914), 76-82; 5 (April
1914), 102-108; 5 (May 1914), 130-136; 5 (June 1914),
160-166; 5 (July 1914), 187-193; 5 (Aug 1914), 216-222;
5 (Sept 1914), 244-249; 5 (Oct 1914), 271-277; 5 (Nov
1914), 300-305; 5 (Dec 1914), 327-332.

1569. "As to God," Forerunner, 5 (Jan 1914), 5-7.

1570. "Pensions for 'Mothers' and 'Widows,'" Forerunner, 5
(Jan 1914), 7-8.

1571. "An Amazing Tyranny," Forerunner, 5 (Jan 1914), 15-19.

1572. "Comment and Review," Forerunner, 5 (Jan 1914), 26-27.
[Comment re. League for the Civic Service of Women;
review of W. L. George, "Feminist Intentions," Atlantic
Monthly, Dec 1913.]

1573. "The Business Side of Matrimony," Physical Culture, 31
(Jan 1914), 13-16.

1574. "Working to Make Black White," Forerunner, 5 (Feb
1914), 33-34.

1575. "'Interviewing,'" Forerunner, 5 (Feb 1914), 34-37.

1576. "As to 'Feminism,'" Forerunner, 5 (Feb 1914), 45.

1577. "Difficulties of Organizing Saleswomen," Forerunner, 5
(Feb 1914), 46-47.

1578. "The Work of the Master," Forerunner, 5 (Feb 1914), 47.

1579. Forerunner, 5 (Feb 1914), 53. [Untitled editorial re.
meaning of the word "mine."]

1580. "Comment and Review," Forerunner, 5 (Feb 1914), 54-56.
[Reviews of A. E. W. Mason, "North of the Tropic of
Capricorn," Metropolitan Magazine, Jan 1914; H. G.
Wells, "Trap to Catch the Sun," Century, Jan 1914;
comments re. "rich men and their new needle,"
"Wisconsin law and Milwaukee doctors."]

1581. "The Women Who Won't Move Forward," Physical Culture,
31 (Feb 1914), 126-128.

1582. "Mourning and Who Wears It," Forerunner, 5 (March

1914), 62-63.

1583. "The Biological Anti-Feminist," Forerunner, 5 (March 1914), 64-67.

1584. "A Cataclysm of Nature," Forerunner, 5 (March 1914), 83.

1585. "Comment and Review," Forerunner, 5 (March 1914), 83-84. [Review of George Middleton, Tradition and Other One-Act Plays of Modern American Life (New York: Henry Holt & Co., 1913).]

1586. "What May We Expect of Eugenics?" Physical Culture, 31 (March 1914), 219-222.

1587. "Socialism and the Race Mind," Forerunner, 5 (April 1914), 89-92.

1588. "Comment and Review," Forerunner, 5 (April 1914), 110-111. [Reviews of Woman's Home Companion, special woman's issue of Medical Review of Reviews, Samuel Merwin, Anthony the Absolute (New York: Century, 1914); What to Read on Suffrage, A Bulletin of the NAWSA, ed. Frances Maule Björkman, and Eugenics: A Selected Bibliography; comments re. Montessori schools and California public schools.]

1589. "Passing of Involuntary Motherhood," Physical Culture, 31 (April 1914), 332-338.

1590. "Immigration, Importation, and Our Fathers," Forerunner, 5 (May 1914), 117-119.

1591. "The 'Noble Animals,'" Forerunner, 5 (May 1914), 120-121.

1592. "These Proud Fathers," Forerunner, 5 (May 1914), 129-130.

1593. "The Unrestricted Hat," Forerunner, 5 (May 1914), 136-138.

1594. "War," Forerunner, 5 (May 1914), 138.

1595. "Comment and Review," Forerunner, 5 (May 1914), 138-140. [Reviews of Ellen Glasgow, Virginia (Garden City: Doubleday, 1913); Mary Johnston, Hagar (Boston: Houghton Mifflin, 1913); Ella Peattie, The Precipice (Boston: Houghton Mifflin, 1914).]

1596. "Marriage: Today, Yesterday, and Tomorrow," Physical Culture, 31 (May 1914), 454-455.

1597. "Gum Chewing in Public," New York Times, 20 May 1914, 12:5. [Letter to editor.]

1598. "'Free Speech,'" Forerunner, 5 (June 1914), 146-148.

1599. "'A Sea Voyage,'" Forerunner, 5 (June 1914), 149-150.

1600. "Bringing People Together," Forerunner, 5 (June 1914), 158-160.

1601. "Comment and Review," Forerunner, 5 (June 1914), 166-168. [Reviews of Social Forces: A Topical Outline with Bibliography (Madison: Wisconsin Suffrage Headquarters, 1914); Owen Johnson, The Salamander (Indianapolis: Bobbs-Merrill, 1914); Floyd Dell, Women as World Builders (Chicago: Forbes, 1913); and Lincoln Steffens, "The Dying Boss," McClure's, May 1914.]

1602. "Romance and Reality in Married Life," Physical Culture, 31 (June 1914), 549-552.

1603. "Swimming," Forerunner, 5 (July 1914), 173.

1604. "'The Perpetuation of the Race,'" Forerunner, 5 (July 1914), 174-175.

1605. "Her Hair," Forerunner, 5 (July 1914), 175-176.

1606. "Professor Langley and the Newspapers," Forerunner, 5 (July 1914), 176-178.

1607. "Our Coal," Forerunner, 5 (July 1914), 185-186.

1608. "Competing with Men," Forerunner, 5 (July 1914), 193-194.

1609. "Comment and Review," Forerunner, 5 (July 1914), 195-196. [Reviews Basil King's serial on divorce, "Letter of the Contract," in McClures, April-June 1914; and James Lane Allen, "A Cathedral Singer," Century, May 1914.]

1610. "Social Parasitism," Forerunner, 5 (Aug 1914), 201-203.

1611. "Hats in Houses," Forerunner, 5 (Aug 1914), 203.

1612. "The Simple Art of Public Speaking," Forerunner, 5 (Aug

1914), 204-205.

1613. "'Pardoned,'" Forerunner, 5 (Aug 1914), 205.

1614. "A Visible Evolution," Forerunner, 5 (Aug 1914), 214-215.

1615. "A 'Sacred Subject,'" Forerunner, 5 (Aug 1914), 215.

1616. "Comment and Review," Forerunner, 5 (Aug 1914), 222-224. [Reviews H. G. Wells, The Passionate Friends (New York: A. L. Burt, 1913); Christine Terhune Herrick, "A Girl's Rights," Woman's Home Companion, July 1914; comments re. prison sentences and animal trainers.]

1617. "Why Nevada Should Win Its Suffrage Campaign in November," Out West, NS 8 (Aug 1914), 73-74.

1618. "Is Feminism Really So Dreadful?" Delineator, 85 (Aug 1914), 6.

1619. "Good for the Women," New York Times, 28 Aug 1914, 8:5.

1620. "A Question of Conscience," Forerunner, 5 (Sept 1914), 229-231.

1621. "'Happiness,'" Forerunner, 5 (Sept 1914), 232-233.

1622. "What are 'Feminine' Qualities?" Forerunner, 5 (Sept 1914), 233-234.

1623. "Village Brains and City Problems," Forerunner, 5 (Sept 1914), 240-242.

1624. "What Should They Do?" Forerunner, 5 (Sept 1914), 243.

1625. "Favorable Symptoms," Forerunner, 5 (Sept 1914), 250.

1626. "The Beginning of the End," Forerunner, 5 (Sept 1914), 250-251.

1627. "From a Hearst Paper," Forerunner, 5 (Sept 1914), 251.

1628. "Comment and Review," Forerunner, 5 (Sept 1914), 252. [Review of Joseph Conrad, Chance (Garden City: Doubleday, 1913); comment re. National Union of Woman Suffrage.]

1629. "Masculism at its Worst," Forerunner, 5 (Oct 1914), 257-258.

1630. "The Higher Law," Forerunner, 5 (Oct 1914), 259-260.

1631. "Feminism or Polygamy," Forerunner, 5 (Oct 1914), 260-261.

1632. "Do Not Waste Emotion," Forerunner, 5 (Oct 1914), 262.

1633. "Feet, Flat Feet and Brains," Forerunner, 5 (Oct 1914), 269.

1634. "The Emotional Sex," Forerunner, 5 (Oct 1914), 270-271. See also CPG, "The 'Emotional Sex' Again," Forerunner, 6 (May 1915), 117.

1635. "Comment and Review," Forerunner, 5 (Oct 1914), 277-279. [Comment re. sex bias in the Springfield Republican; review of Katherine Cecil Thurston, Max: A Novel (New York: A. L. Burt, 1910).]

1636. "War Waste," Forerunner, 5 (Nov 1914), 285-286.

1637. "Constructive Internationalism," Forerunner, 5 (Nov 1914), 286-289.

1638. "Why 'Worse'?" Forerunner, 5 (Nov 1914), 290-291.

1639. "Gifts and Good Taste," Forerunner, 5 (Nov 1914), 298-299.

1640. "War and the Duel," Forerunner, 5 (Nov 1914), 299-300.

1641. "Comment and Review," Forerunner, 5 (Nov 1914), 306-308. [Reviews of Madeline Z. Doty, "Maggie Martin, 933," Century, Oct 1914; Mary Heaton Vorse, "A Child's Heart," Century, Oct 1914; Ernst von Wolzagen, The Third Sex (New York: Macaulay, 1914); Jennie L. Wilson, The Legal and Political Status of Women in the U.S. (Cedar Rapids: Torch Press, 1912); comments re. hate songs and socialism.]

1642. "The Safe Side of Feminism," Pictorial Review, 16 (Nov 1914), 6.

1643. "Instead of a Story," Forerunner, 5 (Dec 1914), 309. [Editorial re. widening of war in Europe.]

1644. "As to World Federation," Forerunner, 5 (Dec 1914), 310-312.

1645. "Pain and Sympathy," Forerunner, 5 (Dec 1914), 312-313.

1646. "A New Impulse in the Woman's Movement," Forerunner, 5 (Dec 1914), 313.

1647. "'What Substitute for War,'" Forerunner, 5 (Dec 1914), 319-321. [Response to editorial by Joseph Lee in Survey, 3 Oct 1914.]

1648. "The Great Change," Forerunner, 5 (Dec 1914), 322-324.

1649. "Neutrality and Interference," Forerunner, 5 (Dec 1914), 324-325.

1650. "War--Peace--Love," Forerunner, 5 (Dec 1914), 333.

1651. "Comment and Review," Forerunner, 5 (Dec 1914), 333-335. [Reviews of "The Archbishop and the Argonaut," Reedy's Mirror, 13 Nov 1914; Annie Nathan Meyer, "The Spur: A Play."]

1652. "Honor--His and Hers," Pictorial Review, 16 (Dec 1914), 10, 61.

1915

1653. "Prayer of the Modern Woman," Designer, 41 (Jan 1915), 6.

1654. "The Dress of Women," Forerunner, 6 (Jan 1915), 20-25; 6 (Feb 1915), 46-51; 6 (March 1915), 75-81; 6 (April 1915), 102-108; 6 (May 1915), 132-138; 6 (June 1915), 159-165; 6 (July 1915), 189-194; 6 (Aug 1915), 215-220; 6 (Sept 1915), 245-250; 6 (Oct 1915), 273-278; 6 (Nov 1915), 302-307; 6 (Dec 1915), 328-334.

1655. "Sunrise and the New Year," Forerunner, 6 (Jan 1915), 1.

1656. "The Power of Freedom," Forerunner, 6 (Jan 1915), 6-7.

1657. "How They Did It," Forerunner, 6 (Jan 1915), 7-9.

1658. "Free Speech in the Schools," Forerunner, 6 (Jan 1915), 9-10.

1659. "A 'Debate' on Suffrage," Forerunner, 6 (Jan 1915), 10-11.

1660. "America and Belgium," Forerunner, 6 (Jan 1915), 18-19.

1661. "'The Written Word,'" Forerunner, 6 (Jan 1915), 25.

1662. "Her 'Charms,'" Forerunner, 6 (Jan 1915), 26.

1663. "A World Beginning," Forerunner, 6 (Jan 1915), 26.

1664. "Comment and Review," Forerunner, 6 (Jan 1915), 27-28.
[Review of G. Hardy Clark and Margaret J. Clark, Home
Training of the Prize Baby (Waterloo, Iowa: privately
printed, 1914); comments re. annulment, munitions, the
war in Europe, subway contractors who ignore the law.]

1665. "Newspaper 'Pogroms,'" Forerunner, 6 (Feb 1915), 33-34.

1666. "Old Religions and New Hopes," Forerunner, 6 (Feb
1915), 34-36.

1667. "My Mother Right or Wrong," Forerunner, 6 (Feb 1915),
45.

1668. "An Anti-Suffrage Meeting," Forerunner, 6 (Feb 1915),
51-52.

1669. "Standardizing Towns," Forerunner, 6 (Feb 1915), 52-54.

1670. "The Woman's Movement for Constructive Peace,"
Forerunner, 6 (Feb 1915), 55.

1671. "Comment and Review," Forerunner, 6 (Feb 1915), 54-55.
[Reviews of A. M. Hutchinson, Once Abroad the Lugger
(New York: Kennerley, 1913); Beatrice Forbes-Robertson
Hale, What Women Want (New York: Stokes, 1914).]

1672. "Why Marriage Will Keep," Pictorial Review, 16 (Feb
1915), 6.

1673. "Mrs. Gilman Asks Evidence: If Failure of Suffrage in
Past Cannot Be Proved, Why Assume It in Future," New
York Times, 14 Feb 1915, VIII, 1:7-8. [Letter to
editor.]

1674. "Mrs. Gilman Speaks Again," New York Times, 14 Feb
1915, section 7, 8:8. [Letter to editor re. suffrage.]

1675. "As to 'War-Brides,'" Forerunner, 6 (March 1915), 61-
63.

1676. "War-Maids and War-Widows," Forerunner, 6 (March 1915),
63-65.

1677. "Freedom of Speech in the Public Schools," Forerunner,
6 (March 1915), 72-74.

1678. "One Effect of the War," Forerunner, 6 (March 1915), 74.

1679. "Comment and Review," Forerunner, 6 (March 1915), 82-84. [Reviews of George Middleton, Possession and Other Plays (New York: Henry Holt, 1915); Upton Sinclair, Sylvia's Marriage (Pasadena: privately printed, 1914); Century, Feb 1915; "Puck as a Suffragist"; comment re. "Beavers and Babies."]

1680. "A Rational Position on Suffrage/At the Request of the New York Times, Mrs. Gilman Presents the Best Arguments Possible in Behalf of Votes for Women," New York Times Magazine, 7 March 1915, pp. 14-15.
    See also "Dignified Woman Debaters," New York Times, 9 March 1915, 8:4.
    Rpt. in Forerunner, 6 (June 1915), 145.

1681. "A Contemptible Trick," Forerunner, 6 (March 1915), 84.

1682. "The Highest Treason," Forerunner, 6 (April 1915), 89-93.

1683. "City-Crabs," Forerunner, 6 (April 1915), 100.

1684. "The Dancing of Isadora Duncan," Forerunner, 6 (April 1915), 101.

1685. "The House-Taster," Forerunner, 6 (April 1915), 108.

1686. "Teaching Practical Philosophy," Forerunner, 6 (April 1915), 109-110.

1687. "Comment and Review," Forerunner, 6 (April 1915), 111-112. [Comments re. venereal diseases, automobile fatalities, professional food services, "another sea serpent"; review of Antoinette Brown Blackwell, The Making of the Universe (Boston: Gorham Press, 1914).]

1688. "The Vision and the Program," Forerunner, 6 (May 1915), 118-120.

1689. "What First?" Forerunner, 6 (May 1915), 120.

1690. "The Gorgeous Exposition," Forerunner, 6 (May 1915), 121-123.

1691. "World Rousers," Forerunner, 6 (May 1915), 131-132.

1692. "Comment and Review," Forerunner, 6 (May 1915), 139-

140. [Comments re. the infant mortality rate, "color music."]

1693. "Should Married Women Work?" San Francisco Bulletin, 8 May 1915, 15:2.
See also "Prize Winner Proves to Be Noted Feminist," San Francisco Bulletin, 13 May 1915, 15:2.

1694. "An Answer to a Letter," Forerunner, 6 (June 1915), 145-148. [Re. suffrage.]

1695. "Teaching 'Morals' in Public Schools," Forerunner, 6 (June 1915), 148-149.

1696. "Worse and More of It," Forerunner, 6 (June 1915), 155-156. [Re. loyalty oaths for teachers.]

1697. "Outlines Before Us: Our Normal Condition," Forerunner, 6 (June 1915), 158-159.

1698. "Addressing the New Voters," Forerunner, 6 (June 1915), 165-167.

1699. "Scientific Promotion," Forerunner, 6 (June 1915), 167. [Review of "Developing and Promoting Men," Saturday Evening Post, 17 April 1915.]

1700. "Comment and Review," Forerunner, 6 (June 1915), 168. [Comment re. threat to rail travel posed by automobile.]

1701. "What the 'Threat of War' Really Means," Pictorial Review, 16 (June 1915), 2.

1702. "Are We Pendulums?" Forerunner, 6 (July 1915), 174-176.

1703. "Jitney, the Giant Killer," Forerunner, 6 (July 1915), 176-177.

1704. "Birth Control," Forerunner, 6 (July 1915), 177-180.

1705. "Taken at its Worst," Forerunner, 6 (July 1915), 187-189.

1706. "Comment and Review," Forerunner, 6 (July 1915), 195-196. [Reviews of Edwin Davies Schoonmaker, The World Storm and Beyond (New York: Century, 1915); Charles A. Ellwood, The Social Problem (New York: Macmillan, 1915); Florence Guertin Tuttle, The Awakening of Woman (New York and Cincinnati: Abington Press, 1915).]

1707. "Charlotte Perkins Gilman Says," New York Tribune, 26
      July 1915, 9:1-2. [Re. Theodore Roosevelt on mothers.]
          See also Margaret Ashley Fairfield, "Mrs. Gilman's
          Prayer," New York Tribune, 1 Aug 1915, 10:4.

1708. "The Woman's Peace Movement," Forerunner, 6 (Aug 1915),
      201-202.

1709. "The 'Buying Power' of Girls," Forerunner, 6 (Aug
      1915), 202-206.

1710. "A Fresh Grievance," Forerunner, 6 (Aug 1915), 214.
      [Re. factory shoes.]

1711. "'Practical Measures,'" Forerunner, 6 (Aug 1915), 221.

1712. "Comment and Review," Forerunner, 6 (Aug 1915), 222-
      224. [Review of Owen Wister, "The Pentecost of
      Calamity," Saturday Evening Post, 3 July 1915; comments
      re. militarism and the Panama-Pacific Exhibition.]

1713. "Coming Changes in Literature," Forerunner, 6 (Sept
      1915), 230-236.

1714. "The Sociologist and the Reformer," Forerunner, 6 (Sept
      1915), 243-244.

1715. "Why Don't We Stop It?" Forerunner, 6 (Sept 1915), 244.

1716. "Comment and Review," Forerunner, 6 (Sept 1915), 250-
      252. [Reviews of Samuel Merwin's serial "The Honey
      Bee," McClure's, Sept 1914-Aug 1915; Henry Sydnor
      Harrison, Angela's Business (Boston and New York:
      Houghton Mifflin, 1915); comments re. strikes by
      ammunition workers and war loans.]

1717. "The College Woman, Feminism and the Birthrate," New
      York Tribune, 5 Sept 1915, section 4, p. 2.
          Rpt. under title "Feminism, College Education and the
          Birthrate" in Forerunner, 6 (Oct 1915), 259-261.

1718. "Let Sleeping Forefathers Lie," Forerunner, 6 (Oct
      1915), 261-263.

1719. "A Re-Grip," Forerunner, 6 (Oct 1915), 263-264.

1720. "Beauty, Physical and Social," Forerunner, 6 (Oct
      1915), 270-271.

1721. "Rest and Power," Forerunner, 6 (Oct 1915), 271-272.

1722. "A Suggestion," Forerunner, 6 (Oct 1915), 272.

1723. "Comment and Review," Forerunner, 6 (Oct 1915), 279.
[Comment re. grammar and review of John D. Barry, The
City of Domes (San Francisco: Newbegin, 1915).]

1724. "An Appeal for Liberty from Women to the Men of New
York," Woman's Journal, 9 Oct 1915, p. 320.

1725. "Do We Want a Political Party for Women?" Forerunner, 6
(Nov 1915), 285-286.

1726. "A Woman's Privilege," Forerunner, 6 (Nov 1915), 286-
287.

1727. "'Social Attentions,'" Forerunner, 6 (Nov 1915), 295-
299.

1728. "Having Faith in Evolution," Forerunner, 6 (Nov 1915),
299-300.

1729. "Beauty from Ashes," Forerunner, 6 (Nov 1915), 300-301.

1730. "A New Association," Forerunner, 6 (Nov 1915), 301.

1731. "Is Childhood Happy?" San Francisco Star, 13 Nov 1915,
p. 13.
Rpt. in Forerunner, 7 (May 1916), 118.

1732. "Without a Husband," Forerunner, 6 (Dec 1915), 314.

1733. "The Power of the Farm Wife," Forerunner, 6 (Dec 1915),
315-319.

1734. "American Unity," Forerunner, 6 (Dec 1915), 326-328.

1735. "Comment and Review," Forerunner, 6 (Dec 1915), 334-
336. [Comments re. the Fuller sisters trio;
newsworthiness of "love affairs"; review of M. A. B.
Arnim, The Pastor's Wife (Garden City: Doubleday,
1914).]

1736. "What Christmas Means," San Francisco Star, 25 Dec
1915, p. 9.

1916

1737. "Growth and Combat," Forerunner, 7 (Jan 1916), 13-18; 7
(Feb 1916), 47-53; 7 (March 1916), 76-82; 7 (April
1916), 105-110; 7 (May 1916), 131-136; 7 (June 1916),

160-165; 7 (July 1916), 188-193; 7 (Aug 1916), 217-222; 7 (Sept 1916), 246-251; 7 (Oct 1916), 274-279; 7 (Nov 1916), 303-308; 7 (Dec 1916), 328-334.

1738. "A Question of the Government?" Forerunner, 7 (Jan 1916), 4-5.

1739. "Assisted Evolution," Forerunner, 7 (Jan 1916), 5.

1740. "American Ships," Forerunner, 7 (Jan 1916), 12-13.

1741. "Suffering and Socialism," Forerunner, 7 (Jan 1916), 18-19.

1742. "A Distinction," Forerunner, 7 (Jan 1916), 19. [Re. differences between the short story and novel.]

1743. "Some Un-Familiar Ways of Living," Forerunner, 7 (Jan 1916), 20-24.

1744. "Mothers and Mothers," Forerunner, 7 (Jan 1916), 24-25.

1745. "The Chautauqua Salute," Forerunner, 7 (Jan 1916), 25.

1746. "Comment and Review," Forerunner, 7 (Jan 1916), 26-27. [Comments re. the Ford Peace Expedition and the war; reviews of Henry Kitchell Webster, The Real Adventure (Indianapolis: Bobbs-Merrill, 1916); and Ernest Poole, The Harbor (New York: Macmillan, 1915).]

1747. "Wanted, A Railroad Cafeteria," Forerunner, 7 (Feb 1916), 33-34.

1748. "The Right Kind of Preparedness," Forerunner, 7 (Feb 1916), 34.

1749. "Patriotism and Humanism," Forerunner, 7 (Feb 1916), 35-37.

1750. "Woman Suffrage and the Woman's Journal," Forerunner, 7 (Feb 1916), 45-46.

1751. "The Honor of Bearing His Name," Forerunner, 7 (Feb 1916), 46-47.

1752. "Announcement," Forerunner, 7 (Feb 1916), 56. [Re. suspension of magazine at close of volume.]

1753. "Comment and Review," Forerunner, 7 (Feb 1916), 53-55. [Comments re. Owen Johnson and Everybody's Magazine;

"the nude in advertising"; the war victories of the allies.]

1754. "The Coming 'Creed,'" Forerunner, 7 (March 1916), 61-64.

1755. "Women's Hair and Men's Whiskers," Forerunner, 7 (March 1916), 64-65.

1756. "Maternity Benefits and Reformers," Forerunner, 7 (March 1916), 65-66.

1757. "The Ford Party and the Newspapers," Forerunner, 7 (March 1916), 73-76.

1758. "Comment and Review," Forerunner, 7 (March 1916), 82-83. [Review of Charles E. Jefferson, "A Sermon to Mothers," Woman's Home Companion, Nov 1915; comments re. suicide, parthenogenesis, and corporal punishment.]

1759. "Others Gave Only Femininity to Their Women Characters," New York Times, 5 March 1916, section 4, p. 3. [Re. Shakespeare.]

1760. "Psychic Jiu-Jitsu," Forerunner, 7 (April 1916), 90-92.

1761. "Danger in the Senate," Forerunner, 7 (April 1916), 99.

1762. "Studies in Social Pathology," Forerunner, 7 (April 1916), 99-104; 7 (May 1916), 119-122; 7 (June 1916), 148-151.

1763. "Comment and Review," Forerunner, 7 (April 1916), 111-112. [Comments re. women workers in England, the German birthrate, and motion pictures; review of Ellen Glasgow, Life and Gabriella (Garden City: Doubleday, 1916).]

1764. "What Feminism Is--and Isn't," Ford Hall Folks, 2 April 1916, pp. 1-2, 4.

1765. "The Four Ages of Woman," Survey, 15 April 1916, pp. 80-81.

1766. "Groups of Babies," Forerunner, 7 (April 1916), 104.

1767. "The Sanctity of Human Life," Forerunner, 7 (May 1916), 128-129.

1768. "Where to 'Begin,'" Forerunner, 7 (May 1916), 136-137.

1769. "Dogs, Pigs, and Cities," Forerunner, 7 (May 1916),
137-138.
See also "Dogs Again," Forerunner, 7 (Sept 1916),
245.

1770. "Comment and Review," Forerunner, 7 (May 1916), 138-
140. [Comments re. the Aero Club of America and the
Survey magazine; reviews of Alice Henry, The Trade
Union Woman (New York and London: Appleton, 1915);
Katharine Anthony, Feminism in Germany and Scandinavia
(New York: Henry Holt & Co., 1915).]

1771. "Among Our Foreign Residents," Forerunner, 7 (June
1916), 145-146.

1772. "Murder on Wheels," Forerunner, 7 (June 1916), 147.

1773. "This 'Self-Development,'" Forerunner, 7 (June 1916),
157-158.

1774. "A Trick Worth Knowing," Forerunner, 7 (June 1916),
165-166.

1775. "Comment and Review," Forerunner, 7 (June 1916), 166-
168. [Comments re. "two fulfillments," circumlocution,
"a striking admission," "the German's pipe," women on
college faculties; review of Meta Stern Lilienthal,
From Fireside to Factory (New York: Rand School,
1916); and magazine Femina.]

1776. "The Mothers' Exchange," Today's Magazine, ca. spring
1916.
MS copy extant in folder 175, CPG Papers.

1777. "Women After the War," Forerunner, 7 (July 1916), 173-
177.

1778. "The Home and the Postoffice," Forerunner, 7 (July
1916), 177-179.

1779. "A Word with the Pacifists on How to End This War,"
Philadelphia Public Ledger, 18 July 1916, 10:6-7.

1780. "The Movies and the Audience," Forerunner, 7 (July
1916), 185.

1781. "Painting Via Literature," Forerunner, 7 (July 1916),
186-187.

1782. "The Gardens," Forerunner, 7 (July 1916), 187-188.

1783. "Comment and Review," Forerunner, 7 (July 1916), 193-196. [Comment re. H. L. Mencken and Theodore Dreiser; reviews of Gerald Stanley Lee, We (Garden City: Doubleday, 1916); and magazine The Masses.]

1784. "The 'Nervous Breakdown' of Women," Forerunner, 7 (Aug 1916), 202-206.

1785. "Manners on a Vacation," Forerunner, 7 (Aug 1916), 207.

1786. "Cartooned 'A Little Deer,' What is Woman Voter's Party," Philadelphia Public Ledger, 8 Aug 1916, 8:5-6.

1787. "The National Woman's Party," Forerunner, 7 (Aug 1916), 214-215.

1788. "Obstacles to Suffrage by States," Forerunner, 7 (Aug 1916), 215-216.

1789. "Comment and Review," Forerunner, 7 (Aug 1916), 222-224. [Comments re. prejudice, a Polish national university, a houseworkers' club; review of Eva Olney Farnsworth, The Art and Ethics of Dress (San Francisco: Paul Elder, 1915).]

1790. "The World Conference We Need," Forerunner, 7 (Sept 1916), 232-234.

1791. "A Body for the World Spirit," Forerunner, 7 (Sept 1916), 235-237.

1792. "Pacifists, Militarists and Money," Forerunner, 7 (Sept 1916), 244.

1793. "Comment and Review," Forerunner, 7 (Sept 1916), 251-252. [Comments re. lynching in Waco, Texas; and public walking.]

1794. "What is Feminism?" Boston Sunday Herald, 3 Sept 1916, magazine section, p. 7.

1795. "The American Social Hygiene Association," Forerunner, 7 (Oct 1916), 257-259.

1796. "The Football Theory," Forerunner, 7 (Oct 1916), 269.

1797. "Peace in Three Pieces," Forerunner, 7 (Oct 1916), 270-271.

1798. "Some Results of Believing," Forerunner, 7 (Oct 1916),

271-272.

1799. "Artist, Illustrator and Cartoonist," Forerunner, 7 (Oct 1916), 272-273.

1800. "These Lovers," Forerunner, 7 (Oct 1916), 273.

1801. "Comment and Review," Forerunner, 7 (Oct 1916), 279-280. [Comments re. "strikes and class legislation" and "monotony and housework"; review of Floyd J. Melvin, Socialism as the Sociological Ideal (New York: Sturgis & Walton Co., 1915).]

1802. "The Milkman and the Public," Forerunner, 7 (Nov 1916), 285-286.

1803. "A Summary of Purpose," Forerunner, 7 (Nov 1916), 286-290. [Reprise of CPG's intent in publishing magazine.]

1804. "The War and Liars," Forerunner, 7 (Nov 1916), 297-300.

1805. "Newspapers and Democracy," Forerunner, 7 (Nov 1916), 300-303; 7 (Dec 1916), 314-318.

1806. "To My Real Readers," Forerunner, 7 (Dec 1916), 326-328.

1807. "Comment and Review," Forerunner, 7 (Dec 1916), 334-336. [Review of George Middleton, The Road Together (New York: Henry Holt & Co., 1916); comments re. women voters, evening dress, reading for women, Christmas, and "the present election" for President.]

1917

1808. "Poverty and Woman," Proceedings of the National Conference of Social Work, (1917), 10-15.

1809. "Jane Smith's Life," Pictorial Review, 18 (May 1917), 2, 82.

1810. "The Housekeeper and the Food Problem," Annals of the American Academy, 74 (Nov 1917), 123-130.

1918

1811. "Concerning Clothes," Independent, 22 June 1918, pp. 478, 483.

1812. "Released Energy of Women," World Outlook, 4 (Sept

1918), 3.

1919

1813. "The Work and Waste of Women," Pictorial Review, 20
(Feb 1919), 11, 38.

1814. "Now That We've Got to Reconstruct the World, Let Us Do
It Right," Pictorial Review, 20 (March 1919), 16, 80.

1815. "A Woman's View of the World's Opportunity to Make
Human Life Mean More," Reconstruction, 1 (March 1919),
78-79.

1816. "Why We Are Going Dry," New York Tribune syndicate,
Louisville Herald, 17 March 1919, 4:3-4.

1817. "The Unfair Sex," New York Tribune syndicate,
Louisville Herald, 18 March 1919, 5:2-3.

1818. "The Foreign Language Press," New York Tribune
syndicate, Louisville Herald, 19 March 1919, 6:4-5.

1819. "Murder on Wheels," New York Tribune syndicate,
Louisville Herald, 20 March 1919, 7:2-3.

1820. "Building Beauty," New York Tribune syndicate,
Louisville Herald, 21 March 1919, 5:3-4.

1821. "A Fair Working Day," New York Tribune syndicate,
Louisville Herald, 22 March 1919, 7:5-6.

1822. "These 'Advanced' Young People," New York Tribune
syndicate, Louisville Herald, 24 March 1919, 5:5-6.

1823. "Society's 'Chores,'" New York Tribune syndicate,
Louisville Herald, 25 March 1919, 5:3-4.

1824. "Venus and Mother," New York Tribune syndicate,
Louisville Herald, 26 March 1919, 5:2-3.

1825. "Looted Art," New York Tribune syndicate, Louisville
Herald, 27 March 1919, 6:2-3.

1826. "Girls and Pockets," New York Tribune syndicate,
Louisville Herald, 28 March 1919, 6:3-4.

1827. "Let the Seller Beware," New York Tribune syndicate,
Louisville Herald, 29 March 1919, 5:2-3.

1828. "Men, Women, Jobs," New York Tribune syndicate,
      Louisville Herald, 31 March 1919, 7:7.

1829. "What Are 'Radicals'?" New York Tribune syndicate,
      Louisville Herald, 1 April 1919, 7:4; Baltimore Sun, 15
      April 1919, 4:5.

1830. "Billions and Grief," New York Tribune syndicate,
      Louisville Herald, 2 April 1919, 6:3-4; Buffalo Evening
      News, 2 April 1919, 12:5-6.
      Rpt. under title "Billions Lost Every Year By Fire"
        in Baltimore Sun, 12 April 1919, 4:4.

1831. "Why We Love Spooks," New York Tribune syndicate,
      Louisville Herald, 3 April 1919, 6:5-6; Buffalo Evening
      News, 3 April 1919, 10:4-6; Baltimore Sun, 7 April
      1919, 4:2.

1832. "Village Farming," New York Tribune syndicate,
      Louisville Herald, 4 April 1919, 6:3-4.

1833. "The Socializing of Education," Public, 5 April 1919,
      pp. 348-349.

1834. "Her Natural Protector," New York Tribune syndicate,
      Louisville Herald, 5 April 1919, 7:5-6; Buffalo Evening
      News, 5 April 1919, 7:7-8.

1835. "Skirts," New York Tribune syndicate, Louisville
      Herald, 7 April 1919, 7:5-6; Buffalo Evening News, 7
      April 1919, 12:5-6.

1836. "Air Traffic and World Union," New York Tribune
      syndicate, Louisville Herald, 8 April 1919, 6:1-2;
      Buffalo Evening News, 8 April 1919, 12:6-8.

1837. "The 'Russian Experiment,'" New York Tribune syndicate,
      Louisville Herald, 9 April 1919, 6:3-4; Buffalo Evening
      News, 9 April 1919, 12:4-5; Baltimore Sun, 10 April
      1919, 4:3.

1838. "This Cooked Food Business," New York Tribune
      syndicate, Louisville Herald, 10 April 1919, 7:4-5.

1839. "Hats with Whiskers," New York Tribune syndicate,
      Buffalo Evening News, 12 April 1919, 9:5-6; Baltimore
      Sun, 1 May 1919, 4:2.

1840. "Knock on Wood," New York Tribune syndicate, Buffalo
      Evening News, 14 April 1919, 12:3-5; Louisville Herald,

17 May 1919, 7:3-4.

1841. "The Last Grave," New York Tribune syndicate,
Louisville Herald, 14 April 1919, 7:2-3; Buffalo
Evening News, 15 April 1919, 25:4-5; Baltimore Sun, 29
April 1919, 4:5.

1842. "Why is a Nation," New York Tribune syndicate,
Louisville Herald, 15 April 1919, 6:3-4; Buffalo
Evening News, 15 April 1919, 19:5-6.

1843. "Wasted Babies," New York Tribune syndicate, Louisville
Herald, 16 April 1919, 7:2-3.

1844. "Peace Rations," New York Tribune syndicate, Louisville
Herald, 17 April 1919, 6:2-3; Buffalo Evening News, 17
April 1919, 7:1-2.

1845. "Mother--Teacher--Citizen," New York Tribune syndicate,
Louisville Herald, 18 April 1919, 3:1-2.

1846. "The Problem of the Disappearing Servant," New York
Tribune syndicate, Louisville Herald, 19 April 1919,
6:1-3.
  Rpt. under title "The Disappearing Servant,"
  Baltimore Sun, 10 June 1919, 4:2-3.

1847. "The Habit of Being Oppressed," New York Tribune
syndicate, Louisville Herald, 21 April 1919, 7:1-2;
Buffalo Evening News, 21 April 1919, 12:4-5; Baltimore
Sun, 28 May 1919, 4:3.

1848. "Do You Like Their Looks?" New York Tribune syndicate,
Louisville Herald, 22 April 1919, 4:2-3; Buffalo
Evening News, 22 April 1919, 12:4-5.

1849. "As to Alimony," New York Tribune syndicate, Louisville
Herald, 23 April 1919, 6:6; Buffalo Evening News, 23
April 1919, 12:4-5; Baltimore Sun, 14 June 1919, 4:5.

1850. "Patience, Laziness, Modesty, or Cowardice?" New York
Tribune syndicate, Louisville Herald, 24 April 1919,
6:3-4; Buffalo Evening News, 24 April 1919, 21:5-6.

1851. "Beefsteak and Geography," New York Tribune syndicate,
Louisville Herald, 25 April 1919, 6:2-3.

1852. "A Pencil and Paper," New York Tribune syndicate,
Louisville Herald, 26 April 1919, 6:5; Buffalo Evening
News, 26 April 1919, 5:6-7.

1853. "Uniform and Livery," New York Tribune syndicate, Louisville Herald, 28 April 1919, 6:5; Baltimore Sun, 14 May 1919, 4:4.

1854. "The Cave Man Theory," New York Tribune syndicate, Louisville Herald, 29 April 1919, 7:2-3; Buffalo Evening News, 29 April 1919, 9:1-2; Baltimore Sun, 5 May 1919, 4:5.

1855. "Harnessed Reformers," New York Tribune syndicate, Louisville Herald, 30 April 1919, 6:2-3; Buffalo Evening News, 30 April 1919, 4:3-4.

1856. "Religion Being Re-Moulded by the Influence of Women," Reconstruction, 1 (May 1919), 148-149.

1857. "The 'Mother's Helper,'" New York Tribune syndicate, Louisville Herald, 1 May 1919, 6:5-6; Buffalo Evening News, 1 May 1919, 14:1-2.

1858. "Noise and Nerves," New York Tribune syndicate, Louisville Herald, 2 May 1919, 6:4; Buffalo Evening News, 2 May 1919, 14:2-3; Baltimore Sun, 2 June 1919, 3:5.

1859. "If I Was a Horse," New York Tribune syndicate, Louisville Herald, 3 May 1919, 6:3-4; Buffalo Evening News, 3 May 1919, 19:1-2.

1860. "Table Manners and Common Sense," New York Tribune syndicate, Louisville Herald, 5 May 1919, 6:5-6; Buffalo Evening News, 5 May 1919, 5:1-2; Baltimore Sun, 31 May 1919, 4:3.

1861. "A Sex Opposition in California," New York Tribune syndicate, Louisville Herald, 6 May 1919, 7:2-3; Buffalo Evening News, 6 May 1919, 13:3-4.

1862. "Is Marriage a Partnership?" New York Tribune syndicate, Louisville Herald, 7 May 1919, 6:2-3; Buffalo Evening News, 7 May 1919, 13:5-6; Baltimore Sun, 20 May 1919, 4:4.

1863. "Can a Child Murder?" New York Tribune syndicate, Louisville Herald, 8 May 1919, 6:3-4.

1864. "Irresistable Changes," New York Tribune syndicate, Louisville Herald, 9 May 1919, 6:2-3.

1865. "A National Union of Woman Citizens," New York Tribune syndicate, <u>Louisville Herald</u>, 10 May 1919, 4:4-5.

1866. "Race Prejudice in Russia," New York Tribune syndicate, <u>Louisville Herald</u>, 12 May 1919, 4:4-5; <u>Baltimore Sun</u>, <u>30 May 1919</u>, 6:6.

1867. "Is There One Divorce to Nine Marriages?" New York Tribune syndicate, <u>Louisville Herald</u>, 13 May 1919, 7:4.

1868. "Why We Are More Foolish Than Other Animals," New York Tribune syndicate, <u>Louisville Herald</u>, 14 May 1919, 7:5-6.

1869. "An Astonishing Advertisement," New York Tribune syndicate, <u>Louisville Herald</u>, 15 May 1919, 7:1-2; <u>Buffalo Evening News</u>, 15 May 1919, 22:3-4.

1870. "The Beast Prison," New York Tribune syndicate, <u>Louisville Herald</u>, 16 May 1919, 6:5-6; <u>Buffalo Evening News</u>, 16 May 1919, 10:2-4.
    Rpt. under title "Managerie are Prisons," <u>Baltimore Sun</u>, 19 May 1919, 4:3.

1871. "What Good is Freedom?" New York Tribune syndicate, <u>Buffalo Evening News</u>, 17 May 1919, 7:6-7.

1872. "Community Schemes," New York Tribune syndicate, <u>Louisville Herald</u>, 19 May 1919, 7:2-3; <u>Buffalo Evening News</u>, 19 May 1919, 17:1-2.

1873. "National Housebuilding," New York Tribune syndicate, <u>Louisville Herald</u>, 20 May 1919, 6:3-4; <u>Buffalo Evening News</u>, 20 May 1919, 17:1-3.

1874. "Some Advantages of 'Visiting,'" New York Tribune syndicate, <u>Louisville Herald</u>, 21 May 1919, 6:2-3; <u>Buffalo Evening News</u>, 21 May 1919, 6:3-4.

1875. "Mind Your Own Business," New York Tribune syndicate, <u>Louisville Herald</u>, 22 May 1919, 6:1-2; <u>Buffalo Evening News</u>, 22 May 1919, 9:1-4; <u>Baltimore Sun</u>, 11 June 1919, 4:2.

1876. "How Young Should a Child Work?" New York Tribune syndicate, <u>Louisville Herald</u>, 23 May 1919, 6:2-3; <u>Buffalo Evening News</u>, 23 May 1919, 4:2-4; <u>Baltimore Sun</u>, 27 May 1919, 4:2.

1877. "Is the Hair of Women Beautiful?" New York Tribune syndicate, <u>Louisville Herald</u>, 24 May 1919, 6:3-4;

Buffalo Evening News, 24 May 1919, 18:4-6.

1878. "Another Foolishness," New York Tribune syndicate, Louisville Herald, 26 May 1919, 7:3-4.

1879. "Common Sense and Sociology," New York Tribune syndicate, Louisville Herald, 27 May 1919, 6:3-4.

1880. "What Work Shall I Choose?" New York Tribune syndicate, Louisville Herald, 28 May 1919, 7:3-4; Baltimore Sun, 4 Aug 1919, 4:7.

1881. "Are We Brothers?" New York Tribune syndicate, Louisville Herald, 29 May 1919, 5:4-5.

1882. "Widow Making," New York Tribune syndicate, Louisville Herald, 30 May 1919, 6:3-4.

1883. "The Influence of Women on Public Life," Public, 31 May 1919, pp. 571-572.

1884. "Mourning and Women," New York Tribune syndicate, Louisville Herald, 31 May 1919, 5:5-6; Buffalo Evening News, 31 May 1919, 9:4-7.

1885. "Permanent Fashions," New York Tribune syndicate, Louisville Herald, 2 June 1919, 5:2-3; Buffalo Evening News, 2 June 1919, 16:7-8.

1886. "If Babies Could Explain," New York Tribune syndicate, Louisville Herald, 3 June 1919, 4:3-4; Baltimore Sun, 20 Sept 1919, 4:4.

1887. "'Summer Furs,'" New York Tribune syndicate, Louisville Herald, 4 June 1919, 6:3-4.

1888. "Have You Had Your Chance?" New York Tribune syndicate, Louisville Herald, 5 June 1919, 7:1-2; Buffalo Evening News, 5 June 1919, 17:1-4; Baltimore Sun, 30 June 1919, 4:4.

1889. "A 'Nickel Out of the Slot' Machine," New York Tribune syndicate, Louisville Herald, 6 June 1919, 8:4-5; Buffalo Evening News, 6 June 1919, 10:1-4.

1890. "Weddings and Foolishness," New York Tribune syndicate, Louisville Herald, 7 June 1919, 7:6-7; Buffalo Evening News, 7 June 1919, 10:3-4.

1891. "Parasites," New York Tribune syndicate, Louisville

Herald, 9 June 1919, 7:3-4; Buffalo Evening News, 9 June 1919, 7:3-4.

1892. "Have Women a Shape?" New York Tribune syndicate, Louisville Herald, 10 June 1919, 7:2-3; Buffalo Evening News, 10 June 1919, 13:2-4.

1893. "The Revelations of Boarding Houses," New York Tribune syndicate, Louisville Herald, 11 June 1919, 6:6-7.

1894. "The 'Farmerette,'" New York Tribune syndicate, Louisville Herald, 12 June 1919, 6:2-3; Buffalo Evening News, 12 June 1919, 16:1-2.

1895. "Killing the Failures," New York Tribune syndicate, Louisville Herald, 13 June 1919, 8:6-7; Buffalo Evening News, 13 June 1919, 7:1-4; Baltimore Sun, 22 July 1919, 4:2.

1896. "The Bride's Job," New York Tribune syndicate, Louisville Herald, 14 June 1919, 7:5-6; Baltimore Sun, 19 June 1919, 4:4.

1897. "Why is 'Art' Unpopular?" New York Tribune syndicate, Louisville Herald, 16 June 1919, 7:4-5; Buffalo Evening News, 16 June 1919, 12:4-5.

1898. "Feminine Vanity," New York Tribune syndicate, Louisville Herald, 17 June 1919, 7:1-2; Baltimore Sun, 23 July 1919, 4:7.

1899. "An 'Open Mind,'" New York Tribune syndicate, Louisville Herald, 18 June 1919, 7:3-4; Baltimore Sun, 21 July 1919, 4:2.

1900. "The City Dog," New York Tribune syndicate, Louisville Herald, 19 June 1919, 7:5-6.

1901. "Two Schools of Feminism," New York Tribune syndicate, Louisville Herald, 20 June 1919, 7:6-7.

1902. "Park Robbers," New York Tribune syndicate, Louisville Herald, 21 June 1919, 5:2-3.

1903. "The Dead Hand," New York Tribune syndicate, Louisville Herald, 23 June 1919, 7:4-5.

1904. "What Would You Like to Wear?" New York Tribune syndicate, Louisville Herald, 24 June 1919, 7:6-7; Buffalo Evening News, 24 June 1919, 20:4-5.

1905. "The 'Heart Interest' and Others," New York Tribune syndicate, Louisville Herald, 25 June 1919, 6:2-3.

1906. "Some Sane City-Keeping," New York Tribune syndicate, Louisville Herald, 26 June 1919, 5:1-2; Buffalo Evening News, 26 June 1919, 20:3-4.

1907. "Fifty 'and Up,'" New York Tribune syndicate, Louisville Herald, 27 June 1919, 7:1-2; Buffalo Evening News, 27 June 1919, 24:7-8.

1908. "Bogus Barriers," New York Tribune syndicate, Louisville Herald, 28 June 1919, 7:1-2; Buffalo Evening News, 30 June 1919, 5:3-8.

1909. "A Pie-Shaped Farm," New York Tribune syndicate, Louisville Herald, 30 June 1919, 7:6-7.

1910. "Respect for Law, and Laws," New York Tribune syndicate, Louisville Herald, 1 July 1919, 9:3-4; Buffalo Evening News, 1 July 1919, 20:3-8.

1911. "The Housewife as a Buyer," New York Tribune syndicate, Louisville Herald, 2 July 1919, 7:1-2.

1912. "Differences in Folks," New York Tribune syndicate, Buffalo Evening News, 2 July 1919, 7:4-5; Louisville Herald, 3 July 1919, 7:1-2.

1913. "The Good Old Fashioned Way," New York Tribune syndicate, Baltimore Sun, 3 July 1919, 4:7; Louisville Herald, 5 July 1919, 5:1-2.

1914. "Parades and Women," New York Tribune syndicate, Louisville Herald, 4 July 1919, 5:2-3; Buffalo Evening News, 5 July 1919, 9:2-3.

1915. "What Philanthropists Might Do," New York Tribune syndicate, Louisville Herald, 7 July 1919, 5:2-3.

1916. "Are We Brothers?" New York Tribune syndicate, Baltimore Sun, 8 July 1919, 4:2.

1917. "Class Conscious Motherhood," New York Tribune syndicate, Louisville Herald, 8 July 1919, 7:3-4; Buffalo Evening News, 9 July 1919, 16:7-8.

1918. "Women's Business--The Old and the New," New York Tribune syndicate, Louisville Herald, 10 July 1919, 7:4-5; Baltimore Sun, 15 Dec 1919, 4:5.

1919. "Is Poverty of Any Use?" New York Tribune syndicate, Louisville Herald, 9 July 1919, 7:2-3; Buffalo Evening News, 14 July 1919, 6:3-4.

1920. "Sliding, Climbing and Sitting Still," New York Tribune syndicate, Louisville Herald, 11 July 1919, 7:3-4; Baltimore Sun, 29 July 1919, 4:4.

1921. "What Young People Are For," New York Tribune syndicate, Louisville Herald, 12 July 1919, 7:2-3; Buffalo Evening News, 12 July 1919, 5:3-4.

1922. "Landlord and His Profits," New York Tribune syndicate, Louisville Herald, 14 July 1919, 7:6-7; Buffalo Evening News, 16 July 1919, 13:3-5; 28 July 1919, 4:2.

1923. "Frailty, Thy Name is Woman," New York Tribune syndicate, Louisville Herald, 15 July 1919, 5:3-4; Buffalo Evening News, 19 July 1919, 9:7-8.

1924. "A Time for All Things," New York Tribune syndicate, Louisville Herald, 16 July 1919, 7:4-5.

1925. "Empty Lots, Roofs, and Children," New York Tribune syndicate, Louisville Herald, 17 July 1919, 6:2-3; Buffalo Evening News, 21 July 1919, 12:4-5.

1926. "Mind Makers," New York Tribune syndicate, Louisville Herald, 18 July 1919, 7:2-3.

1927. "Martyrdom and Achievement," New York Tribune syndicate, Louisville Herald, 19 July 1919, 7:6-7; Buffalo Evening News, 23 July 1919, 9:4-5.

1928. "Hints on Taxes," New York Tribune syndicate, Buffalo Evening News, 22 July 1919, 12:4-5.

1929. "Watch Their Ankles," New York Tribune syndicate, Louisville Herald, 22 July 1919, 7:6-7; Buffalo Evening News, 24 July 1919, 19:3-4.

1930. "That 'Pendulum' Idea," New York Tribune syndicate, Louisville Herald, 23 July 1919, 7:1-2; Baltimore Sun, 3 Sept 1919, 4:5.

1931. "The Summer Camp," New York Tribune syndicate, Louisville Herald, 24 July 1919, 7:3-4.
    Rpt. under title "About Summer Camps," Buffalo Evening News, 25 July 1919, 6:3-4.

1932. "Our 'Poor Human Intellect,'" New York Tribune syndicate, Louisville Herald, 25 July 1919, 7:3-4.

1933. "A 'Hope Chest' Worth While," New York Tribune syndicate, Louisville Herald, 26 July 1919, 7:3-4; Buffalo Evening News, 30 July 1919, 6:3-5; Baltimore Sun, 9 Aug 1919, 4:4.

1934. "Innocent-Looking Dangers," New York Tribune syndicate, Louisville Herald, 28 July 1919, 7:3-4.

1935. "The Housing and the Servant Problem," New York Tribune syndicate, Louisville Herald, 29 July 1919, 7:6-7; Buffalo Evening News, 29 July 1919, 10:4-5; Baltimore Sun, 12 Aug 1919, 4:4.

1936. "School Teachers and Justice," New York Tribune syndicate, Louisville Herald, 30 July 1919, 7:1-2; Buffalo Evening News, 31 July 1919, 7:1-4.

1937. "Worrying About the World," New York Tribune syndicate, Louisville Herald, 31 July 1919, 7:2-3; Buffalo Evening News, 1 Aug 1919, 5:3-4.

1938. "Are Women More Beautiful Than Men?" New York Tribune syndicate, Louisville Herald, 1 Aug 1919, 6:2-3; Buffalo Evening News, 4 Aug 1919, 7:4-5.

1939. "'Seeing Life,'" New York Tribune syndicate, Louisville Herald, 2 Aug 1919, 5:4-5; Buffalo Evening News, 2 Aug 1919, 16:2-3.

1940. "Glory and Women Folks," New York Tribune syndicate, Louisville Herald, 4 Aug 1919, 7:5-6; Buffalo Evening News, 5 Aug 1919, 6:2-4.

1941. "Step by Step," New York Tribune syndicate, Louisville Herald, 5 Aug 1919, 6:4-5; Buffalo Evening News, 6 Aug 1919, 12:4-5; Baltimore Sun, 23 Aug 1919, 4:4.

1942. "Should All Girls Learn to Cook," New York Tribune syndicate, Louisville Herald, 6 Aug 1919, 7:3-4.

1943. "Picnic Pigs," New York Tribune syndicate, Louisville Herald, 7 Aug 1919, 6:1-2; Baltimore Sun, 30 Aug 1919, 4:4.

1944. "City Hall No. 600," New York Tribune syndicate, Louisville Herald, 8 Aug 1919, 6:6-7.

1945. "Finished Streets," New York Tribune syndicate, Louisville Herald, 9 Aug 1919, 6:5-6.

1946. "Mrs. Demos," New York Tribune syndicate, Louisville Herald, 11 Aug 1919, 3:4-5; Buffalo Evening News, 13 Aug 1919, 9:4-8.

1947. "What is Happiness?" New York Tribune syndicate, Louisville Herald, 12 Aug 1919, 6:6-7; Baltimore Sun, 27 Sept 1919, 4:7.

1948. "Movies and the Mind," New York Tribune syndicate, Louisville Herald, 13 Aug 1919, 6:1-2; Buffalo Evening News, 14 Aug 1919, 7:1-3; Baltimore Sun, 26 Aug 1919, 4:4.

1949. "Blaming the Women," New York Tribune syndicate, Louisville Herald, 15 Aug 1919, 7:1-2; Buffalo Evening News, 15 Aug 1919, 10:3-8.

1950. "His Own Labor," New York Tribune syndicate, Louisville Herald, 14 Aug 1919, 7:3-4; Buffalo Evening News, 16 Aug 1919, 6:7-8.

1951. "Is Progress a Delusion?" New York Tribune syndicate, Louisville Herald, 16 Aug 1919, 5:1-2; Buffalo Evening News, 18 Aug 1919, 7:4-6.

1952. "Child-Marriage, Girl-Marriage, Woman-Marriage," New York Tribune syndicate, Louisville Herald, 18 Aug 1919,5:2-3; Buffalo Evening News, 19 Aug 1919, 12:4-8; Baltimore Sun, 21 Aug 1919, 4:7.

1953. "Practicing What You Preach," New York Tribune syndicate, Buffalo Evening News, 20 Aug 1919, 7:2-3; Baltimore Sun, 17 Sept 1919, 4:4.

1954. "How Big is a Village?" New York Tribune syndicate, Louisville Herald, 20 Aug 1919, 6:2-3; Buffalo Evening News, 21 Aug 1919, 23:1-2.

1955. "Why Women Are Restless," New York Tribune syndicate, Louisville Herald, 21 Aug 1919, 7:1-2; Buffalo Evening News, 22 Aug 1919, 12:5-6.

1956. "Teaching Children to Think," New York Tribune syndicate, Louisville Herald, 22 Aug 1919, 4:3-4.

1957. "Hot Weather Tricks," New York Tribune syndicate, Buffalo Evening News, 23 Aug 1919, 15:4-5; Louisville

Herald, 6 Sept 1919, 7:1-2.

1958. "Children and Colts," New York Tribune syndicate,
Louisville Herald, 25 Aug 1919, 6:6-7.

1959. "Suppose You Were Dead," New York Tribune syndicate,
Louisville Herald, 26 Aug 1919, 12:2-3; Buffalo Evening
News, 26 Aug 1919, 7:2-4; Baltimore Sun, 24 Nov 1919,
4:4.

1960. "Trolley Traveling," New York Tribune syndicate,
Louisville Herald, 27 Aug 1919, 6:3-4.

1961. "Credit for Mrs. Lemuel," New York Tribune syndicate,
Louisville Herald, 28 Aug 1919, 5:1-2; Buffalo Evening
News, 28 Aug 1919, 6:2-8.

1962. "The Beauty of the Earth," New York Tribune syndicate,
Louisville Herald, 29 Aug 1919, 9:5-6; Buffalo Evening
News, 29 Aug 1919, 7:2-4.

1963. "We Don't Care to Be Well," New York Tribune syndicate,
Louisville Herald, 30 Aug 1919, 6:6-7; Buffalo Evening
News, 30 Aug 1919, 14:7-8; Baltimore Sun, 7 Oct 1919,
4:2.

1964. "What Are Our 'Rights'?" New York Tribune syndicate,
Louisville Herald, 1 Sept 1919, 6:2-3.

1965. "Too Much Mother," New York Tribune syndicate,
Louisville Herald, 2 Sept 1919, 7:3-4.

1966. "Not Enough Mother," New York Tribune syndicate,
Louisville Herald, 3 Sept 1919, 7:2-3; Buffalo Evening
News, 5 Sept 1919, 24:1-3; Baltimore Sun, 9 Oct 1919,
4:4.

1967. "Society's 'Hang Over,'" New York Tribune syndicate,
Louisville Herald, 4 Sept 1919, 6:3-4.

1968. "That Powdered Nose," New York Tribune syndicate,
Louisville Herald, 5 Sept 1919, 8:3-4.

1969. "Why Slap the Baby?" New York Tribune syndicate,
Louisville Herald, 8 Sept 1919, 3:5-6; Baltimore Sun,
20 Oct 1919, 4:2.

1970. "What is Good Philosophy?" New York Tribune syndicate,
Louisville Herald, 11 Sept 1919, 7:2-3; Baltimore Sun,
25 Oct 1919, 4:5.

1971. "Are You For the 'Meter-Liter-Gram'?" New York Tribune syndicate, Louisville Herald, 9 Sept 1919, 7:5-6; Buffalo Evening News, 9 Sept 1919, 18:1-3.

1972. "Does Beauty Pay?" New York Tribune syndicate, Louisville Herald, 12 Sept 1919, 9:3-4; Buffalo Evening News, 12 Sept 1919, 17:1-4.

1973. "Wasted Dirt," New York Tribune syndicate, Louisville Herald, 13 Sept 1919, 5:4-5.

1974. "Who Are 'They'?" New York Tribune syndicate, Louisville Herald, 15 Sept 1919, 5:6-7; Baltimore Sun, 15 Oct 1919, 4:2.

1975. "These Bachelor Girls," New York Tribune syndicate, Louisville Herald, 16 Sept 1919, 6:4-5; Buffalo Evening News, 16 Sept 1919, 9:5-7; Baltimore Sun, 11 Oct 1919, 4:2.

1976. "Is Labor a Curse?" New York Tribune syndicate, Louisville Herald, 17 Sept 1919, 4:2-3.

1977. "Why Private Property is Right," New York Tribune syndicate, Louisville Herald, 18 Sept 1919, 7:6-7.

1978. "Our Food Habits," New York Tribune syndicate, Louisville Herald, 19 Sept 1919, 9:3-4.

1979. "When to Go to the Doctor," New York Tribune syndicate, Louisville Herald, 20 Sept 1919, 10:5-6.

1980. "Love and Time," New York Tribune syndicate, Louisville Herald, 22 Sept 1919, 7:6-7; Baltimore Sun, 1 Nov 1919, 4:5-6.

1981. "The Story 'With a Purpose,'" New York Tribune syndicate, Louisville Herald. 23 Sept 1919, 7:5-6.

1982. "Teaching and Nursing," New York Tribune syndicate, Louisville Herald, 24 Sept 1919, 6:3-4.

1983. "Egoism and Patriotism," New York Tribune syndicate, Louisville Herald, 26 Sept 1919, 9:1-2.

1984. "Those Evenings at Home," New York Tribune syndicate, Louisville Herald, 27 Sept 1919, 5:2-3.

1985. "The City and the Kitchen," New York Tribune syndicate, Louisville Herald, 29 Sept 1919, 7:3-4.

1986. "Do Women Need Names?" New York Tribune syndicate, Louisville Herald, 30 Sept 1919, 9:2-3; Baltimore Sun, 4 Dec 1919, 4:2.

1987. "What is Going to Happen to Marriage?" Pictorial Review, 21 (Oct 1919), 21, 31.

1988. "An Untouched Romance," New York Tribune syndicate, Louisville Herald, 1 Oct 1919, 9:5-6.

1989. "Catching Tomorrow," New York Tribune syndicate, Louisville Herald, 2 Oct 1919, 7:4-5; Baltimore Sun, 22 Oct 1919, 4:6-7.

1990. "The Drag of Yesterday," New York Tribune syndicate, Louisville Herald, 3 Oct 1919, 6:4-5.

1991. "What Did You Expect?" New York Tribune syndicate, Louisville Herald, 4 Oct 1919, 6:2-3.

1992. "The People's Hall," New York Tribune syndicate, Louisville Herald, 6 Oct 1919, 7:3-4.

1993. "Stretching Our Minds," New York Tribune syndicate, Louisville Herald, 7 Oct 1919, 9:3-4; Baltimore Sun, 26 Nov 1919, 4:2.

1994. "The Hand That Rocks the Frying Pan," New York Tribune syndicate, Louisville Herald, 8 Oct 1919, 8:1-2.

1995. "Is It 'Human' to Be Selfish?" New York Tribune syndicate, Louisville Herald, 9 Oct 1919, 5:4-5; Baltimore Sun, 11 Nov 1919, 4:5.

1996. "The Weaker Vessel," New York Tribune syndicate, Louisville Herald, 10 Oct 1919, 7:4-5.

1997. "What is the Duty of Women?" New York Tribune syndicate, Louisville Herald, 11 Oct 1919, 7:3-4.

1998. "Pockets and Bags," New York Tribune syndicate, Louisville Herald, 13 Oct 1919, 5:4-5.

1999. "'You Can't Alter Human Nature,'" New York Tribune syndicate, Louisville Herald, 14 Oct 1919, 9:5-6.

2000. "Tree Farming," New York Tribune syndicate, Louisville Herald, 15 Oct 1919, 8:6-7.

2001. "Is Woman a Mystery?" New York Tribune syndicate,

Louisville Herald, 16 Oct 1919, 7:3-4.

2002. "'Loving' Animals," New York Tribune syndicate, Louisville Herald, 17 Oct 1919, 9:5-6.

2003. "The Sanctity of Human Life," New York Tribune syndicate, Louisville Herald, 18 Oct 1919, 7:2-3.

2004. "Why Fuss About Death?" New York Tribune syndicate, Louisville Herald, 20 Oct 1919, 7:4-5; Baltimore Sun, 4 Nov 1919, 4:5.

2005. "Private Home with Public Service," New York Tribune syndicate, Louisville Herald, 21 Oct 1919, 6:1-2.

2006. "The Head and the Hair," New York Tribune syndicate, Louisville Herald, 22 Oct 1919, 8:1-2.

2007. "Nursemaids," New York Tribune syndicate, Louisville Herald, 24 Oct 1919, 6:3-4.

2008. "As to Kissing," New York Tribune syndicate, Louisville Herald, 25 Oct 1919, 5:4-5; Baltimore Sun, 10 Nov 1919, 4:7.

2009. "Feeding the Baby," New York Tribune syndicate, Louisville Herald, 27 Oct 1919, 7:5-6.

2010. "The Coal Age," New York Tribune syndicate, Louisville Herald, 28 Oct 1919, 7:3-4.

2011. "Couldn't You Make a Better World," New York Tribune syndicate, Louisville Herald, 29 Oct 1919, 7:4-5. Rpt. under title "Could You Make a Better World?" in Baltimore Sun, 1 Dec 1919, 4:2.

2012. "Enjoying Yourself," New York Tribune syndicate, Louisville Herald, 30 Oct 1919, 7:2-3; Baltimore Sun, 19 Nov 1919, 4:3.

2013. "The Bloom of Innocence," New York Tribune syndicate, Louisville Herald, 31 Oct 1919, 8:1-2.

2014. "Civic Pride," New York Tribune syndicate, Louisville Herald, 1 Nov 1919, 6:4-5.

2015. "Do Women Dress to Please Men?" New York Tribune syndicate, Louisville Herald, 3 Nov 1919, 6:5-6; Baltimore Sun, 9 Dec 1919, 4:3-4.

2016. "Unnecessary Evils," New York Tribune syndicate, Louisville Herald, 4 Nov 1919, 7:5-6.

2017. "Ennobling Domestic Service," New York Tribune syndicate, Louisville Herald, 5 Nov 1919, 6:1-2.

2018. "Carrying Sorrow," New York Tribune syndicate, Louisville Herald, 6 Nov 1919, 7:2-3.

2019. "Cupid and Love," New York Tribune syndicate, Louisville Herald, 7 Nov 1919, 6:4-5.

2020. "Social Inventors," New York Tribune syndicate, Louisville Herald, 8 Nov 1919, 5:3-4.

2021. "What is 'Conscience'?" New York Tribune syndicate, Louisville Herald, 10 Nov 1919, 7:6-7.

2022. "Pork, Plums and Budgets," New York Tribune syndicate, Louisville Herald, 11 Nov 1919, 8:2-3.

2023. "Can Parents Be Friends?" New York Tribune syndicate, Louisville Herald, 13 Nov 1919, 8:2-3.

2024. "A Social Clinic," New York Tribune syndicate, Louisville Herald, 14 Nov 1919, 8:4-5.

2025. "A 'Fallen' Woman," New York Tribune syndicate, Louisville Herald, 15 Nov 1919, 7:2-3.

2026. "The Greatest Comfort on Earth," New York Tribune syndicate, Louisville Herald, 17 Nov 1919, 7:2-3.

2027. "Dolls and Babies," New York Tribune syndicate, Louisville Herald, 18 Nov 1919, 7:1-2.

2028. "The Human Voice," New York Tribune syndicate, Louisville Herald, 19 Nov 1919, 7:3.

2029. "The Block That 'Buckled,'" New York Tribune syndicate, Louisville Herald, 21 Nov 1919, 11:3-4.

2030. "Lingerie and Laundry," New York Tribune syndicate, Louisville Herald, 22 Nov 1919, 9:3-4.

2031. "The Helpers and the Hinderers," New York Tribune syndicate, Louisville Herald, 24 Nov 1919, 7:6-7.

2032. "Heels Again," New York Tribune syndicate, Louisville Herald, 25 Nov 1919, 7:4-5.

2033. "How About Lying?" New York Tribune syndicate, Louisville Herald, 26 Nov 1919, 6:6-7.

2034. "Comrades in Service," New York Tribune syndicate, Louisville Herald, 27 Nov 1919, 8:2-3.

2035. "Love in the Dinner," New York Tribune syndicate, Louisville Herald, 28 Nov 1919, 7:3-4.

2036. "The Head and the Hat," New York Tribune syndicate, Louisville Herald, 29 Nov 1919, 12:2-3.

2037. "Are You an Ingrate?" New York Tribune syndicate, Louisville Herald, 1 Dec 1919, 7:2-3.

2038. "Eight Hours in the Kitchen," New York Tribune syndicate, Louisville Herald, 2 Dec 1919, 6:4-5; Baltimore Sun, 6 Dec 1919, 4:2-3.

2039. "If Wishes Were Horses," New York Tribune syndicate, Louisville Herald, 3 Dec 1919, 6:4-5.

2040. "The Pig and the Cannibal," New York Tribune syndicate, Louisville Herald, 4 Dec 1919, 6:3-4.

2041. "One in Nine," New York Tribune syndicate, Louisville Herald, 6 Dec 1919, 8:2-3.

2042. "The Glory of Living," New York Tribune syndicate, Louisville Herald, 10 Dec 1919, 6:5-6.

2043. "Pictures and Poppycock," New York Tribune syndicate, Louisville Herald, 11 Dec 1919, 7:3-4.

2044. "Ghastly News," New York Tribune syndicate, Louisville Herald, 13 Dec 1919, 7:6-7.

2045. "Women as Women," New York Tribune syndicate, Louisville Herald, 16 Dec 1919, 7:1-2.

2046. "What Keeps Women Back Most," New York Tribune syndicate, Louisville Herald, 17 Dec 1919, 6:3-4.

2047. "Anarchists and Jokes," New York Tribune syndicate, Louisville Herald, 18 Dec 1919, 6:1-3.

2048. "Plaintiff, Counsel, Judge and Executioner," New York Tribune syndicate, Louisville Herald, 19 Dec 1919, 7:3-4.

2049. "The Last Struggle," New York Tribune syndicate, Louisville Herald, 20 Dec 1919, 7:2-3.

2050. "He-ness, She-ness and Childishness," New York Tribune syndicate, Louisville Herald, 22 Dec 1919, 7:2-3.

2051. "Once Upon a Time--There Will Be," New York Tribune syndicate, Louisville Herald, 23 Dec 1919, 7:5-6.

2052. "Near-Mindedness," New York Tribune syndicate, Louisville Herald, 24 Dec 1919, 7:1-2.

2053. "Better Than Santa Claus," New York Tribune syndicate, Louisville Herald, 25 Dec 1919, 15:6-7.

2054. "Compared with Rabbits," New York Tribune syndicate, Louisville Herald, 26 Dec 1919, 7:4-5.

2055. "How Many Things Do You Eat?" New York Tribune syndicate, Louisville Herald, 27 Dec 1919, 5:4-5.

2056. "Common Knowledge," New York Tribune syndicate, Louisville Herald, 29 Dec 1919, 4:6-7.

2057. "The Strength of Women," New York Tribune syndicate, Louisville Herald, 30 Dec 1919, 6:2-3.

2058. "Judging People," New York Tribune syndicate, Louisville Herald, 31 Dec 1919, 7:3-4.

1920

2059. "Community Conservation of Women's Strength," Proceedings of the International Conference of Women Physicians, 1 (1920), 257-264.
See also discussion pp. 264-267.
See also item 2261.

2060. Testimonial in Debs and the Poets, ed. Ruth Le Prade (Pasadena: Upton Sinclair, 1920), p. 45.

2061. "Introduction" to the ninth edition of Women and Economics. London: G. P. Putnam's Sons, 1920, pp. xi-xiii.
Rpt. in New York: Gordon Press, 1975.

2062. "Beginning Again," New York Tribune syndicate, Louisville Herald, 1 Jan 1920, 7:4-5.

2063. "One Day's Loving," New York Tribune syndicate,

Louisville Herald, 2 Jan 1920, 5:5-6.

2064. "Looking for Leaders," New York Tribune syndicate, Louisville Herald, 8 Jan 1920, 7:4-5.

2065. "The Eternal Masculine," New York Tribune syndicate, Louisville Herald, 9 Jan 1920, 8:6-7.

2066. "Is Love Enough?" New York Tribune syndicate, Louisville Herald, 12 Jan 1920, 4:5-6.

2067. "Customer, Client, Patient, Patron, Employer," New York Tribune syndicate, Louisville Herald, 13 Jan 1920, 7:5-6.

2068. "House-Ridden," New York Tribune syndicate, Louisville Herald, 14 Jan 1920, 7:2-3.

2069. "Second-Hand Furniture," New York Tribune syndicate, Louisville Herald, 15 Jan 1920, 5:2-3.

2070. "The Woman Must Choose," New York Tribune syndicate, Louisville Herald, 16 Jan 1920, 8:5-6.

2071. "The People's Power," New York Tribune syndicate, Louisville Herald, 17 Jan 1920, 7:3-4.

2072. "'Talking Shop,'" New York Tribune syndicate, Louisville Herald, 19 Jan 1920, 7:4-5.

2073. "Self-Expression," New York Tribune syndicate, Louisville Herald, 20 Jan 1920, 7:3-4.

2074. "Vengeance and Justice," New York Tribune syndicate, Louisville Herald, 23 Jan 1920, 3:3-4.

2075. "Youth, Age and Women," New York Tribune syndicate, Louisville Herald, 24 Jan 1920, 5:3-4.

2076. "Which Way Are Women Going?" San Francisco Chronicle, 25 Jan 1920, magazine section, p. 1.

2077. "The Terrible Tongue," New York Tribune syndicate, Louisville Herald, 26 Jan 1920, 7:1-2.

2078. "House-Bound," New York Tribune syndicate, Louisville Herald, 27 Jan 1920, 6:5-6.

2079. "Believing Things," New York Tribune syndicate, Louisville Herald, 28 Jan 1920, 7:3-4.

2080. "Shopping Ethics," New York Tribune syndicate, Louisville Herald, 29 Jan 1920, 7:5-6.

2081. "Social Primer," New York Tribune syndicate, Louisville Herald, 30 Jan 1920, 7:6-7.

2082. "A Shapeless Mass," New York Tribune syndicate, Louisville Herald, 31 Jan 1920, 7:2-3.

2083. "A Woman's Party," Suffragist, 8 (Feb 1920), 8-9.

2084. "An Easy Duty," New York Tribune syndicate, Louisville Herald, 2 Feb 1920, 7:6-7.

2085. "To End the Slums," New York Tribune syndicate, Louisville Herald, 3 Feb 1920, 4:5-6.

2086. "The Wolf and the Star," New York Tribune syndicate, Louisville Herald, 4 Feb 1920, 6:5-6.

2087. "A Woman's Complaint," New York Tribune syndicate, Louisville Herald, 5 Feb 1920, 7:2-3.

2088. "From Now On," New York Tribune syndicate, Louisville Herald, 6 Feb 1920, 7:4-5.

2089. "The Cost and the Price of Living," New York Tribune syndicate, Louisville Herald, 7 Feb 1920, 7:3-4.

2090. "Would You Like It?" New York Tribune syndicate, Louisville Herald, 9 Feb 1920, 5:4-5.

2091. "'In My Time,'" New York Tribune syndicate, Louisville Herald, 10 Feb 1920, 9:2-3.

2092. "A Question for Men," New York Tribune syndicate, Louisville Herald, 11 Feb 1920, 9:6-7.

2093. "'The Peoples of America,'" New York Tribune syndicate, Louisville Herald, 12 Feb 1920, 12:5-6.

2094. "An Extinct Specimen," New York Tribune syndicate, Louisville Herald, 13 Feb 1920, 12:3-4.

2095. "'Exiling Dissenters,'" New York Tribune syndicate, Louisville Herald, 14 Feb 1920, 6:4.

2096. "What is America?" New York Tribune syndicate, Louisville Herald, 17 Feb 1920, 6:3-4.

2097. "Tired Business Women," New York Tribune syndicate, Louisville Herald, 19 Feb 1920, 7:4-5.

2098. "'The Slate,'" New York Tribune syndicate, Louisville Herald, 20 Feb 1920, 7:4-5.

2099. "Marriage-Plus," New York Tribune syndicate, Louisville Herald, 21 Feb 1920, 5:2-3.

2100. "Feminine Charm," New York Tribune syndicate, Louisville Herald, 23 Feb 1920, 4:6-7.

2101. "Author and Writer," New York Tribune syndicate, Louisville Herald, 24 Feb 1920, 7:1-2.

2102. "The Historic View," New York Tribune syndicate, Louisville Herald, 26 Feb 1920, 7:4-5.

2103. "Her Back," New York Tribune syndicate, Louisville Herald, 27 Feb 1920, 7:3-4.

2104. "Solid Ground," New York Tribune syndicate, Louisville Herald, 28 Feb 1920, 7:3-4.

2105. "New Missionaries," New York Tribune syndicate, Louisville Herald, 1 March 1920, 7:2-3.

2106. "War Gains," New York Tribune syndicate, Louisville Herald, 4 March 1920, 10:2-3.

2107. "A Vision of Clothes," New York Tribune syndicate, Louisville Herald, 5 March 1920, 9:2-3.

2108. "A Man-Fancier," New York Tribune syndicate, Louisville Herald, 6 March 1920, 5:3-4.

2109. "The Round-Square Pain," New York Tribune syndicate, Louisville Herald, 8 March 1920, 7:1-2.

2110. "A Little Stranger," New York Tribune syndicate, Louisville Herald, 9 March 1920, 7:3-4.

2111. "A New Feeding Car," New York Tribune syndicate, Louisville Herald, 11 March 1920, 6:5-6.

2112. "Usury and Profits," New York Tribune syndicate, Louisville Herald, 12 March 1920, 8:6-7.

2113. "Stories About Women," New York Tribune syndicate, Louisville Herald, 13 March 1920, 5:3-4.

2114. "Snow Removal," New York Tribune syndicate, <u>Louisville Herald</u>, 15 March 1920, 5:6-7.

2115. "State Wrongs," New York Tribune syndicate, <u>Louisville Herald</u>, 19 March 1920, 9:4-5.

2116. "'Of Interest to Women,'" New York Tribune syndicate, <u>Louisville Herald</u>, 20 March 1920, 5:3-4.

2117. "A Platform for Women," New York Tribune syndicate, <u>Louisville Herald</u>, 22 March 1920, 7:6-7.

2118. "Where 'Movies' Lead," New York Tribune syndicate, <u>Louisville Herald</u>, 23 March 1920, 7:3-4.

2119. "Incentive to What?" New York Tribune syndicate, <u>Louisville Herald</u>, 25 March 1920, 8:2-3.

2120. "Is Labor a Curse," New York Tribune syndicate, <u>Louisville Herald</u>, 26 March 1920, 8:5-6.

2121. "Working Children," New York Tribune syndicate, <u>Louisville Herald</u>, 27 March 1920, 5:4.

2122. "Real America," New York Tribune syndicate, <u>Louisville Herald</u>, 29 March 1920, 6:5-6.

2123. "A Proud Grandma," New York Tribune syndicate, <u>Louisville Herald</u>, 1 April 1920, 9:2-3.

2124. "A New Theme for Drama," New York Tribune syndicate, <u>Louisville Herald</u>, 2 April 1920, 9:6-7.

2125. "Proof by Miracle," New York Tribune syndicate, <u>Louisville Herald</u>, 3 April 1920, 5:7.

2126. "These Awful Atoms," New York Tribune syndicate, <u>Louisville Herald</u>, 5 April 1920, 7:6-7.

2127. "An Altar Shunned," New York Tribune syndicate, <u>Louisville Herald</u>, 6 April 1920, 7:3-4.

2128. "As to Memory," New York Tribune syndicate, <u>Louisville Herald</u>, 10 April 1920, 5:3-4.

2129. "Whatever Else We Lose, We Must Keep the Home," <u>Woman Citizen</u>, 19 June 1920, pp. 72-74.
    See also replies by Lulu Daniel Harder in Woman Citizen, 17 July 1920, pp. 179-180; by Julia M. Husbands in <u>Woman Citizen</u>, 7 Aug 1920, p. 252; and

Marian Murdock in <u>Woman</u> <u>Citizen</u>, 7 Aug 1920, p. 253.

2130. "Applepieville," <u>Independent</u>, 25 Sept 1920, pp. 365, 393-395.

2131. "Blunders About Women," New York <u>Evening</u> <u>Post</u> <u>Literary</u> <u>Review</u>, 30 Oct 1920, p. 8. [Review of <u>Arabella</u> <u>Kenealy</u> <u>and</u> <u>L.</u> R. C. P. Dublin, <u>Feminism</u> <u>and</u> <u>Sex-Distinction</u> (New York: E. P. Dutton, 1920).]

2132. "Woman's Outlook for 1921," <u>San</u> <u>Francisco</u> <u>Chronicle</u>, 26 Dec 1920, magazine section, <u>p.</u> 1.
     Rpt. in <u>Philadelphia</u> <u>North</u> <u>American</u>, 2 Jan 1921, magazine section, p. 1.

1921

2133. "Should Women Take Alimony?" <u>Woman</u> <u>Citizen</u>, 5 Feb 1921, pp. 953-954.

2134. "Making Towns Fit to Live In," <u>Century</u>, 102 (July 1921), 361-366.
     Rpt. in <u>Dallas</u> <u>Morning</u> <u>News</u>, 24 June 1921, 4:1-2.

1922

2135. "Back of Birth Control," <u>Birth</u> <u>Control</u> <u>Review</u>, 6 (March 1922), 31-33.
     See also reply by F. W. Stella Browne in <u>Birth</u> <u>Control</u> <u>Review</u>, 6 (March 1922), 33-34.

2136. "Do Women Dress to Please Men?" <u>Century</u>, 103 (March 1922), 651-655.
     Reviewed in <u>New</u> <u>York</u> <u>Times</u> <u>Book</u> <u>Review</u> <u>and</u> <u>Magazine</u>, 26 Feb 1922, section 3, p. 9.

2137. "Vanguard, Rearguard and Mudguard," <u>Century</u>, 104 (July 1922), 348-353.
     Reviewed in <u>New</u> <u>York</u> <u>Times</u>, 9 July 1922, section 2, 4:4.

2138. "The Problem of the Unhappy Woman," <u>Beautiful</u> <u>Womanhood</u>, 1 (Oct 1922), 10, 64.

2139. "Cross-Examining Santa Claus," <u>Century</u>, 105 (Dec 1922), 169-174.
     Reviewed in <u>Literary</u> <u>Digest</u>, 16 Dec 1922, pp. 32-33.

1923

2140. "Do You Know Beauty When You See It?" Beautiful
Womanhood, 2 (March 1923), 12-13, 68.

2141. "His Religion and Hers," Century, 105 (March 1923),
676-683; 105 (April 1923), 855-861.
Reviewed in Literary Digest, 12 May 1923, pp. 30-31.
See also item 2142.

2142. His Religion and Hers: A Study of the Faith of Our
Fathers and the Work of Our Mothers. New York and
London: Century Co., 1923. 300 pp.
Rpt. in British edition in London: T. Fisher Unwin,
1924. Rpt. in Westport, Conn.: Hyperion Press, 1976.
Reviewed by W.S.S. in Christian Register, 8 Nov 1923,
p. 1070.
Reviewed in Booklist, 20 (Dec 1923), 82.
Reviewed by Amy Wellington in Literary Review, 1 Dec
1923, p. 303.
Reviewed by D.F.G. in Boston Transcript, 8 Dec 1923,
p. 3.
Reviewed in Woman Citizen, 29 Dec 1923, p. 27.
Reviewed by Hildegarde Fillmore in Bookman, 58 (Jan
1924), 575.
Reviewed in Dial, 76 (March 1924), 290.
Reviewed in Christian Work, 29 March 1924, pp. 405-
406.
Reviewed by William Pepperell Montague in Birth
Control Review, 8 (June 1924), 178.
See also item 2141.

2143. "If You Are Queer--and Know It," Survey, 15 March 1923,
pp. 773-774.

2144. "The New Generation of Women," Current History, 18 (Aug
1923), 731-737.

2145. "Is America Too Hospitable?" Forum, 70 (Oct 1923),
1983-1989.

1924

2145. "Toward Monogamy," Nation, 11 June 1924, pp. 671-673.
Reviewed in Congregationalist, 25 Sept 1924, p. 389.
Rpt. in Our Changing Morality, ed. Freda Kirchweg
(New York: Albert and Charles Boni, 1930), pp. 53-
66.

2146. "The Old and the New," New York Evening Post Literary

Review, 1924. [Review of Stuart P. Sherman, My Dear
Cornelia (Boston: Atlantic Monthly Press, 1924).]

1925

2147. "Wash-Tubs and Woman's Duty," Century, 110 (June 1925),
152-159.

2148. "The Nobler Male," Forum, 74 (July 1925), 19-21.

2149. "What Our Children Might Have," Century, 110 (Oct
1925), 706-711.
Rpt. in Visual Review, (1926), 3-8.

2150. "Mind-Stretching," Century, 111 (Dec 1925), 217-224.

1926

2151. "These Too, Too Solid Ghosts," Forum, 75 (Feb 1926),
238-244.

2152. "American Radicals," New York Jewish Daily Forward, 1
Aug 1926, p. 1.

2153. "Public Library Motion Pictures," Annals of the
American Academy, 128 (Nov 1926), 143-145.

1927

2154. "Woman's Achievements Since the Franchise," Current
History, 27 (Oct 1927), 7-14.
Reviewed in New York Times, 25 Sept 1927, section 2,
20:1.
Excerpted in Readings in the Family, ed. Ernest R.
Groves and Lee M. Brooks (Chicago and Philadelphia:
J. B. Lippincott Co., 1934), pp. 146-149.

2155. "Progress Through Birth Control," North American
Review, 224 (Dec 1927), 622-629.

1928

2156. Letter to William R. Thurston, in "The Great Secret,"
supplement to Thurston's Philosophy of Marriage (New
York: Traymore Press, 1928), pp. 3-4.
Copy extant in folder 270, CPG Papers.

2157. "Divorce and Birth Control," Outlook, 25 Jan 1928, pp.
130-131.

2158. "Thrills, Common and Uncommon," Forum, 80 (July 1928), 97-102.

1929

2159. "Feminism and Social Progress," in Problems of Civilization, ed. Baker Brownell (New York: D. Van Nostrand, 1929), pp. 115-142.

2160. "Sex and Race Progress," in Sex in Civilization, ed. V. F. Calverton and Samuel D. Schmalhausen (New York: Macaulay, 1929), pp. 109-123.

2161. "Unity is Not Equality," World Unity, 4 (Aug 1929), 418-420.

2162. "Fashion, Beauty and Brains," Outlook, 7 (Aug 1929), 578-579.

1931

2163. "Parasitism and Civilized Vice," in Woman's Coming of Age, ed. Samuel D. Schmalhausen and V. F. Calverton (New York: Liveright, 1931), pp. 110-126.

1932

2164. "Birth Control, Religion and the Unfit," Nation, 27 Jan 1932, pp. 108-109.

1935

2165. The Living of Charlotte Perkins Gilman: An Autobiography. With a foreword by Zona Gale. New York and London: Appleton-Century, 1935. xxxviii + 341 pp. Rpt. in New York: Arno Press, 1972; and New York: Harper & Row, 1975.
    Reviewed in New York Herald Tribune, 14 Oct 1935, p. 13.
    Reviewed in Books, 20 Oct 1935, p. 7.
    Reviewed by Clara Gruening Stillman in New York Herald Tribune Books, 20 Oct 1935, section 7, p. 7.
    Reviewed in Boston Transcript, 23 Oct 1923, p. 3.
    Reviewed in News Week, 26 Oct 1935, p. 40.
    Reviewed in Booklist, 32 (Nov 1923), 63.
    Reviewed by L. B. H. in Springfield Republican, 10 Nov 1935, p. 7E.
    Excerpted in Amerikanische Turnzeitung, 10 Nov 1935, p. 15.
    Reviewed in Special Libraries, 26 (Nov 1935), 301.

Reviewed in <u>Independent</u> <u>Woman</u>, 14 (Nov 1935), 381.
Reviewed in <u>Pasadena Star-News</u>, 30 Nov 1935, p. 8.
Reviewed in <u>Review of Reviews</u>, 92 (Dec 1935), 2.
Reviewed by M. R. Bruere in <u>Survey Graphic</u>, 25 (Jan 1936), 50.
Reviewed in <u>New York Times Book Review</u>, 28 June 1936, p. 15.
Reviewed by Harriet Howe in <u>Equal Rights: Independent Feminist Weekly</u>, 12 Sept 1936, pp. 221-222.
Excerpted in <u>The Oven Birds</u>, ed. Gail Parker (New York: Doubleday & Co., 1972), pp. 353-387.

2166. "The Right to Die," <u>Forum</u>, 94 (Nov 1935), 297-300.
Excerpted in <u>Literary Digest</u>, 18 Sept 1937, p. 22.

Undated

2167. "The Best from the Poorest," New York <u>Evening Post</u>.
Rpt. in <u>Forerunner</u>, 7 (Oct 1916), 260-262.

2168. "'Woman Suffrage Would Unsex Women,'" in <u>Twenty-five Answers to Antis</u> (New York: NAWSA, n.d.), p. 3.

2169. "A Leisure League for Mothers."
Copy signed CPG extant in vol. 1, CPG Papers.

2170. "There is No Hurry."
Copy signed CPG extant in folder 248, CPG Papers.

2171. "Her Visioning of Growth/Due Salutations to Our Great-Great-Grandchildren."
Copy signed CPG extant in folder 255, CPG Papers.

2172. "Two Old-Fashioned Games."
Copy signed CPG extant in folder 255, CPG Papers.

2173. "Traveling at Home."
Copy signed CPG extant in folder 255, CPG Papers.

Part II

Selected Biographical Sources

LECTURE REPORTS

1890

2174. "Club News," Weekly Nationalist, 21 June 1890, p. 6. [Re. "On Human Nature."]

1891

2175. "News from the Clubs," New Nation, 7 Feb 1891, p. 34. [Re. "Nationalism and the Virtues."]

2176. "News from the Clubs," New Nation, 28 Feb 1891, p. 83. [Re. "Nationalism and Love."]

2177. "News from the Clubs," New Nation, 14 March 1891, p. 115. [Re. "Nationalism and Religion."]

2178. "In a New Sphere," San Francisco Call, 17 March 1891, 2:2. [Re. "The Coming Woman."]

2179. "With Women Who Write," San Francisco Examiner, 17 March 1891, 3:3. [Re. "The Coming Woman."]

2180. "News from the Clubs," New Nation, 28 March 1891, p. 147. [Re. "Who Owns the Children?"]

2181. "News from the Clubs," New Nation, 25 April 1891, p. 211. [Re. "Dress Reform" and "Society and the Baby."]

2182. "Pacific Coast Press Notices," Woman's Journal, 25 April 1891, p. 130. [Re. "The Coming Woman."]

2183. "'The Real Woman,'" San Francisco Call, 30 May 1891, 2:2. [Re. "The Real Woman."]

2184. "News from the Clubs," New Nation, 31 May 1891, p. 259.
[Re. "Nationalism and the Arts."]

1892

2185. "The New Nation Club, Oakland," New Nation, 23 Jan
1892, p. 58. [Re. series of Nationalist lectures.]

2186. "The Human Paradox," San Francisco Call, 24 April 1892,
12:4. [Re. "An Old Baby," "A Married Child," and
"Heaven Underfoot."]

2187. "Safeguards Suggested for Social Evils," San Francisco
Call, 20 Dec 1892, 8:4.

1893

2188. Ambrose Bierce, "Prattle," San Francisco Examiner, 23
July 1893, 6:5-6. [Re. "She Who is to Come."]

2189. "Women Writers," San Francisco Call, 21 Sept 1893,
10:3-4. [Re. keynote address of PCWPA convention.]

2190. "An Authors' Day," San Francisco Call, 22 Sept 1893,
4:1. [Re. "The World's Voices."]

1894

2191. "Announcement," Impress, 1 (July 1894), 2. [Re. series
of "Talks on Social Questions."] See also Impress, 1
(Aug 1894), 6.

2192. Impress, 6 Oct 1894, p. 7. [Re. "Journalism."]

1895

2193. "All the Comforts of a Home," San Francisco Examiner,
22 May 1895, p. 9. [Re. "Simplicity and Decoration."]

2194. "Home and Art at the Woman's Congress," San Francisco
Call, 22 May 1895, 9:7-10:1. [Re. "Simplicity and
Decoration."]

1896

2195. "The Washington Convention," Woman's Journal, 15 Feb
1896, pp. 49, 50. [Lectures re. California.]

2196. Henry B. Blackwell, "Educated Motherhood," Woman's
Journal, 15 Feb 1896, p. 52. [Re. "Educated

Motherhood."]

2197. Woman's Journal, 22 Feb 1896, p. 58. [Re. "The
      Spiritual Significance of Democracy, and Woman's
      Relation to It."]
          See also History of Woman Suffrage, ed. Susan B.
      Anthony and Ida Husted Harper (Indianapolis:
      Hollenbeck Press, 1902), vol. 4, pp. 258-259.

2198. "Woman Suffrage and Motherhood," Woman's Journal, 29
      Feb 1896, p. 66. [Re. "The Ballot as an Improver of
      Mankind."]
          See also History of Woman Suffrage, ed. Susan B.
      Anthony and Ida Husted Harper (Indianapolis:
      Hollenbeck Press, 1902), vol. 4, pp. 266-267.

2199. "Third Congress of Coast Women," San Francisco
      Examiner, 5 May 1896, p. 16. [Re. "The Beginnings of
      Government."]

2200. Henry B. Blackwell, "Mrs. Charlotte Perkins Stetson,"
      Woman's Journal, 30 May 1896, p. 172. [Lecture on the
      principles of American government.]
          See also item 1033.

2201. "New England Anniversary Meeting," Woman's Journal, 6
      June 1896, pp. 181, 184. [Re. the "selfishness of
      women."]

                          1897

2202. "The National Convention," Woman's Journal, 27 Feb
      1897, pp. 65-66. [Re. "Duty and Honor."]
          See also History of Woman Suffrage, ed. Susan B.
      Anthony and Ida Husted Harper (Indianapolis:
      Hollenbeck Press, 1902), vol. 4, pp. 277-278.

2203. "The Ballot and the Nursery/Charlotte Perkins Stetson
      Talks on the 'Home Duties' and 'Public Affairs' of
      Women," New York Tribune, 9 June 1897, 5:6.

2204. "Concerning Women," Woman's Journal, 4 Sept 1897, p.
      281. [Re. "The Social Organism."]

2205. "Woman Suffrage League," Boston Advertiser, 10 Nov
      1897, 8:1. [Re. "The Economic Basis of the Woman
      Question."]

1898

2206. Woman's Journal, 22 Jan 1898, p. 25; Woman's Journal, 29 Jan 1898, p. 40. [Re. "The Economic Basis of the Woman Question."]

2207. "Bellamy Memorial Meeting," American Fabian, 4 (June 1898), 3.

2208. "Equal Suffrage Day at Mechanics' Fair," Woman's Journal, 5 Nov 1898, p. 357. [Re. lecture on government.]
    See also Woman's Column, 5 Nov 1898, p. 1.

1899

2209. "An Evening with Kipling," Goldsboro, N.C., Daily Argus, 14 March 1899, 4:2.

2210. "Lecture on Public Ethics," New York Times, 23 April 1899, 20:7. [Re. "Public Ethics."]

2211. Woman's Journal, 6 May 1899, p. 137. [Lectures before Political Equality Club and Walt Whitman Fellowship of Boston.]

2212. Woman's Journal, 14 Oct 1899, p. 321. [Re. "Our Country."]

2213. "Mrs. Stetson Welcomed," New York Tribune, 20 April 1899, 7:2. [Re. "What a Just Economic System Would Do For Women."]

2214. "Talks with Clubwomen," Chicago Times-Herald, 12 Nov 1899, supplement, section 3, pp. 1-2. [Re. English women.]

1900

2215. In Women in Education, vol. 2 of International Congress of Women of 1899, ed. Countess of Aberdeen (London: T. Unwin Fisher, 1900), p. 12. [Re. "Parental Responsibility."]

2216. In Women in Professions, vol. 3. of International Congress of Women of 1899, ed. Countess of Aberdeen (London: T. Unwin Fisher, 1900), pp. 155-156. [Re. "The Art of Poetry with Regard to Women."]

2217. In Women in Industrial Life, vol. 6 of International

Congress of Women of 1899, ed. Countess of Aberdeen
(London: T. Unwin Fisher, 1900), p. 109. [Re.
"Scientific Training of Domestic Servants."]

1902

2218. "The Ideal Mother/Her Place in the World as Defined by
Charlotte P. Gilman," New York Tribune, 13 March 1902,
7:2. [Re. "Woman in the Social Fabric."]

2219. "Society and the Child," Brooklyn Eagle, 11 Dec 1902,
8:4.

1903

2220. "Woman and Work/Popular Fallacy That They Are a Leisure
Class, Says Mrs. Gilman," New York Tribune, 26 Feb
1903, 7:1. [Re. "Women and Work."]

2221. "Women and Duty/Specialists to Help Mothers Bring Up
Children Advocated," Work/Popular Fallacy That They Are
a Leisure Class, Says Mrs. Gilman," New York Tribune,
12 March 1903, 7:1. [Re. professional child care.]

2222. Woman's Journal, 18 April 1903, pp. 122-123. [Re.
"Duties of Today."]
See also History of Woman Suffrage, ed. Ida Husted
Harper (New York: National American Woman Suffrage
Association, 1922), vol. 5, p. 71.

2223. Woman's Journal, 25 April 1903, p. 130. [On
educational qualification to vote.]

2224. "'Woman Created First,'" New York Tribune, 17 Oct 1903,
7:4. [Re. androcentrism.]

1904

2225. Woman's Journal, 5 March 1904, pp. 76-77. [Re. "A New
Light on the Woman Question."]
See also History of Woman Suffrage, ed. Ida Husted
Harper (New York: National American Woman Suffrage
Association, 1922), vol. 5, pp. 92-93.

1905

2226. "Straight Talk by Mrs. Gilman is Looked For," San
Francisco Call, 16 July 1905, 33:2.
See also "Noted Woman Suffragist Speaks at the
Alhambra," San Francisco Call, 17 July 1905, 4:6.

[Re. "America's Place Today."]

2227. Woman's Journal, 2 Sept 1905, p. 139. [Re. "Woman's World."]
See also History of Woman Suffrage, ed. Ida Husted Harper (New York: National American Woman Suffrage Association, 1922), vol. 5, p. 149.

1908

2228. "Higher Marriage Mrs. Gilman's Plea," New York Times, 29 Dec 1908, 2:3. [Re. "How Do Home Conditions React on the Family?"]
See also item 1305.

1909

2229. "Think Husbands Aren't Mainstays," New York Times, 7 Jan 1909, 9:5. [Re. debate with Anna Howard Shaw, CPG in affirmative on question "Is the wife supported by her husband?"]

2230. "Three Women Leaders in Hub," Boston Post, 7 Dec 1909, 1:1-2 and 14:5-6. [Re. suffrage.]

2231. "Collectivists Hear Charlotte P. Gilman," New York Call, 8 Dec 1909, 2:1. [Re. child labor.]

1910

2232. "Author Demands Woman Suffrage," San Francisco Chronicle, 14 Nov 1910, 12:3. [Re. "Woman's Place in Civilization."]

2233. "Warless World When Women's Slavery Ends," San Francisco Examiner, 14 Nov 1910, 4:1. [Re. "Woman's Place in Civilization."]

1911

2234. "Noted Woman to Deliver Lecture," San Francisco Call, 7 Nov 1911, 11:5.
See also "Mrs. Gilman Talks on Place of Woman in Social Movement," San Francisco Call, 11 Nov 1911, 15:6.

2235. "Lecture Given by Mrs. Gilman," San Francisco Call, 15 Nov 1911, 7:3. [Re. "The Society--Body and Soul."]

1913

2236. "Says Our Women Are Ill-Informed/Mrs. Gilman Finds That English Women Know and Care More About Public Matters/But Ours Want to Learn," New York Times, 20 May 1913, 4:3. [Re. "English and American Women."]
See also item 1528.

2237. "Mrs. Gilman Assorts Sins," New York Times, 3 June 1913, 3:8. [Re. "Assorted Sins."]

1914

2238. "Adam the Real Rib, Mrs. Gilman Insists," New York Times, 19 Feb 1914, 9:3. [Re. "The Biological Base of the Larger Feminism."]
See also item 2260.

2239. "Feminists Ask for Equal Chance," New York Times, 21 Feb 1914, 18:1-2. [Re. "The Right of Women to Specialize in Home Industries."]

2240. "Adam Made from Rib of Eve, Newest Theory Offered by Suffragist as Result of Discoveries," Boston Post, 22 Feb 1914, 36:1-2. [Re. "The Biological Base of the Larger Feminism."]

2241. "Mrs. Gilman Tilts at Modern Women," New York Times, 26 Feb 1914, 9:3. [Re. "The Economic Relation of Men and Women: The Effect of Making Marriage a Profession."]
See also "Women and Men and Money," New York Times, 27 Feb 1914, 10:5.
See also Lavinia Leitch, "Marrying for Money," New York Times, 1 March 1914, II, 14:5; and Oliver C. Morse, "The Indian as Exception," New York Times, 7 March 1914, 10:5.

2242. "'Man Makes Money to Get Love,' Says Mrs. Gilman/'Women Make Love to Get Money in Marriage,'" New York American, 26 Feb 1914, 5:2. [Re. "The Economic Relation of Men and Women: The Effect of Making Marriage a Profession."]

2243. "Cupid is Scorned by Mrs. Gilman," New York Times, 5 March 1914, 8:8. [Re. "'Love,' Love, and Marriage."]

2244. "Hard Words for Wicked Papers," New York Times, 6 March 1914, 20:1-2. [Re. freedom of the press and The Masses.]

2245. "Mrs. Gilman Swats Home-Cooking Ideal," New York Times,
12 March 1914, 8:8. [Re. "The Home: Past, Present,
and Future."]
    See also Henry T. Finck, "As to Home Cooking," New
        York Times, 14 March 1914, 10:6; R. A. Dix and
        M. H., "Old Fashioned Homes," New York Times, 16
        March 1914, 8:5.
    See also "'Home' Means Everything and Nothing," New
        York Times, 16 March 1914, 8:4.

2246. "Feminist Dooms 'Home Cooking,'" New York Tribune, 12
March 1914, 9:3-4. [Re. "The Home: Past, Present, and
Future."]

2247. "Mrs. Gilman Seeks Wider Motherhood," New York Times,
19 March 1914, 8:8. [Re. "Motherhood: Personal and
Social."]

2248. "Women's Weakness Due to Education," New York Times, 26
March 1914, 10:8. [Re. "The Normal Woman and the
Coming World."]
    See also "Proofs for the Suffragists," New York
        Times, 27 March 1914, 10:3-4.
    See also Olive L. Reamy, "Women Who Do Men's Work,"
        New York Times, 29 March 1914, IV, 4:6.

2249. "Mrs. Gilman's Scorn Strikes 'Masculism,'" New York
Times, 2 April 1914, 11:1-2. [Re. first lecture in
"Our Male Civilization" series.]
    See also "A Feminist Revision of History," New York
        Times, 3 April 1914, 10:5.
    See also W. H. Sampson, "Not All Man's Fault," New
        York Times, 3 April 1914, 10:6; and William K.
        Lane, "Paris and Helen," New York Times, 4 April
        1914, 14:6.

2250. "Mrs. Gilman Calls Science to Witness," New York Times,
9 April 1914, 10:8. [Re. second lecture in "Our Male
Civilization" series.]
    See also "200 Women May Pounce on Press," New York
        Tribune, 9 April 1914, 5:5.

2251. "Women Denounce War with Mexico," New York Times, 24
April 1914, 6:1. [CPG among speakers who denounce
invasion of Mexico and arrest of Mary "Mother" Jones in
Colorado coal war.]

2252. "Opposed to Militarism," New York Times, 18 Dec 1914,
15:1. [CPG and others address Columbia Univ. students
on doctrine of preparedness.]

1915

2253. "Advocates a 'World City,'" New York Times, 6 Jan 1915, 15:5. [Re. arbitration of diplomatic disputes by an international agency.]

2254. "Split on War and Votes/Women Forget Great Conflice in Discussing Suffrage," New York Times, 20 Feb 1915, 7:3. [CPG and others address Woman Suffrage Party meeting at Cooper Union on "Women and War."]

2255. "War Has Ended Old Subservience of Women, is Belief," Oregon Journal, 28 March 1915, 2:8.

2256. "Women Ridicule Security League," New York Times, 16 June 1915, 4:6. [CPG and others condemn doctrine of preparedness.]

2257. "Woman the Slave Exhorted to Rebel," New York Times, 29 Sept 1915, 14:1. [Re. "Woman's Work."]

1917

2258. "The Listener," Boston Transcript, 14 April 1917, section 3, 3:5. [Announcement of lecture series.]

1918

2259. "Great Duty for Women After War," Boston Post, 26 Feb 1918, 2:7. [Re. "The World War and Its Effect on Women."]

2260. "Describes Man as the 'Whole Thing,'" New York Times, 5 March 1918, 11:3. [Re. "The Biological Base of the Larger Feminism."]
    See also item 2238.

1919

2261. "Mrs. Gilman Urges Hired Mother Idea," New York Times, 23 Sept 1919, 36:1-2. [Re. "Community Conservation of Women's Strength"]
    See also Woman Citizen, 4 Oct 1919, pp. 448-449.
    See also item 2059.

1920

2262. "Eulogize Susan B. Anthony," New York Times, 16 Feb 1920, 15:6. [CPG and others eulogize Anthony on the centenary of her birth.]

1921

2263. "Walt Whitman Dinner," New York Times, 1 June 1921, 16:7. [CPG speaks at annual meeting of Whitman Society of New York.]

1926

2264. "Fiction of America Being Melting Pot Unmasked by Charlotte Perkins Gilman," Dallas Morning News, 15 Feb 1926, 9:7-8 and 15:8. [Re. "Americans and Non-Americans."]

SKETCHES, BIOGRAPHIES, AND OBITUARIES

1891

2265. Gertrude Franklin Atherton, "The Literary Development of California," Cosmopolitan, 10 (Jan 1891), esp. 272. Excerpted in Nationalist, 3 (Feb 1891), 491.

2266. "Women in Literature," San Francisco Call, 15 March 1891, 3:2.

2267. "Di Vernon" [Eliza D. Keith], "Charlotte Perkins Stetson," San Francisco News Letter, 28 March 1891, p. 5.

1893

2268. "Charlotte Perkins Stetson," San Francisco Call, 28 May 1893, 6:7.

1897

2269. "Charlotte Perkins Stetson: A Daring Humorist of Reform," American Fabian, 3 (Jan 1897), 1-3.

2270. Eugene Hough, "The Work and Influence of Charlotte Perkins Stetson in the Labor Movement," American Fabian, 3 (Jan 1897), 12.

1898

2271. The Labour Annual, ed. Joseph Edwards, 4 (1898), 207.

2272. Helen Campbell, "Famous Persons at Home--Charlotte Perkins Stetson," Time and the Hour, 16 April 1898, pp. 7-8.
Excerpted in Bookman, 12 (Nov 1900), 204-206.

1899

2273. "Charlotte Perkins Stetson," Current Literature, 25 (Feb 1899), 115-116.

2274. "Men, Women and Events," Cosmopolitan, 27 (Aug 1899), 453-455.

2275. "Stetson, Charlotte Perkins," Who's Who in America 1899-1900, 1st ed. (Chicago: A. N. Marquis, 1899), p. 891.

1900

2276. Short Stories About Clever People Whom You Ought to Know (Chicago: Hollister Bros., 1900), pp. 22-23.

1904

2277. "The Lounger," Critic, 44 (March 1904), 195-196. Rpt. in Woman's Journal, 19 March 1904, p. 90.

2278. "Mrs. Charlotte Perkins Gilman," Current Literature, 36 (May 1904), 511.

1905

2279. Florence Edgar Hobson, "Charlotte Perkins Gilman: An Appreciation and a Criticism," London New Age, 2 March 1905, p. 138.

1906

2280. "Gilman, Charlotte Perkins Stetson," National Cyclopaedia of American Biography, vol. 13 (New York: James T. White & Co., 1906), pp. 212-213.

1910

2281. "Charlotte Perkins Gilman," Progressive Woman, 3 (Feb 1910), 11.

1911

2282. Rosika Schwimmer, "Charlotte Perkins-Gilman," Kvinden og Samfundet (Copenhagen), 15 Juni 1911, pp. 118-120.

2283. "Charlotte Perkins Gilman, Public Speaker, Advanced Thinker," Pictorial Review, 13 (Oct 1911), 14.

1923

2284. James L. Hughes, "World Leaders I Have Known/Charlotte Perkins Gilman," Canadian Magazine, 61 (Aug 1923), 335-338.

2285. Alexander Black, "The Woman Who Saw It First," Century, 107 (Nov 1923), 33-42.

1926

2286. "Charlotte Perkins Gilman," Visual Review, 1 (1926), 2.

2287. Susa Young Gates, "Charlotte Perkins Gilman," Deseret News, 30 April 1927, section 3, 5:4-5.

1930

2288. Amy Wellington, Women Have Told: Studies in the Feminist Tradition (Boston: Little, Brown, and Co., 1930), pp. 115-131.

1934

2289. "Among the Prophets," Boston Sunday Globe, editorial and news section, 15 July 1934, 4:1-2.

1935

2290. "Death Takes Noted Poet," Pasadena Star-News, 19 Aug 1935, p. 2.

2291. "Charlotte Gilman Dies to Avoid Pain," New York Times, 20 Aug 1935, 44:2-4. [Obituary.]
     See also "Mrs. Catt Defends Mrs. Gilman's Suicide," New York Times, 21 Aug 1935, 21:7.

2292. "Charlotte Gilman Kills Herself, Backing Suicide for Incurables," New York Herald Tribune, 20 Aug 1935, 1:5-6 and 11:1-2. [United Press obituary.]
     See also "Mrs. Catt Backs Mrs. Gilman on Right of Suicide," New York Herald Tribune, 21 Aug 1935, 17:3.

2293. "Mrs. Gilman, Author, Takes Her Own Life," Hartford Courant, 20 Aug 1935, 1:4 and 4:5. [Associated Press obituary.]
     See also "Mrs. Gilman's Body is to be Cremated," Hartford Courant, 21 Aug 1935, 3:8.

2294. "Mrs. Charlotte Perkins Gilman, Poet and Lecturer, Leaves Note She Prefers Chloroform to Cancer," San Antonio Express, 20 Aug 1935, 2:2-3. [Associated Press obituary.]

2295. "Woman, Once Rated First in U.S., Dies to Promote Wiser Views on Suicide," Dallas Times-Herald, 20 Aug 1935, 2:5-6. [International News Service obituary.]

2296. "Poet Ends Life as Duty," San Francisco Chronicle, 20 Aug 1935, 10:6. [Obituary.]

2297. "Mrs. Charlotte Gilman, Poet, Lecturer, Dies," Dallas Morning News, 20 Aug 1935, 2:1. [Obituary.]

2298. "Mrs. Charlotte Gilman, Poet, Ends Her Life," Chicago Tribune, 20 Aug 1935, 1:5-6.

2299. "Charlotte Perkins Gilman," Publishers' Weekly, 24 Aug 1935, p. 514. [Obituary.]

2300. "The Right to Die," Survey, 71 (Sept 1935), 274. [Obituary.]

2301. "A Tribute of Gratitude," Equal Rights, 1 Oct 1935, p. 4. [Obituary.]

2302. Zona Gale. "Foreword" to The Living of Charlotte Perkins Gilman (New York and London: Appleton-Century, 1935), pp. xiii-xxxviii.
    Excerpted in Nation, 25 Sept 1935, pp. 350-351.

2303. August Ruedy, "Interesting Letters from Charlotte Perkins Gilman," Amerikanische Turnzeitung, 10 Nov 1935, pp. 12-13; 24 Nov 1935, pp. 10-11; 8 Dec 1935, pp. 9-10; and 22 Dec 1935, pp. 7-8.

1936

2304. Harriet Howe, "Charlotte Perkins Gilman--As I Knew Her," Equal Rights: Independent Feminist Weekly, 5 Sept 1936, pp. 211-216.

1938

2305. Harriet Howe, "A Tribute to Charlotte Perkins Gilman," Equal Rights, 1 July 1938, p. 286.

1939

2306. Harriet Howe, "The Personality of Charlotte Perkins Gilman," Equal Rights, 25 (Oct 1939), 118.

1944

2307. Mary Wilhelmine Williams, "Gilman, Charlotte Perkins Stetson," Dictionary of American Biography, Supplement 1 (New York: Scribner's, 1944), p. 346.

1963

2308. Robert E. Riegel, American Feminists (Lawrence: Univ. Press of Kansas, 1963), pp. 163-173.

1973

2309. James L. Cooper and Sheila McIsaac Cooper, The Roots of American Feminist Thought (Boston: Allyn & Bacon, Inc., 1973), pp. 177-192.

1977

2310. Judith Nies, Seven Women (New York: Viking Press, 1977), pp. 126-145.

1979

2311. Carol Berkin, "Private Woman, Public Woman: The Contradictions of Charlotte Perkins Gilman," in Women in America: A History, ed. Ruth Berkin and Mary Beth Norton (Boston: Houghton Mifflin, 1979), pp. 150-173.

1980

2312. Mary A. Hill, Charlotte Perkins Gilman: The Making of a Radical Feminist 1860-1896 (Philadelphia: Temple Univ. Press, 1980). 362 pp.
    Reviewed by Millicent Bell in New York Review of Books, 17 April 1980, pp. 10-14.
    Reviewed by Anne Firor Scott in Reviews in American History, 8 (Dec 1980), 442-447.
    Reviewed by Lois W. Banner in American Historical Review, 86 (April 1981), 463.
    Reviewed by Mary Ellis Gibson in Signs, 6 (Summer 1981), 753-757.

2313. Mary Beth Pringle, "Charlotte Perkins Stetson Gilman," American Women Writers (New York: Ungar, 1980), vol.

2, pp. 131-133.

2314. Barbara Scott Winkler, Victorian Daughters: The Lives and Feminism of Charlotte Perkins Gilman and Olive Schreiner, Michigan Occasional Paper No. 13 (Ann Arbor: Univ. of Michigan, 1980). 78 pp.

2315. Mary A. Hill, "Charlotte Perkins Gilman: A Feminist's Struggle with Womanhood," Massachusetts Review, 21 (Fall 1980), 503-526.

1981

2316. Richard F. Snow, "Charlotte Perkins Gilman," American Heritage, 32 (Oct-Nov 1981), 46-47.

MANUSCRIPTS AND RELATED DOCUMENTS

Manuscripts

2317. Charlotte Perkins Gilman Collection, Arthur and
Elizabeth Schlesinger Library on the History of Women
in America, Radcliffe College, Cambridge, Mass. 343
folders of letters, clippings, and photographs; as well
as 77 holograph diaries, notebooks, and account books;
and 5 oversize folders. See also the Beecher-Stowe
Papers, folders 410-420, vol. 3, and oversize vol. 3.
Inventory in The Schlesinger Library: The Manuscript
Inventories and the Catalogs of the Manuscripts, Books,
and Pictures (Boston: G. K. Hall & Co., 1973), vol. 3,
pp. 513-519. Rpt. in 2nd edition (Boston: G. K. Hall
& Co., 1984), vol. 9, pp. 379-386.

2318. Rhode Island Historical Society, Providence, R.I. 32
letters from CPS to Martha A. Lane, 1879-1890.

2319. Bancroft Library, Univ. of California, Berkeley, Cal.
24 letters from CPG, including 2 to her mother and 17
to Anne H. Martin, and 2 related documents, 1888-1920.

2320. Houghton Library, Harvard Univ., Cambridge, Mass. 21
letters from CPG to various correspondents, including 5
to W. D. Howells and 1 to Jacob Blanck, 1890-1932.

2321. Vassar College Library, Vassar College, Poughkeepsie,
N.Y. 6 letters from CPG to Martha Whitney, 1890-1903.

2322. Horrmann Library, Wagner College, Staten Island, N.Y.
3 letters from CPS to Edwin Markham, 1892-1894.

2323. Butler Library, Columbia Univ., New York, N.Y. 5
letters from CPG, with 1 to Brander Matthews, 1 to
E. C. Stedman, 1 to Lincoln Steffens, and 2 to Curtis
Hidden Page, 1892-1910.

2324. Huntington Library, San Marino, Cal. 13 letters from

CPG to various correspondents, including 2 to Mary
Austin, 2 to Charles F. Lummis, and 1 to Ida H. Harper;
and 1 letter from Lummis to CPG, 1893-1925.

2325. John Hay Library, Brown Univ., Providence, R.I. 33
letters from CPG, including 26 to Lester Frank Ward,
and 1 holograph poem, 1896-1914.

2326. Sophia Smith Collection, Smith College, Northampton,
Mass. 9 letters from CPG to correspondents including
Margeret Sanger, Ernestine and Herbert Mills, 1896-
1934.

2327. Humanities Research Center, Univ. of Texas at Austin.
8 letters from CPG, including 1 to Charlotte A. Hedge,
1899-1910. 4 manuscript poems, ca. 1904-1910.

2328. Univ. of Rochester Library, Univ. of Rochester,
Rochester, N.Y. 11 letters from CPG and 3 carbons of
letters to CPG, mostly correspondence with Emma
Biddlecom Sweet, 1903-1907.

2329. Wollman Library, Barnard College, New York, N.Y. 3
letters from CPG, 2 to Curtis Hidden Page, 1904-1934.

2330. The Stowe, Beecher, Hooker, Seymour, Day Memorial
Library and Historical Foundation, Hartford, Conn. 14
letters from CPG to 2 of her Day cousins, 1905-1935.
Typescript of "A Study in Ethics," 1933. 1 typescript
poem "Hyenas," 1927. 20 other letters by various
correspondents which refer to CPG, 1877-1938.

2331. Morristown National Historical Park, Morristown, N.J.
1 letter from CPG to "Mr. Walker," 1 Feb 1905.

2332. Department of Special Collections, Research Library,
Univ. of California at Los Angeles, Los Angeles, Cal.
1 letter from CPG to "Mr. Mills," 28 April 1905.

2333. Rare Book Room, University Library, Univ. of Illinois
at Urbana-Champaign. 1 letter from CPG to H. G. Wells,
1 Jan 1907. 6 documents in Putnam's records re.
British sales of Women and Economics and Concerning
Children.

2334. Bailey-Howe Library, Univ. of Vermont, Burlington, Vt.
1 letter from CPG to John Spargo, 23 Sept 1908.

2335. Fruitlands Museum, Prospect Hill, Harvard, Mass. 1
letter from CPG to George W. Cooke, 21 Dec 1909.

2336. Lilly Library, Indiana Univ., Bloomington, Ind. 6 letters from CPG, including 4 to Upton Sinclair, 1910-1930.

2337. Sterling Memorial Library, Yale Univ., New Haven, Conn. 1 letter from CPG to Simeon E. Baldwin, 2 April 1916.

2338. Newberry Library, Chicago, Ill. 2 letters from CPG, 1916-1928.

2339. Starr Library, Middlebury College, Middlebury, Vt. 1 letter from CPG to Marguerite Wilkinson, 22 May 1917.

2340. Miller Library, Colby College, Waterville, Me. 1 letter from CPG to Phyllis W. McIntyre, 20 Nov 1917.

2341. Manuscripts Division, Library of Congress, Washington, D.C. Several letters from CPG to Carrie Chatman Catt, Carrie Chatman Catt Papers. Several letters from CPG to Alice Stone Blackwell, 1923-1935, in the National American Woman Suffrage Association Records. 1 carbon of letter from "Miss Paul" and CPG reply, Dec 1914, in the Charlotte Perkins Gilman file, Miscellaneous Manuscripts Collection. 2 letters from CPG to Benjamin Huebsch, 1912-1932, in the Papers of Benjamin Huebsch, Box 10.

2342. Alderman Library, Univ. of Virginia, Charlottesville, Va. 1 letter from CPG to Glen W. Blodgett, 5 Sept 1928.

Related Documents

2343. Dartmouth College Library, Dartmouth College, Hanover, N.H. 4 letters from Richard Hovey to Herbert Small which mention CPG, 1897-1898.

2344. Berg Collection, New York Public Library, New York, N.Y. 2 readers' reports to T. Fisher Unwin, English publishers of Women and Economics, including one report by G. K. Chesterton, ca. 1899.

2345. Beinecke Rare Book and Manuscript Library, Yale Univ., New Haven, Conn. 1 letter from Ernest Thompson Seton to CPG, 19 March 1901.

2346. Milton S. Eisenhower Library, Johns Hopkins Univ., Baltimore, Md. Undated letter from "McF." to [George H.?] Gilman re. CPG.

MISCELLANEOUS

1891

2347. "Literary Workers," San Francisco Call, 12 March 1891,
4:3. [Editorial re. forthcoming PCWPA convention.]
See also "Adjourned," San Francisco Call, 19 March
1891, 2:1-2.

2348. "The Unitarian Reception," Oakland Times, 1 April 1891,
3:6. [CPS at reception for Edward Everett Hale and
W. R. Alger.]

2349. Clara Spalding Brown, "Pacific Coast Woman's Press
Association," Woman's Journal, 18 April 1891, p. 128.
[Report of PCWPA convention attended by CPS.]

2350. "California Literary Genius," San Francisco Alta
California, 26 April 1891, 4:1-2. [Promotes CPS as the
foremost young California writer.]

2351. "The Working Women," Oakland Times, 26 May 1891, 3:5.

2352. "P.C.W.P.A.," Pacific Rural Press, 19 Sept 1891, p.
249. [CPS on program of annual convention.]

2353. Ambrose Bierce, "Prattle," San Francisco Examiner, 4
Oct 1891, 6:5. [Derisive comment re. PCWPA in general
and CPS in particular.]
See also reply in Woman's Journal, 10 Jan 1892, p.
20.

2354. Oakland Tribune, 13 Oct 1891, 4:4. [Re. poetry.]

1892

2355. "Had Ideas of Her Own/Providence Artist Seeks Divorce
from His Too Practical Wife," Boston Globe, morning
edition, 18 Dec 1892, 2:3.

See also "Bellamyism, or OEhology?" Boston Globe,
morning edition, 19 Dec 1892, 4:2; evening edition,
19 Dec 1892, 9:1-2. [Editorial re. divorce.]
See also "'Is No One's Business,'" Boston Globe, 20
Dec 1892, morning edition, 7:3. [Interview with
CPS re. divorce.]

2356. "The Wife and the Writer," San Francisco Examiner, 19
Dec 1892, 3:1-3. [Report that CWS has filed for
divorce from CPS.]

2357. "Nationalists on Marriage," Boston Herald, 20 Dec 1892,
4:8.

2358. "Preferred Literature to Marriage," New York Times, 20
Dec 1892, 2:2.

2359. "Artist Stetson's Divorce," Philadelphia Press, 20 Dec
1892, 1:2.

2360. "Stetson Objects to Reform. His Wife's Plans for
Bettering the Universe Annoy Him," San Francisco
Examiner, 20 Dec 1892, 1:3-4. [Interview with CWS.]
See also "Women of Brains as Wives," San Francisco
Examiner, 25 Dec 1892, 6:2-3. [Editorial.]

2361. Ambrose Bierce, "Prattle," San Francisco Examiner, 25
Dec 1892, 6:6. [CWS should "have based his suit for
separation upon the quality of (CPS's) writing."]

1893

2362. "Mrs. Stetson Defended," San Francisco Call, 6 Jan
1893, 6:2. [Reprint of CWS letter in defense of CPS.]

2363. Ambrose Bierce, "Prattle," San Francisco Examiner, 10
Sept 1893, 6:4. [Derisive comment re. "Col. Charlotte"
Stetson.]

2364. "Journalists' Day," San Francisco Call, 23 Sept 1893,
10:1-2. [CPS at PCWPA convention.]

2365. Ambrose Bierce, "Prattle," San Francisco Examiner, 12
Nov 1893, 6:4. [Re. "Col. Charlie Perkins-Stetson,"
her poetry, and her essay on "The Labor Movement."]

1894

2366. "Turn About," Oakland Tribune, 1 March 1894, 2:2. [Re.
divorce.]

2367. "Lives Grown Apart," Oakland Enquirer, 2 March 1894, 1:7. [Re. divorce.]

2368. "A Cook-Stove Throne," San Francisco Examiner, 2 March 1894. [Re. divorce.]
See also "She Gives Him to Another," San Francisco Examiner, 4 March 1894, 12:1-2.]

2369. Helen Campbell, "Woman's Congress of the Midwinter Fair," Outlook, 16 June 1894, p. 1099. [CPS helped to organize west coast congress.]

2370. "Married in Providence/Quiet Wedding of Artist Stetson and Miss Channing," San Francisco Call, 19 June 1894, 8:5.

2371. Ambrose Bierce, "Prattle," San Francisco Examiner, 11 Nov 1894, 6:5. [Derisive comment re. Impress.]

1895

2372. "Next Woman's Congress," San Francisco Call, 5 Jan 1896, 18:4.

2373. Ambrose Bierce, "Prattle," San Francisco Examiner, 28 April 1895, 6:5. [Derisive comment re. demise of Impress.]

2374. "Mrs. Stetson is Honored," San Francisco Examiner, 19 May 1896, 8:5. [Re. Woman's Congress.]

2375. Helen Campbell, "Pacific Coast Woman's Congress," Woman's Journal, 22 June 1895, p. 194. [Re. CPG at the second Congress.]

1896

2376. "Nelly Bly with the Female Suffragists," New York World, 26 Jan 1896, p. 4. [Re. CPS at national convention of the NAWSA in Washington, D.C.]

2377. Alice Stone Blackwell, "The National Convention," Woman's Journal, 1 Feb 1896, p. 36. [Re. CPS at national convention of the NAWSA in Washington, D.C.]

2378. "Stetson Reception," Topeka State Journal, 13 June 1896, p. 6. [Re. CPS on lecture tour.]

1899

2379. "Evolution in Education," Southern Educational Journal, 12 (March 1899), 182-183. [Re. CPS as educator.]

2380. "Notable Woman Visiting Utah," Deseret Evening News, 27 Nov 1899, 8:4-5. [Re. CPS on lecture tour.]

2381. "Mrs. Stetson is in Town/She Expresses Her Views in an Interview with Miriam Michelson," San Francisco Bulletin, 12 Dec 1899, 1:6-7 and 2:1.

1900

2382. Charles F. Lummis, "In Western Letters," Land of Sunshine, 12 (March 1900), 302. [CPS in writing Human Work.]

2383. Charles F. Lummis, "In Western Letters," Land of Sunshine, 12 (May 1900), 348-350. [General comment re. the sociology of CPS.]

2384. "Takes a Second Chance in Lottery of Marriage," San Francisco Examiner, 19 June 1900, 4:3-4. [Re. remarriage.]

2385. Charles F. Lummis, "In Western Letters," Land of Sunshine, 13 (July 1900), 89. [Re. remarriage.]

2386. "Philosophy and Physiology," Bookman, 12 (Oct 1900), 99. [Re. remarriage.]

1902

2387. History of Woman Suffrage, ed. Susan B. Anthony and Ida Husted Harper (Indianapolis: Hollenbeck Press, 1902), vol. 4, passim.

1903

2388. Olive Muir Fuller, "Mrs. Gilman Defended by a Civitas Member," Brooklyn Eagle, 28 Feb 1903, 10:4.

1905

2389. "Mrs. Gilman To Go To Portland," Woman's Journal, 29 April 1905, p. 66. [CPG to attend NAWSA convention in Portland, Ore.]

1906

2390. Upton Sinclair, The Jungle (Garden City: Doubleday, 1906), chap. 31. [Alludes to CPG.]

2391. Lester F. Ward, "The Past and Future of the Sexes," Independent, 8 March 1906, p. 541. [Re. CPG as a "cosmic" thinker.]

1907

2392. "No Servants Soon," New York Tribune, 19 Dec 1907, 5:5. [Re. I. M. Rubinow. See also item 2394.]

1909

2393. "Light on Socialism," New York Times, 23 Jan 1909, 8:1-2. [Editorial re. CPG.]

2394. I. M. Rubinow, "Woman and Economic Dependence," American Journal of Sociology, 14 (March 1909), 618. [Re. the middle-class bias of CPG's reform proposals.] See also item 2392.

2395. Anita C. Block, "A New Magazine by a Woman," New York Call, 22 Oct 1909, 5:2. [Re. Forerunner.] See also New York Call, 8 Nov 1909, 5:2.

2396. "Magazines," Christian Register, 9 Dec 1909, p. 1339. [Review of Forerunner.]

1910

2397. "The Lounger," Putnam's, 7 (Jan 1910), 501. [Review of Forerunner.]

1911

2398. "Mrs. Gilman," Woman's Journal, 16 Sept 1911, p. 295. [Announcement of lecture tour.]

1912

2399. Josephine Conger-Kaneko, Progressive Woman, 6 (Oct 1912), 7. [Review of Forerunner.]

1913

2400. Ellen Key, "Education for Motherhood," Atlantic Monthly, 112 (July 1913), 49-50. [Critique of CPG's proposed reforms.]

2401. "Three Won't Back New Coppee Play," New York Times, 30 Sept 1913, 3:5. [CPG withdraws as sponsor of "The Guilty Man."]

1914

2402. "Raise 'Free Love' Cry," New York Times, 25 May 1914, 11:5. [CPG quoted out of context by anti-suffragists.]

2403. "Teacher-Mothers Look to Mitchel," New York Times, 17 Nov 1914, 9:1. [CPG and others call on mayor of New York on behalf of teacher-mothers in city.]

2404. "'War Stops Literature,' Says W. D. Howells," Oregon Journal, 13 Dec 1914. [Howells alludes to CPG.]

1915

2405. Vella Winner, "Noted Lecturer is Exponent of Wider Feminist Movement," Oregon Journal, 28 March 1915, 2:5-8.

2406. "Mrs. Gilman, Writer, Here," San Francisco Examiner, 4 April 1915, 8:7. [CPG to visit Panama-Pacific Exhibition.]

2407. Bessie Beatty, "Would You Know Feminist Truths? Hear Mrs. Gilman," San Francisco Bulletin, 26 April 1915, 11:1.

1916

2408. Clara E. Laughlin, Reminiscences of James Whitcomb Riley (New York and Chicago: Revell Co., 1916), pp. 51-52. [Riley on In This Our World and CPS.]

2409. "Even Barbers Rebel at Shearing Women," New York Times, 16 March 1916, 13:3. [Protest against CPG's suggestion that women cut their hair.]

1920

2410. "$25,000 for Proof League Means War," New York Times, 16 Oct 1920, 2:3. [CPG endorses proposal for League of Nations.]

1921

2411. Mary Austin, "American Women and the Intellectual Life," Bookman, 53 (Aug 1921), 484. [Allusion to CPG.]

1922

2412. History of Woman Suffrage, ed. Ida Husted Harper (New York: National American Woman Suffrage Association, 1922), vol. 5, passim.

1925

2413. Emanuel Haldeman-Julius, "Walter Hurt Proposes a Woman," Haldeman-Julius Weekly, 19 Dec 1925, p. 3.

1926

2414. The Intimate Papers of Colonel House, ed. Charles Seymour (Boston and New York: Houghton Mifflin, 1926), vol. 1, pp. 120-121. [Woodrow Wilson enjoys CPS's poem "A Conservative."]

1927

2415. "Noted Writer is Visiting in City," Pasadena Star-News, 18 Feb 1927, p. 11.

1928

2416. T. V. Smith, The American Philosophy of Equality (Chicago: Univ. of Chicago Press, 1928), p. 298. [Re. Women and Economics.]

1929

2417. Carey McWilliams, Ambrose Bierce: A Biography (New York: Albert & Charles Boni, 1929), p. 156. [CPG on Bierce.]

1931

2418. Fred Lewis Pattee, "The Twenty Best American Short Stories," Golden Book, 13 (Jan 1931), 82. [Re. "The Yellow Wall-paper."]

1933

2419. "Zona Gale Lists Her Nine Women Immortals," New York

World-Telegram, 15 Feb 1933, p. 21. [CPG listed.]

2420. Rosika Schwimmer, *New York Times Book Review*, 3 Sept 1933, 13:5. [Letter to editor criticizes failure of International Woman Writers conferences to include any books by CPG on list of 100 best books by American women.]

1934

2421. "Writer is Welcomed Back to City," Pasadena *Star-News*, 3 Nov 1934, p. 6.

1936

2422. Edward Alsworth Ross, *Seventy Years of It: An Autobiography* (New York: Appleton-Century, 1936), pp. 60, 243-244. [Alludes to CPG.]

2423. "The Courage She Gave," *Equal Rights: Independent Feminist Weekly*, 5 Sept 1936, p. 210. [Editorial tribute to CPG one year after her death.]

1944

2424. Mary Gray Peck, *Carrie Chapman Catt* (New York: H. W. Wilson Co., 1944), pp. 130, 139, 454-455. [Re. CPG on 1904 International Congress of Women in Berlin and other topics.]

1982

2425. Charles C. Eldredge, *Charles Walter Stetson: Color and Fantasy* (Lawrence: Spencer Museum of Art, 1982), esp. pp. 25-49. [Biographical sketch of CWS with frequent reference to CPS.]

Part III

SELECTED CRITICISM

2426. Allen-Robinson, Polly Wynn. "The Social Ethics of Charlotte Perkins Gilman." Ph.D. dissertation, Harvard Univ., 1978.

2427. "Charlotte Perkins Gilman's Dynamic Social Philosophy." Current Literature, 51 (July 1911), 67-70.

2428. Degler, Carl N. "Charlotte Perkins Gilman on the Theory and Practice of Feminism." American Quarterly, 8 (Spring 1956), 21-39.
     Rpt. in Our American Sister, ed. Jean E. Friedman and William G. Shade (Boston: Allyn and Bacon, 1973), pp. 197-218.

2429. --------. "Introduction" to Women and Economics. New York: Harper & Row, 1966, pp. vi-xxxv.

2430. Dell, Floyd. Women as World Builders. Chicago: Forbes, 1913, pp. 22-29.
     See also item 1601.

2431. Doyle, William. "Charlotte Gilman and the Cycle of Feminist Reform." Ph.D. dissertation, Univ. of California, Berkeley, 1960.

2432. Filene, Peter Gabriel. Him/Her/Self: Sex Roles in Modern America. New York and London: Harcourt, Brace & Jovanovich, 1974, pp. 63-65 and passim.

2433. Gilbert, Sandra, and Susan Gubar. The Madwoman in the Attic: The Woman Writer and the Nineteenth-Century Imagination. New Haven, Conn.: Yale Univ. Press, 1979, pp. 89-92. [Analysis of "The Yellow Wallpaper."]

2434. Gornick, Vivian. "Twice Told Tales." Nation, 23 Sept 1978, pp. 278-281. [Analysis of "The Yellow Wall-paper."]

2435. Hayden, Dolores. "Charlotte Perkins Gilman and the Kitchenless House." Radical History Review, 21 (Fall 1979), 225-247.

2436. Hedges, Elaine R. "Afterword" to The Yellow Wall-paper. Old Westbury, N.Y.: Feminist Press, 1973, pp. 37-63.

2437. Kennard, Jean K. "Convention Coverage, or How to Read Your Own Life." New Literary History, 13 (Autumn 1981), 69-88. [Analysis of "The Yellow Wall-paper."]

2438. Kessler, Carol Farley. "Brittle Jars and Bitter Jangles: Light Verse by Charlotte Perkins Gilman." Regionalism and the Female Imagination, 4 (Winter 1979), 35-43.

2439. Kolodny, Annette. "A Map for Rereading: or, Gender and the Interpretation of Literary Texts." New Literary History, 11 (Spring 1980), esp. 455-460.

2440. Lane, Ann J. "The Fictional World of Charlotte Perkins Gilman." Introduction to The Charlotte Perkins Gilman Reader. New York: Pantheon, 1980, pp. ix-xlii.

2441. -------. "Introduction" to Herland. New York: Pantheon, 1979, pp. v-xxiv.

2442. MacPike, Loralee. "Environment as Psychopathological Symbolism in 'The Yellow Wallpaper.'" American Literary Realism, 8 (Summer 1975), 286-288.

2443. Magner, Lois. "Women and the Scientific Idiom: Textual Episodes from Wollstonecraft, Fuller, Gilman, and Firestone." Signs, 4 (Autumn 1978), esp. 68-77.

2444. O'Neill, William. Everyone Was Brave. New York: Quadrangle, 1969, esp. pp. 38-44, 130-133. [Useful survey of relationship between Gilman's life and published work.]

2445. Pearson, Carol. "Coming Home: Four Feminist Utopias and Patriarchal Experience." In Future Females: A Critical Anthology. Ed. Marleen S. Barr. Bowling Green, Ohio: Bowling Green State Univ. Popular Press, 1981, pp. 63-70. [Re. Herland.]

2446. Porter, Mary A. "Charlotte Perkins Gilman: A Feminist Paradox." Ph.D. dissertation, McGill Univ., 1975. See also item 2312.

2447. Porterfield, Amanda. Feminine Spirituality in America. Philadelphia: Temple Univ. Press, 1980, pp. 171-180. [General comments re. Women and Economics, The Home, and "The Yellow Wall-paper."]

2448. Potts, Helen Jo. "Charlotte Perkins Gilman: A Humanist Approach to Feminism." Ph.D. dissertation, North Texas State Univ., 1975.

2449. Schöpp-Schilling, Beate. "'The Yellow Wallpaper': A Rediscovered 'Realistic' Story." American Literary Realism, 8 (Summer 1975), 284-286.

2450. Schramm, Sarah Slavin. Plow Women Rather Than Reapers: An Intellectual History of Feminism in the United States (Metuchen, N.J., and London: Scarecrow Press, 1979), pp. 37-39, 97-98, 267-269, 387-389, and passim.

2451. Spacks, Patricia Meyer. The Female Imagination. New York: Knopf, 1975, pp. 208-218. [Excellent analysis of Living.]

2452. Stern, Madeleine B. "Introduction" to the reprint edition of the Forerunner. New York: Greenwood, 1968, vol. 1, [pp. iii-x].

2453. Wood, Ann Douglas. "'The Fashionable Diseases': Women's Complaints and Their Treatment in Nineteenth-Century America." Journal of Interdisciplinary History, 4 (Summer 1973), esp. 41-44. [Analysis of Gilman's treatment by S. Weir Mitchell in 1887 and Gilman's later treatment of this theme in "The Yellow Wall-paper."]
    Rpt. in Clio's Consciousness Raised: New Perspectives in the History of Women, ed. Mary S. Hartman and Lois W. Banner (New York: Harper & Row, 1974), pp. 1-22.

PERSONAL NAME INDEX

Browne, F. W. Stella 2135
Brownell, Baker 2159
Bruere, Martha Bensley 1527, 2165
Bruere, Robert 1527
Bucke, Richard Maurice 835
Buhle, Mari Jo 313
Burnett, Frances Hodgson 799
Burroughs, John 811

Caffyn, Kathleen M. 855
Calverton, V. F. 2160, 2163
Campbell, Helen 828, 836, 897, 2272, 2369, 2375
Canning, Lisbeth 69
Carlsberg, Frigga 1095
Carnegie, Andrew 822, 1161
Carpenter, Edward 835
Carroll, Lewis 1462
Cary, Edward 959
Catt, Carrie Chapman 2291-2292, 2341
Chambliss, Edgar 1389
Chancellor, Louise Beecher 1405
Channing, Grace Ellery 783, 909, 2369
Chesterton, G. K. 1456, 1487, 2344
Chettle, H. F. 170
Childs, Jessie D. 1341
Chopin, Kate 1045
Clark, G. Hardy 1664
Clark Margaret J. 1664
Clark, Thomas Curtis 62, 140, 185, 272, 353
Clarke, Helen A. 170, 1045
Clausen, Emma 21, 39, 50, 60, 61, 74, 86, 140, 162, 173
Clemens, Samuel L. 523, 835
Cleveland, Grover 910
Cockerell. T.D.A. 1381
Coit, Stanton 1359
Conger-Kaneko, Josephine 68, 544, 1268, 1448, 2399
Conrad, Joseph 1628
Cooke, George W. 2335
Cooley, Alice Kingsbury 861
Coolbrith, Ida 942
Cooper, James L. 1045, 2309

Cooper, Sheila McIsaac 1045, 2309
Coppee, Francois 2401
Cott, Nancy 1045
Cross, E. A. 505
Culley, Margaret 1045
Curtis, George William 959
Cushman, Ralph Spaulding 157

Davidson, John 18, 44, 72, 77, 130, 170
Davies, H. Walford 161
Daviess, Maria Thompson 1493
Davis, John 791
Dawson, Emma Frances 935
de Aguirre, Gertrude G. 989
Debs, Eugene V. 976, 2060
Degler, Carl 1045, 2428-2429
DeLana, Alice 69, 154
Dell, Floyd 566, 1601, 2430
deLong, Helen 185
Dewey, John 844
Dickens, Charles 519
Dix, R. A. 2245
Dock, Lavinia 1374
Dole, Nathan 697
Doty, Madeline Z. 1641
Doyle. Arthur Conan 934
Doyle, William 2431
Dreiser, Theodore 1783
Drescher, Martin 158
Dublin, L.R.C.P. 2131
Dunbar, Olivia H. 1095
Duncan, Isadora 1684

Edwards, Joseph 2271
Ehrmann, Max 1433
Eldredge, Charles C. 2425
Eliot, George 516
Ellis, Havelock 981
Ellwood, Charles A. 1706
Ely, Richard T. 787, 834
Emerson, Ralph Waldo 107
Evans, E. E. 82

Fairfield, Margaret Ashley 1707
Farnsworth, Eva Olney 1789
Faustman, Alma 1381
Ferber, Edna 1480

DATE DUE

DEMCO, INC. 38-2931